I0793612

IMAGES
of America

YORKTOWN

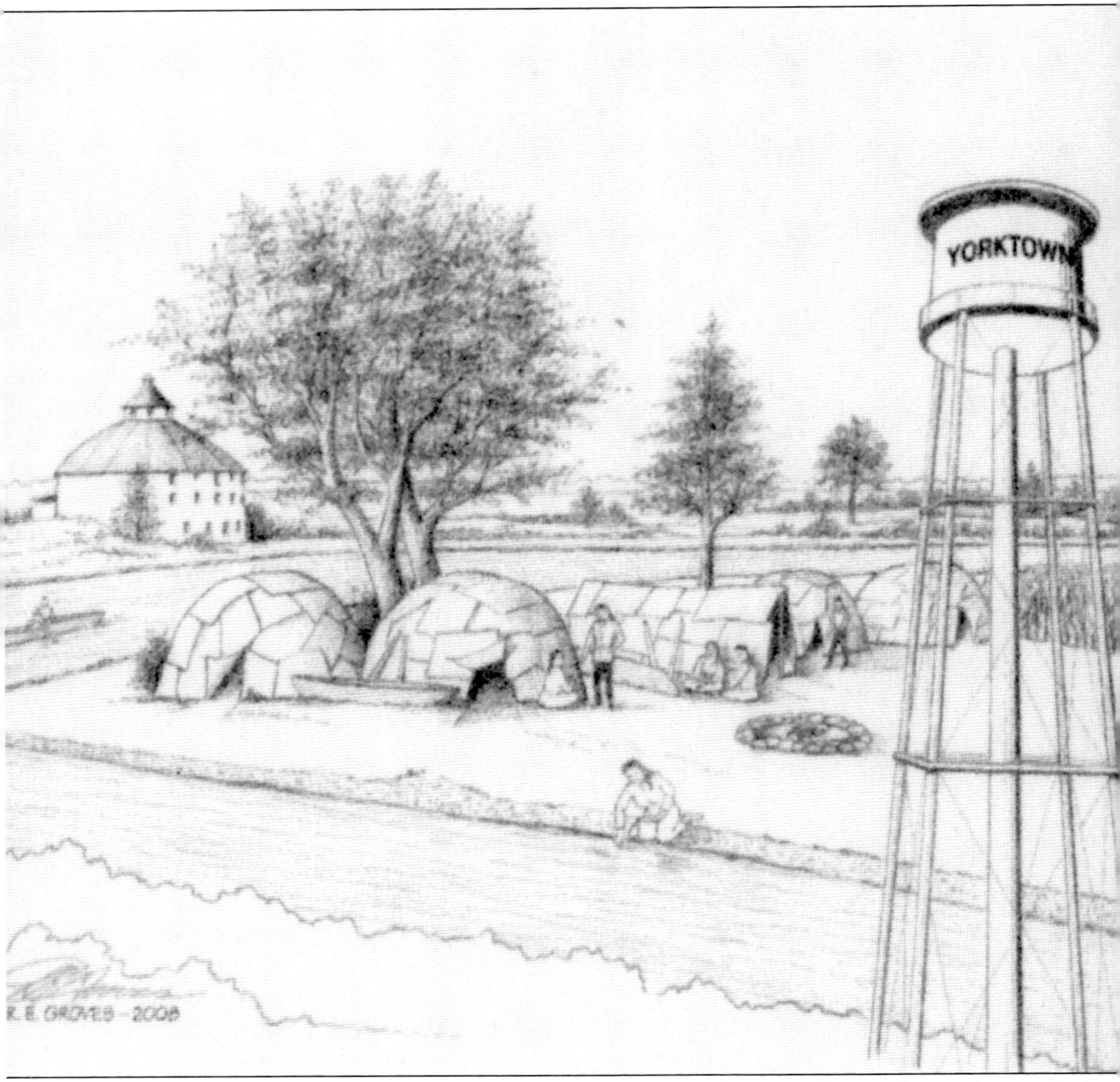

Local artist Ron Groves's drawing depicts some historical icons. The small, mostly rounded structures are wigwams, the type of home Delaware Indians would build for themselves. The round barn, no longer standing, was on the Marion Hofherr farm. The water tower stood tall above the town as if to welcome one home from a journey. (Ron Groves.)

On the Cover: Mark Broadwater (left), a local banker, and Rue (center) and Clyde "Doc" Byerly, owners of Byerly's Drug Store, pose in front of their business. The drugstore was located on the northeast corner of Smith and Walnut Streets. Byerly's carried the normal medical needs, sold tickets for the local bus routes, and had a soda fountain featuring flavored Cokes and a variety of ice-cream treats. (Susan Clevenger.)

IMAGES
of America

YORKTOWN

Becky Monroe and John Shideler

ARCADIA
PUBLISHING

ISBN 978-1-4671-1503-2

Published by Arcadia Publishing
Charleston, South Carolina

Printed in the United States of America

Library of Congress Control Number: 2015942947

For all general information, please contact Arcadia Publishing:
Telephone 843-853-2070
Fax 843-853-0044
E-mail sales@arcadiapublishing.com
For customer service and orders:
Toll-Free 1-888-313-2665

Visit us on the Internet at www.arcadiapublishing.com

Dedicated to those who have gone before us and their heirs, who have been kind enough to donate their family treasures to the Yorktown–Mount Pleasant Township Historical Alliance.

Contents

Acknowledgments 6

Introduction 7

1. Smith Street and Beyond 9
2. Churches 33
3. Homes, Friends, and Families 41
4. Nearby Neighbors 63
5. Local Heroes 73
6. Clubs and Activities 83
7. Taking a Tour 95
8. Learning the ABCs 103

About the Yorktown–Mount Pleasant Township Historical Alliance 127

Acknowledgments

Big thank-yous go to Shirley Pearson for the many hours she spent editing the written document and to Dave Parkison for coming on board at the last minute to help with all phases of the preproduction.

The following individuals and organizations also deserve special thanks: Shirley Masters, Marilyn Swander, Tim Spangler, Marsha Spratt, Judy St. John, Dale Stephenson, Larry Stewart, Betty Thurman, Paul Vise, Phil White, Don Williams, Rhonda Williams, Laurie Swartz, Barbara Young, Sarah Belle Applegate estate, Corey Sears, Ball State University Archives and Special Collections, John Boyle, Sue Burger, Susan Clevenger, Brian Couch, Wendell Conner, Bob Daugherty, Jerry K Davis, Marian Donovan, Bob Ellis, Betty Mae Fisher, Shawn Gray, Don Guinn, Independent Order of Odd Fellows No. 345, Jeff Koneker, Sherry Lake, Paula Lennington, Yorktown Lions Club, Marsh Supermarkets, Dick Grimes, Ron Groves, Billie Grubbs, Marcelle Hatton, Lois Ann Henderson, Yorktown–Mt. Pleasant Township Historical Alliance (YMPTHA), Kathy Mattingly, Bruce Monroe, Evelyn Morrow, Phyllis Myer, Mark Parkison, Yorktown Police Department, Bea Porter estate, Jim Proudfoot, Terry Reed, Ron Richcreek, Janice Ross, Marylou Schmidt, and Sheila Sheward.

INTRODUCTION

Yorktown is located in Mount Pleasant Township, Delaware County, Indiana. The first residents of record were Native Americans known as the Delaware Indians, who were members of the Miami tribe. The Delawares were a nomadic people and moved their village according to season. They normally stayed along the White River or Buck Creek where they could hunt and fish year-round. The Delawares lived in wigwams, structures with rounded tops.

One of the first white settlers to enter Mount Pleasant Township was David Hellis, who purchased land in 1822. Except for a few, the local Indians were friendly and helped the new settlers plant and harvest their crops. Following the signing of the Miami Treaty, the Native Americans were forced off the land and moved west. Only a few members of the Delaware tribe remained.

During the period 1824–1925, a young Oliver H. Smith was serving as the prosecuting attorney for the Third Judicial District. The nearby Mount Pleasant Township was not in his district, but he purchased a large amount of land here and platted the original town of Yorktown. The plat was drawn in 1836 and recorded in 1837. At that time, Smith owned the majority of the land within the boundaries of Yorktown but soon began selling lots and participating in the operation of several early businesses. Until recently, it was believed the name Yorktown came from the York Indians, a branch of the Delaware. Recent research has revealed that there were no York Indians. It appears that a group of Indians composed of three different tribes moved to Indiana from New York and settled here with the Delaware. As a result, they were referred to as Yorks. He adopted the name and labeled his early plat York-Town.

A mill of one type or another is normally one of the first businesses to operate in a community. Yorktown was no different. There has been a good deal of confusion as to the whereabouts of the mills here. Most early property documentations show the mill on Canal Street but recent research has shown that there were indeed three mills. Some property maps should have shown other mills instead of the Canal Street mill. Another mill was located on the east side of Mill Street and north of the railroad tracks. The third one was found west of Buck Creek and south of Cornbread Road at the end of Hemingway Street. Another cause for confusion is the fact that some of the same people were involved in the operation of more than one mill.

Both Oliver Smith and judge David Kilgore were active in local government and the community, but they also had great foresight in the future of the railroad. With their encouragement and the support of area residents, by 1848 the Indianapolis and Bellefontaine Railroad began constructing a line through Mount Pleasant Township and running through Yorktown. This system provided direct access to Indianapolis and Muncie, as well as other parts of the state.

Farming was the primary source of income for many years. Mount Pleasant Township had its share of large, successful farms. Following the discovery of natural gas in 1886, several factories were established, which gave families another method of support. After the gas supply began to dwindle, operations at several of the factories slowed and even ceased. The Skillen-Gooden Glass Factory, which relied on the natural gas, burned and did not reopen. This left a lot of people without jobs. Many of the more adventurous went to West Virginia to work in the coal mines. In most cases, that did not work well and they returned to Yorktown to seek other employment.

Following World War II, the housing industry in the area was at an all-time high. Several small additions were developed in which most of the houses were single-story ranch style. A lot of farmland was lost to these additions, and once again, people were forced to seek jobs in other industries.

Along with the housing boom, there was a need for the business community to expand, which caused the development of spotty business areas. Some areas would consist of only one business, such as a service station or small shopping areas.

The polio epidemic hit the area in the late 1940s and early 1950s. Several families lost loved ones to this terrible disease. Others were lucky enough to survive the crippling disease—some with lifelong disfigurement. Others had no visible signs of having been ill.

Baby boomers caused an increase in population, and the walls of the Yorktown School were stretched to overflowing. Plans were soon made to build a new school for elementary through high school grades on property located at the northeast corner of Highway 32 and Yorktown-Gaston Road, now affectionately known as Tiger Drive. The fall of 1955 saw an unusual change in the pattern of school while the new school was being built. The overcrowded students were divided into two groups; grades seven through twelve attended school in the morning and grades one through six went in the afternoon. Later that year, ordinary schedules were resumed, and when the elementary students left for Christmas break, each put all of his or her items in a paper bag marked with a name and left it on the desk. Following break, they reported to the new school and entered their classrooms to find their belongings on their new desks. Classes returned to a regular schedule.

The population of the entire area continued to increase; in 1969, both Pleasant View Elementary and Yorktown High School were ready to welcome students. Our school system now consists of Pleasant View (kindergarten through second grade), Yorktown Elementary (grades three through five), Yorktown Middle School (grades six through eight), and Yorktown High School.

Over the years, several new developments have been annexed into the town of Yorktown. In 2011, the governing body became very aggressive and voted to annex the remainder of Mount Pleasant Township, which became effective in 2013.

One

Smith Street and Beyond

It is not known exactly when Oliver H. Smith arrived in the area, but he platted the town of Yorktown in 1836. Buck Creek runs along the east side of Yorktown and northward, flowing into the White River. The river runs along the north side of town. Smith knew the location was ideal. The first businesses to pop up in the area were a mill and a general store where merchants, farmers, and traders had easy access to supplies.

A merchant's book published in 1915 indicates the Overmire Company had been in business for over 30 years, taking its origins here back to at least 1885. Records indicate that the Overmires had three successive general stores, each time moving to a larger location. General stores provided meats, produce, canned goods, heating and cookstoves, and dry goods consisting of household items, fabrics, and so forth. When families moved, they usually left a lot of large household belongings behind simply because wagons, either flat or covered, were not big enough to take everything with them.

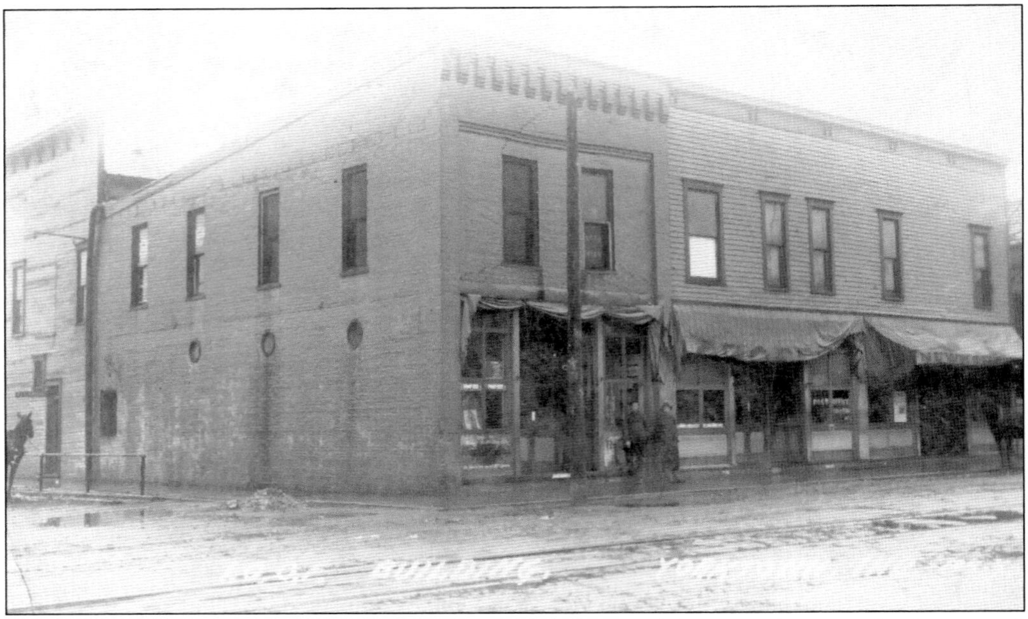

The photographs on this page show a portion of the original business district, which was well established by 1890. In 1913, fire destroyed the general store, post office, and Newhouse Grocery. Dr. Carl Wright and the Odd Fellows lodge occupied the second stories of these buildings. The structures on the left side of the lower photograph were rebuilt after the fire. The ones farther down the block had been built prior to the fire but were not yet occupied. Located in the rebuilt section were a drugstore, grocery, automobile repair shop, restaurant, and pool hall. Businesses occupied sections on the street level while the Odd Fellows lodge and some professional offices occupied the upper floor. The basement level also had space for businesses that were accessed by stairways at the front of the buildings. (Above, Jeff Koenker; below, Ball State University Archives and Special Collections.)

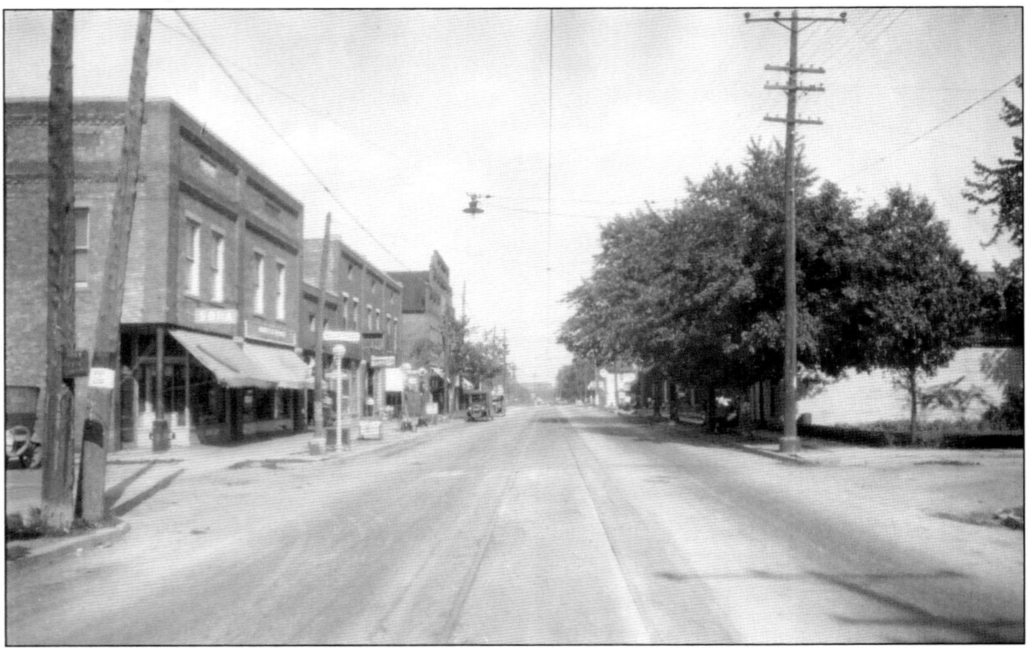

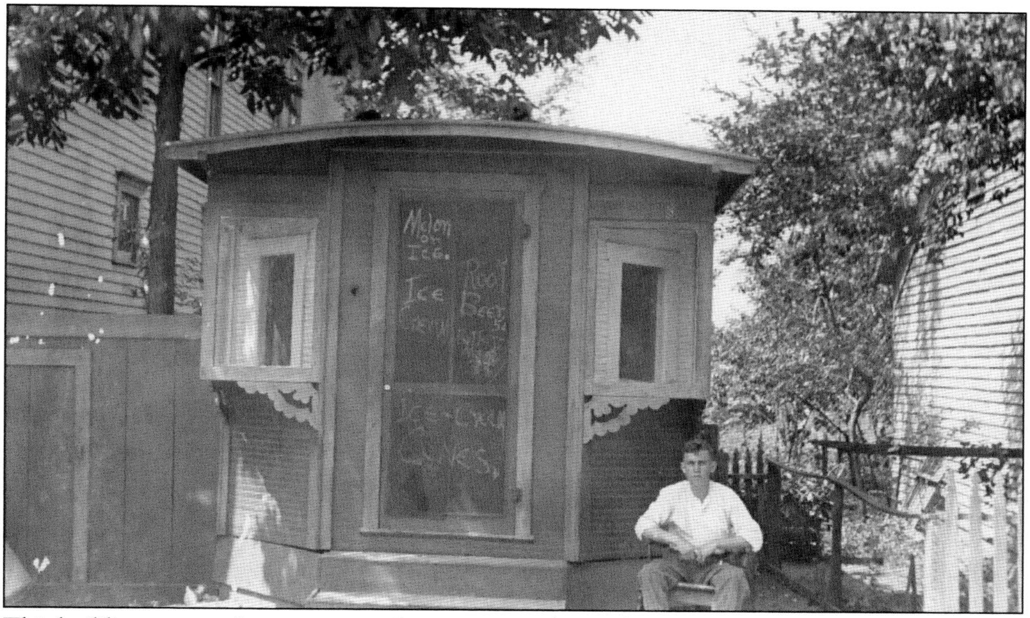

This building appears be some type of wagon. It was located east of the original business buildings and operated by Hubert "Bob" Parkinson. Featured items at this early-day convenience store were melon, ice cream, root beer, butter, and milk. Prior to this time period, the building served as a restaurant. The structure was removed prior to 1913, when the Odd Fellows built on this site. (Mark Parkinson.)

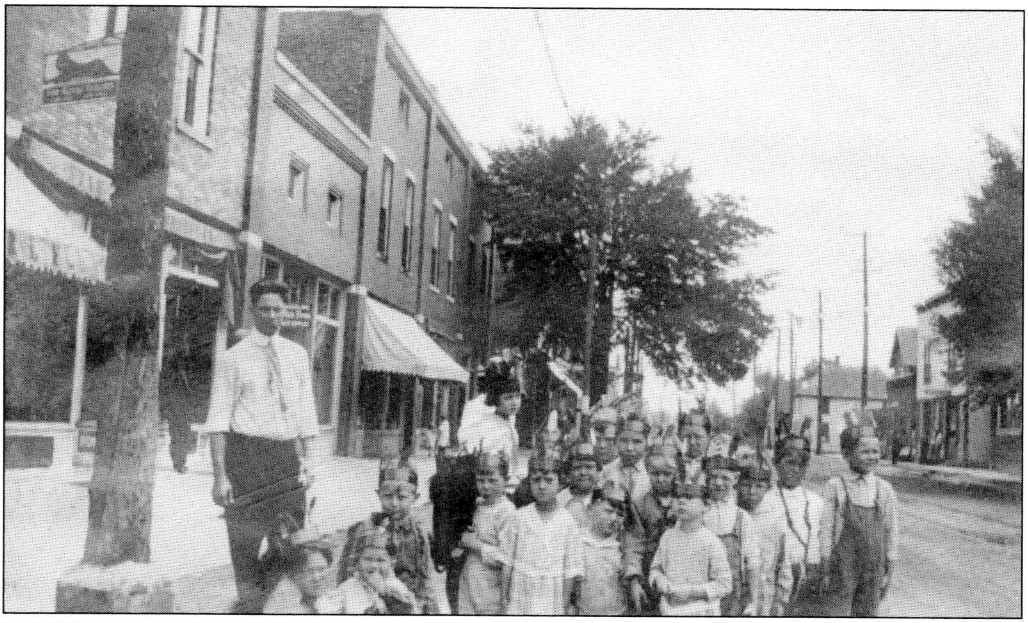

In 1917, a group of small children visits the downtown business area. The children appear to be wearing some sort of hats, perhaps celebrating an upcoming holiday. Shown on the opposite side of the street in the background is a two-story building that served as a hotel as well as two houses farther down the block. (YMPTHA.)

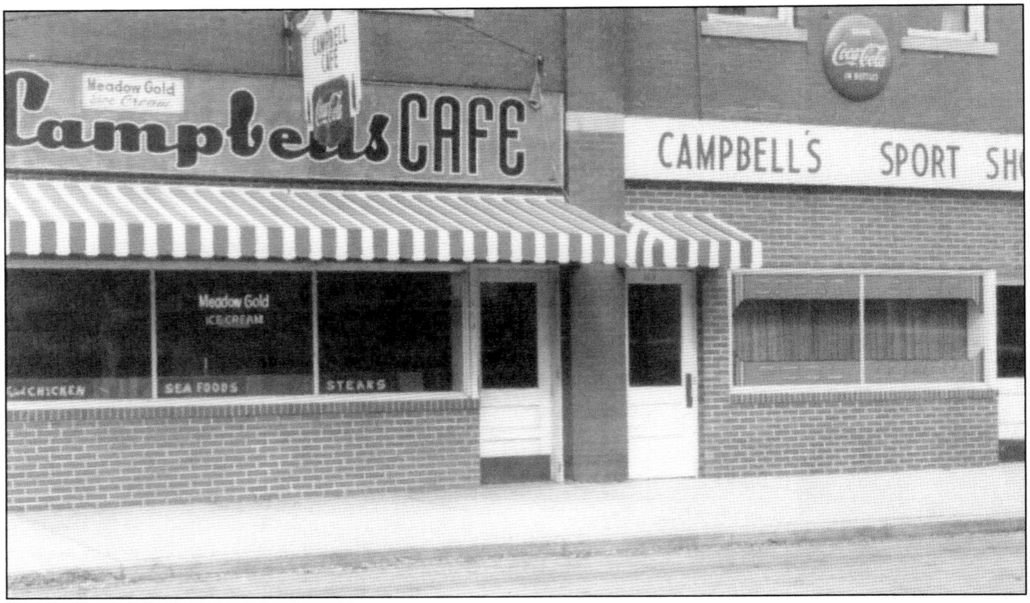

Prior to being Campbell's Café, this business was known as Garrison's Café, operated by Ralph Garrison. Later, the café was operated by Floshia Sears-Campbell and her son Earland "Shike" Sears. Campbell's was well known for its homemade pies. The adjacent sport shop was a pool hall run by Freeman and Shike Sears. The current business here is Osborn's Country Kitchen. (Marsha Spratt.)

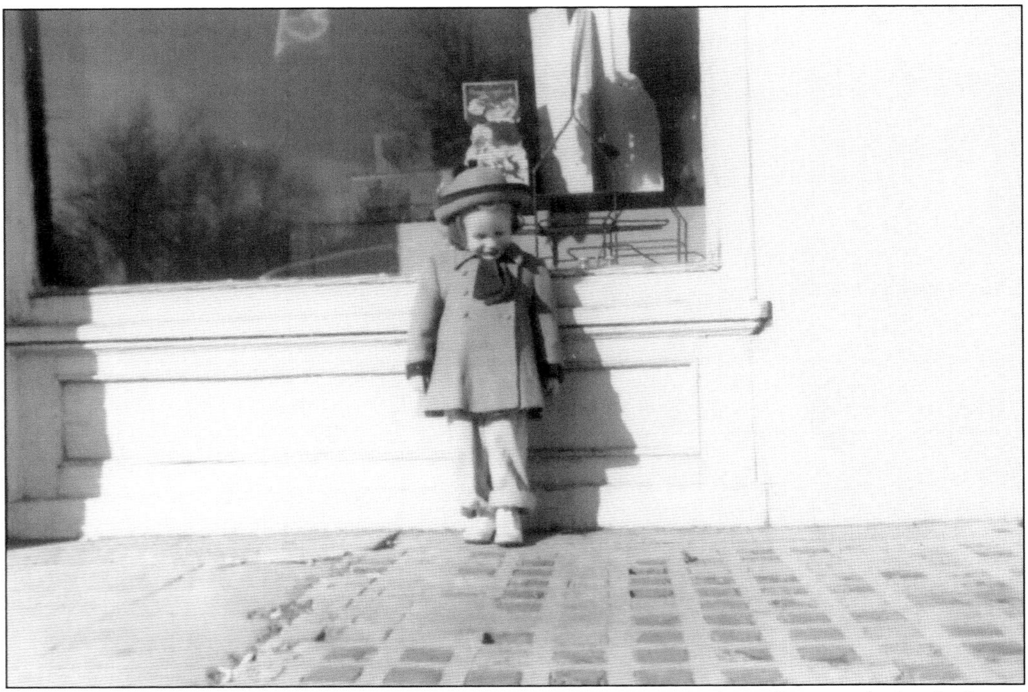

Marsha Sears, granddaughter of Floshia Sears-Campbell, is shown looking down at the bricked-over area used to seal off one of the stairways leading to the basement levels of some of the businesses on Smith Street. Marsha said she feared the bricks with glass centers would fall in if she stepped on them. (Marsha Spratt.)

Bud Estep (third from left) and friends watch downtown shoppers. They are standing between Applegate's Grocery and a small automobile repair shop on the north side of Smith Street. There is a reflection in the window of a Texaco gas pump that stood in front the repair shop. Located in the back was a large rolling door to allow automobiles access to the garage. (YMPTHA.)

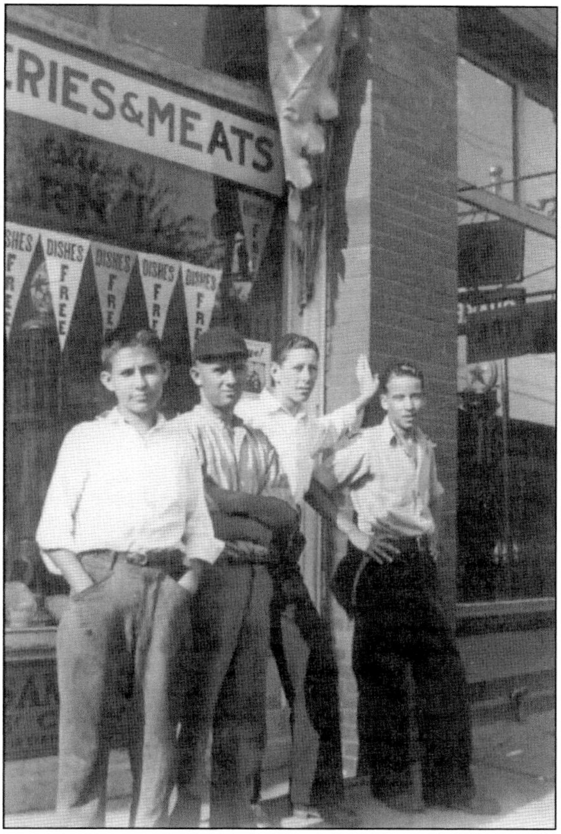

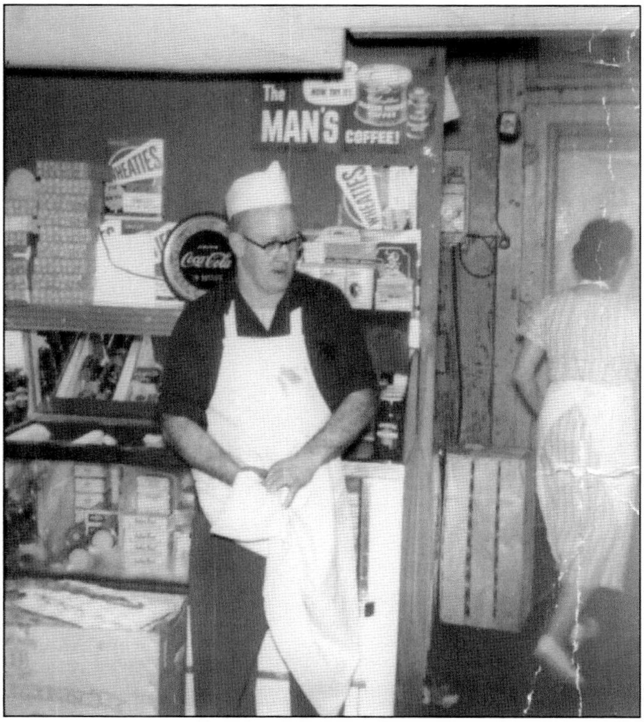

Alan Ross stands inside his original grocery store in downtown Yorktown in the early 1950s. The site had been home to both the Applegate and Linda Lee's grocery stores. Notice the advertisement in the background stating that the coffee advertised is a "Man's Coffee." (Janice Ross.)

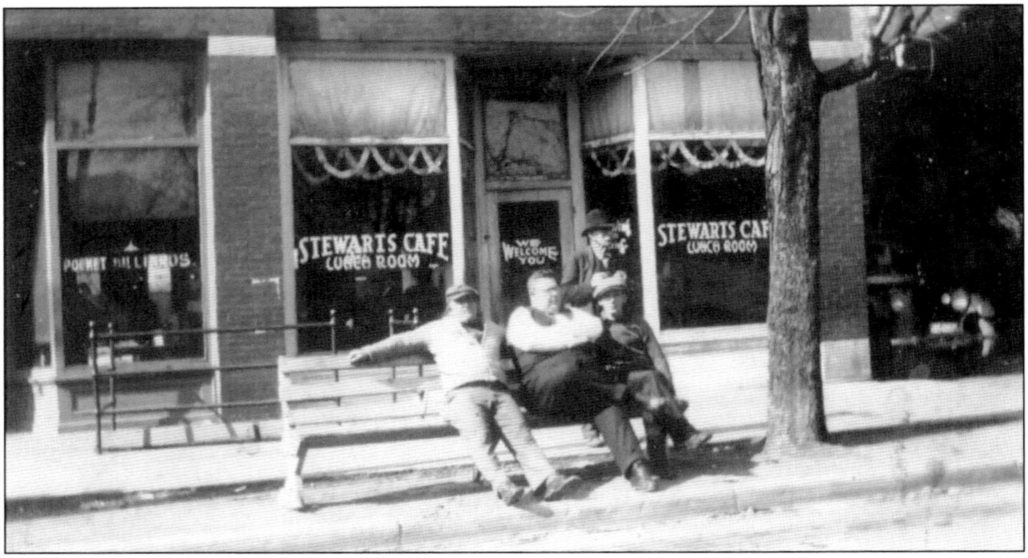

Taylor Stewart, owner of Stewart's Café, and friends are pictured here visiting outside the restaurant in the late 1920s. The iron guardrail in front of the café surrounded a stairwell that led to the basement. The basement housed other businesses and a teen center with a jukebox, card tables, and other furnishings. The exterior stairs were boarded up in the 1950s and all but forgotten. (YMPTHA.)

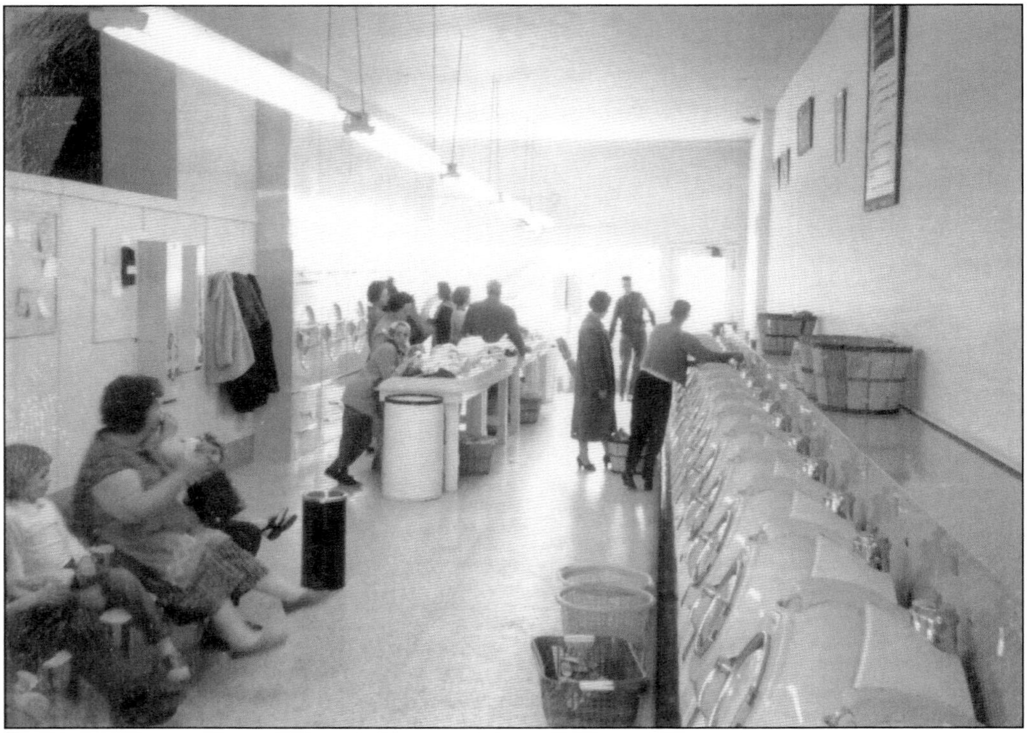
In the late 1950s and early 1960s, the Yorktown Laundry occupied the building that is currently home to the Yorktown Historical Alliance. Washing machines cost 25¢ and drying cost 10¢ for 10 minutes, giving customers plenty of time to chat. The laundry provided a place for people to socialize while catching up on the washing. (Bob Daugherty.)

The three-story building in the background was built by the Overmire family and also owned by George Parkison. Later, it became Prillaman's Hardware and Furniture Store. Over time, the building has housed a general store, hardware store, and a used-furniture store. It is currently divided into apartments. Pictured in the foreground are Clyde Neff (left) and Victor McKibben. (Janice Ross.)

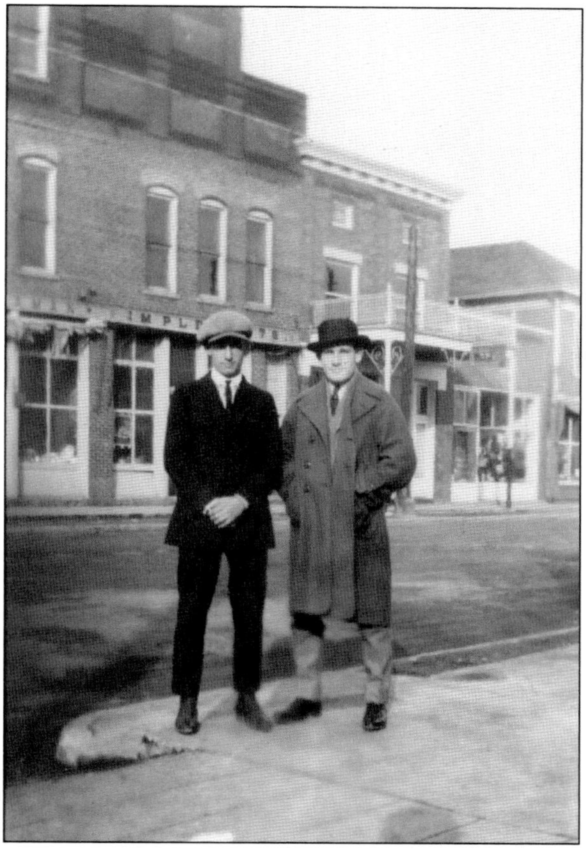

Mauck's Café sat on the north side of Smith Street and served everything from pork chops and salmon cakes to freshly baked bread from its built-in brick oven in the back of the building. This structure was home for many years to the Oasis Tavern, known around town as Gus's, and currently is the Hideout Lounge. Pictured are, from left to right, Stella Rush, Joe Mauck, and Jane Stewart (YMPTHA.)

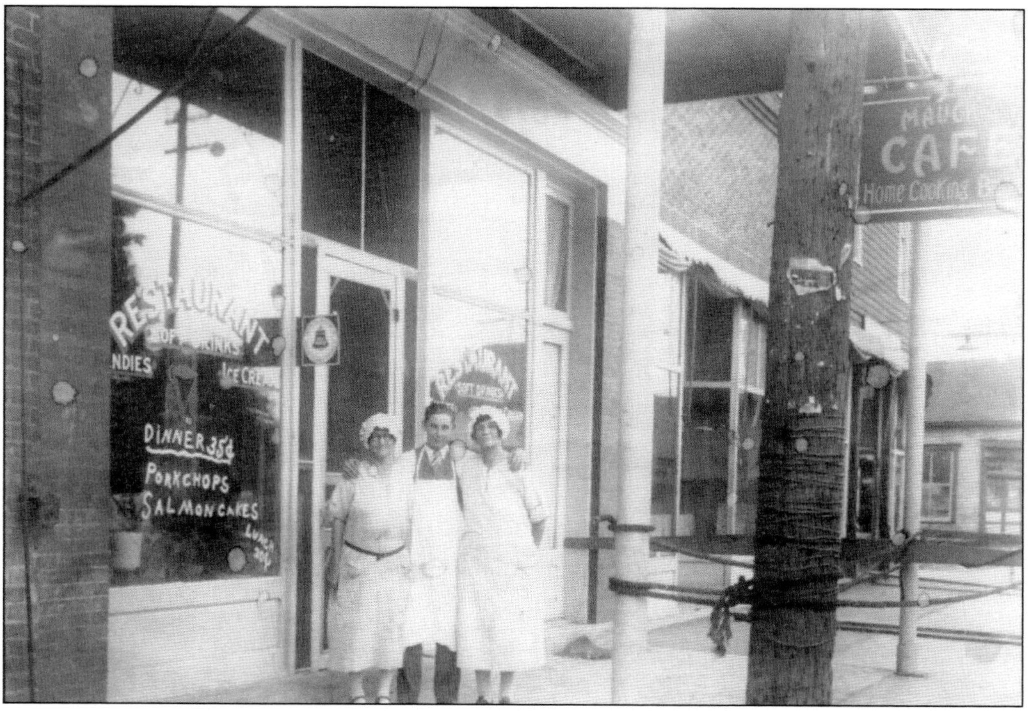

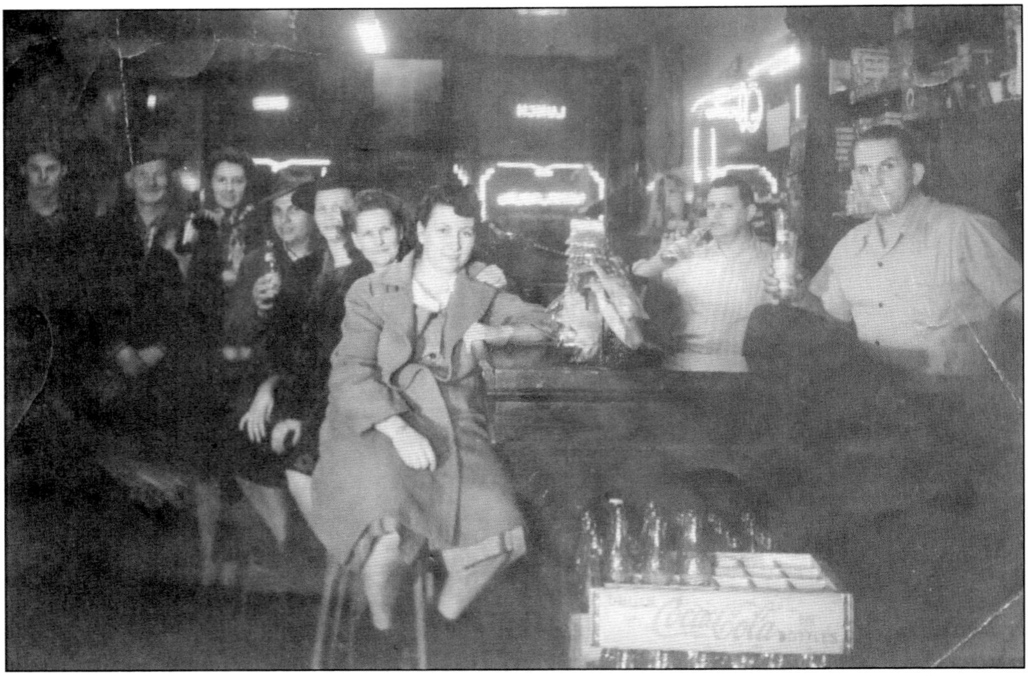

The Oasis Tavern was a popular lunch place for Yorktown residents. Better remembered as Gus's, the tavern served hamburgers that locals still fondly remember, often referred to as "the best thing they'd ever eaten." It was run by brothers Gus and Leo Donovan. Gus (right) and John Belcher (second from right) are shown here with several members of the Donovan family. The Hideout Lounge and Grill now occupies that lot. (YMPTHA.)

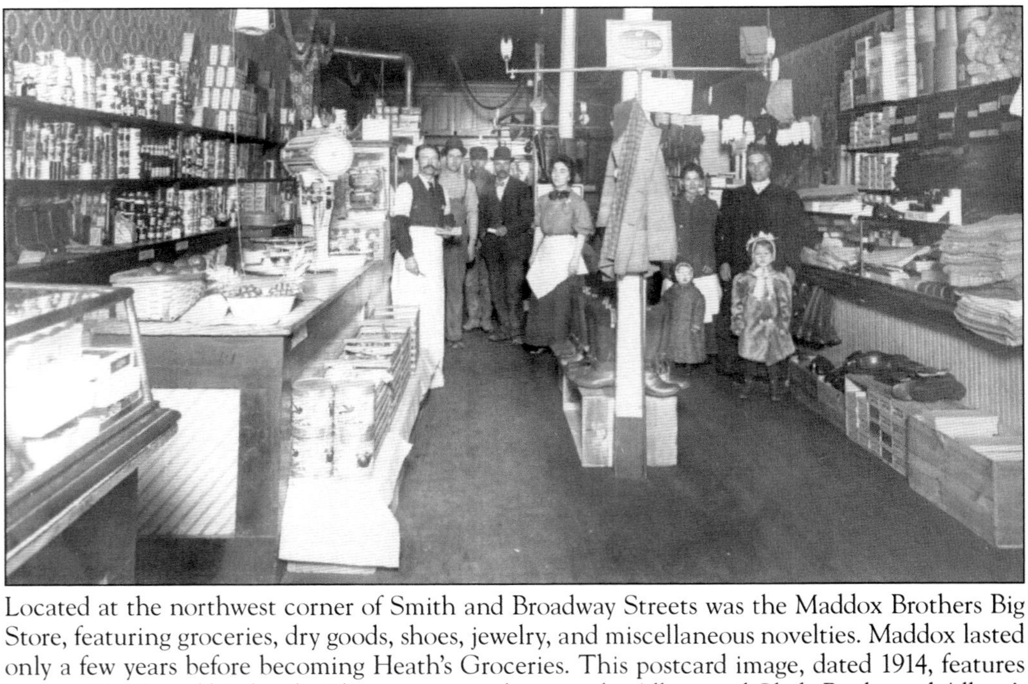

Located at the northwest corner of Smith and Broadway Streets was the Maddox Brothers Big Store, featuring groceries, dry goods, shoes, jewelry, and miscellaneous novelties. Maddox lasted only a few years before becoming Heath's Groceries. This postcard image, dated 1914, features Merritt Heath and his family. The grocery was later run by Albert and Clyde Boyle, and Albert's family lived in the upper level. (Sue Burger.)

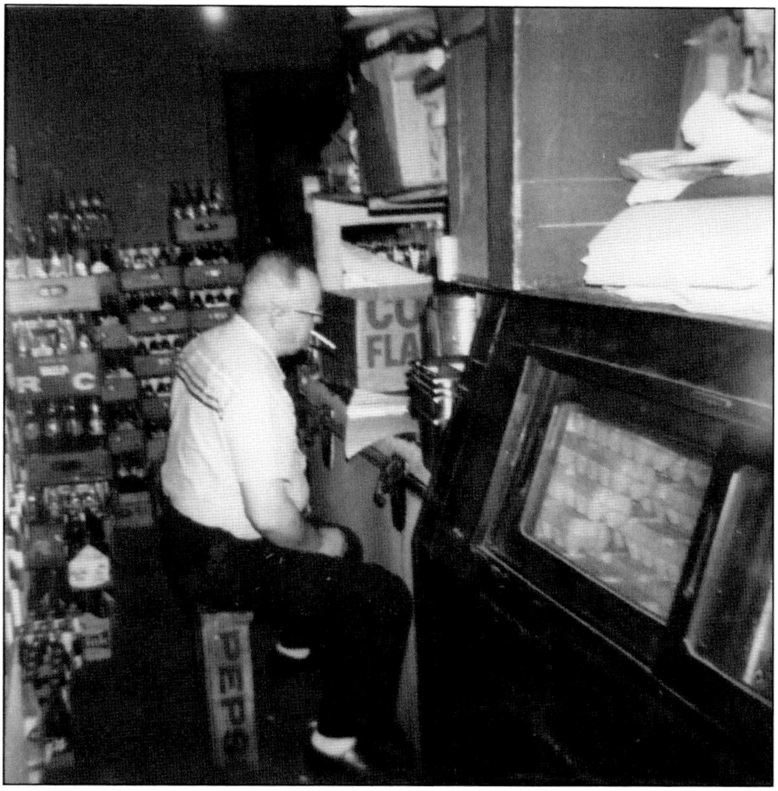

In 1967, Ralph McShurley, owner of one of the downtown grocery stores, uses a Pepsi case as a stool while he sits behind the meat counter reading the newspaper and smoking. This store still stands at the northwest corner of Smith and Broadway Streets and has been a grocery, a bakery, an antique shop, and many others. Ralph was known for giving newlyweds their first week's supply of groceries. (Marcelle Hatton.)

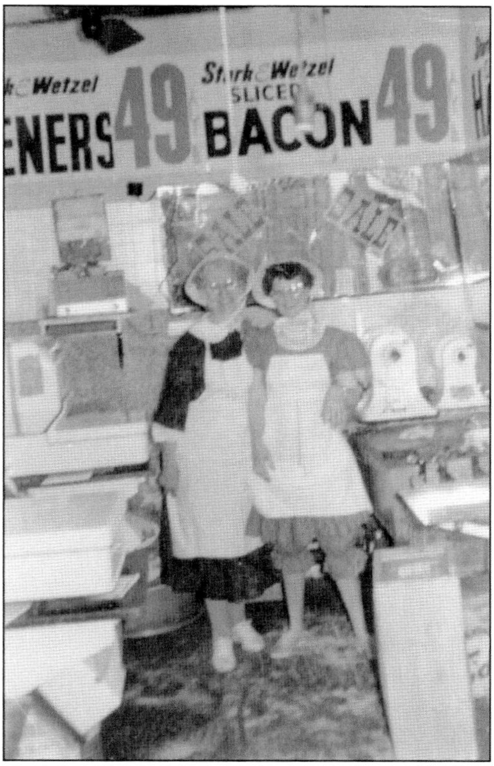

Florence Cross (left) and Marcelle Hatton are dressed as pioneers and ready to celebrate Yorktown's Old Fashioned Days at Ralph's Market in 1967. Notice the price of hot dogs and bacon. Most of the meat was cut to order, and young children were always offered a hot dog. (Marcel Hatton.)

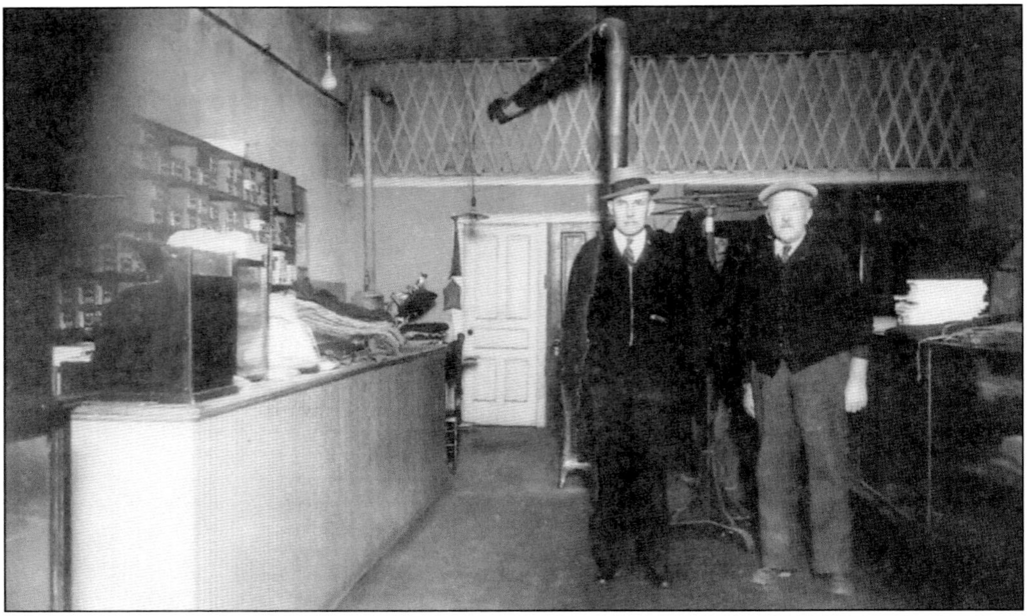

Brothers Harry and Marvin Case are shown inside their clothing and variety store. This business occupied the space that currently serves as a family dining area for the Hideout Lounge, and for many years it was occupied by the Wilhoit family. Wilhoit's featured Firestone brand items and specialized in the sale and repair of radios and televisions. (YMPTHA.)

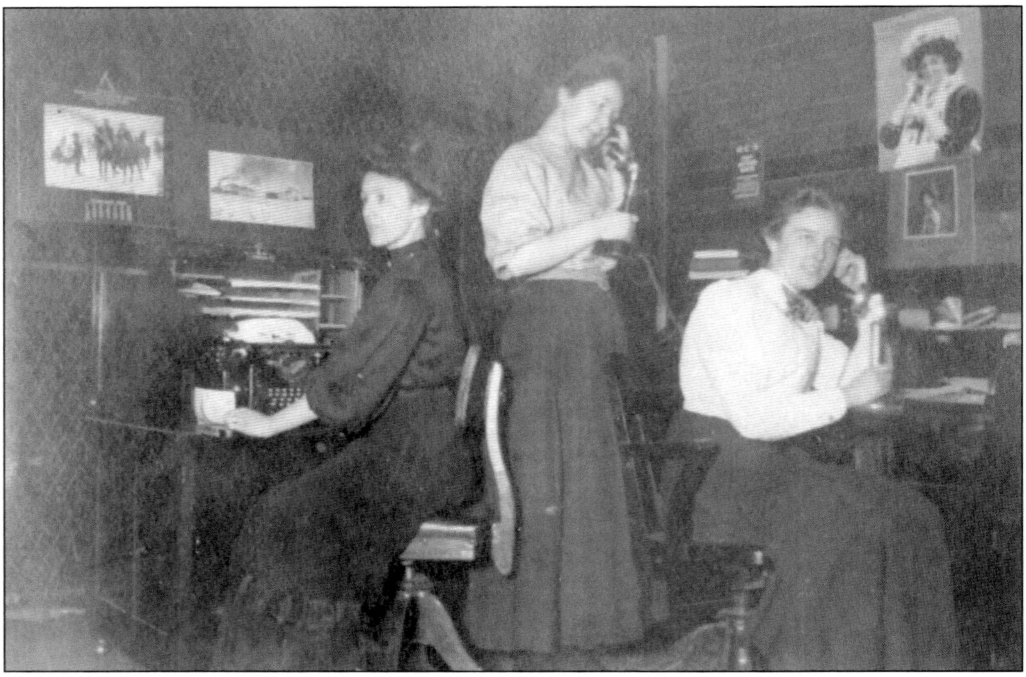

The early telephone exchange was located inside the interurban office. Here, the women not only handled the switchboard, but they also addressed the needs of the interurban customers by selling tickets and managing the shipping. Ruth Dickerson is featured in the center of this c. 1910 photograph. The other operators are unidentified. Later, the telephone exchange was moved to a small house at the intersection of Market and Canal Streets. (Shirley Pearson.)

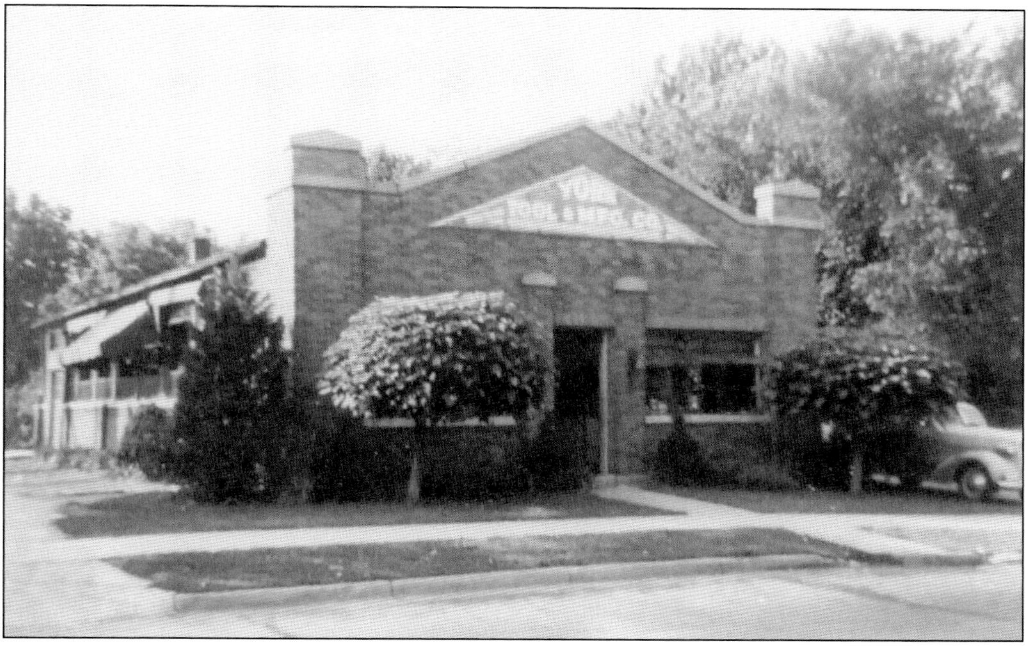

York Tool and Manufacturing served Yorktown residents for decades. Founded by Howard Warfel in 1920, the company specialized in punches, dies, gauges, and the like. In 1947, the business was bought by Howard Gregory, who changed the name in 1957 to Yorktown Tool & Die Corporation. The large addition on the east side of the building was to accommodate a diaper-folding operation on behalf of Procter & Gamble. (YMPTHA.)

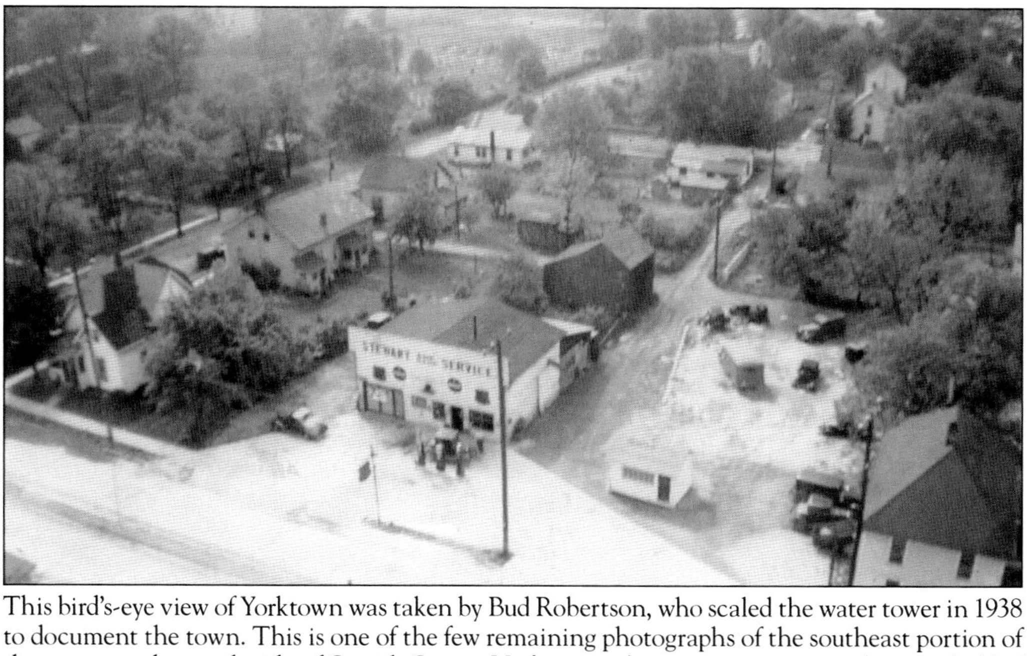

This bird's-eye view of Yorktown was taken by Bud Robertson, who scaled the water tower in 1938 to document the town. This is one of the few remaining photographs of the southeast portion of the town on the south side of Smsith Street. Unfortunately, every structure in the near half of the photograph has either burned or been torn down and replaced. (YMPTHA.)

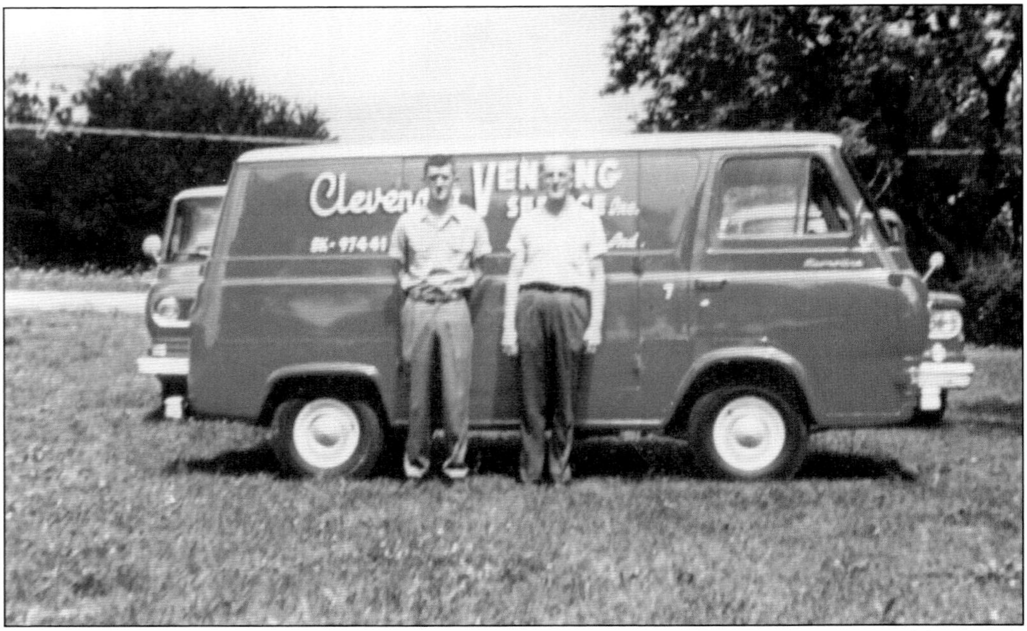

Clevenger Vending started operations in 1956 at the home of Mark Clevenger. Pictured here with Mark (right) is his son Don. From their home base, they relocated to a warehouse at the corner of Elm and Smith Streets. After outgrowing this building, they moved to Canal Street and finally settled just south of the railroad and west of Broadway. Clevenger's remained a family-operated business until it closed in 2007. (Susan Clevenger.)

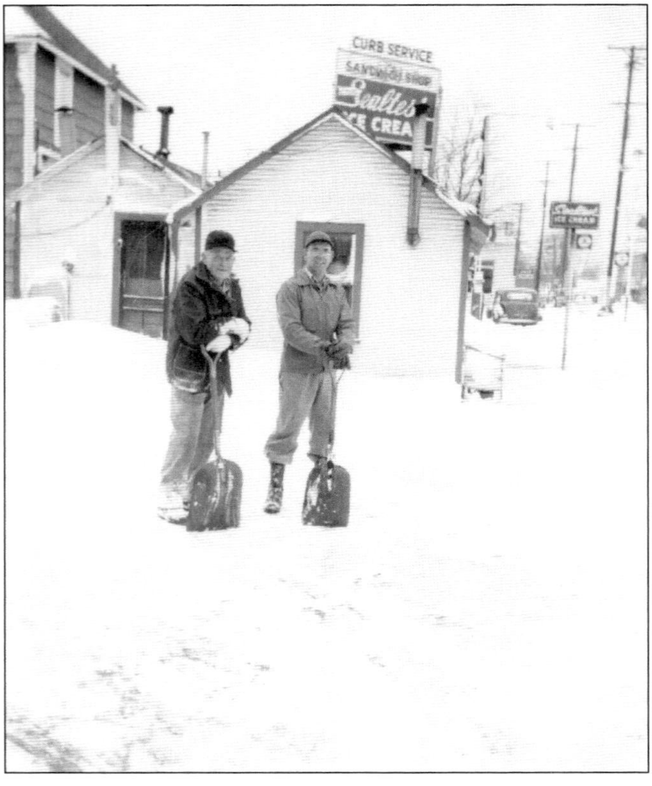

Fred Payne (left) and Tom Lennis are pictured here shoveling snow from the parking lot in front of the Standard Station that sat along Smith Street just west of Elm Street. Fred was the owner and operator during this era. Taylor Stewart and Carl Ogle were also owners of this business. The smaller buildings behind Tom and Fred are a restaurant and, beyond that, another service station. (Lois Henderson.)

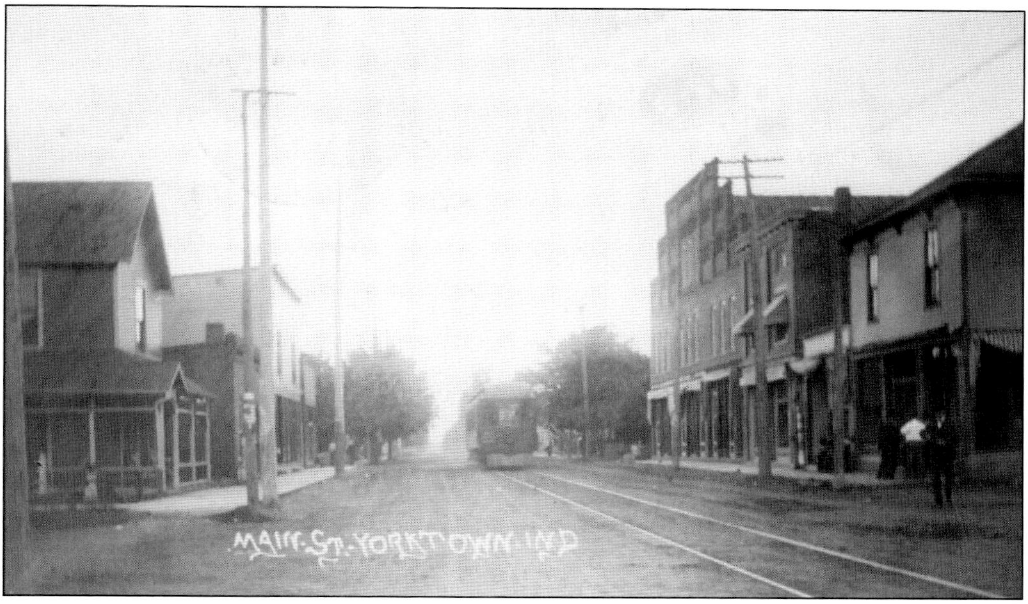

Sometime prior to 1938, the house pictured in the lower left of this photograph at Broadway and Smith Streets was purchased by Elmer and Lillian Ellis and moved to Cornbread Road, where it remains today. This home served the Ellis family until Elmer and Lillian passed away. After the house was moved, the ever-popular Dickie Mouse was built at this corner; it is now known as Mr. Mouse. (YMPTHA.)

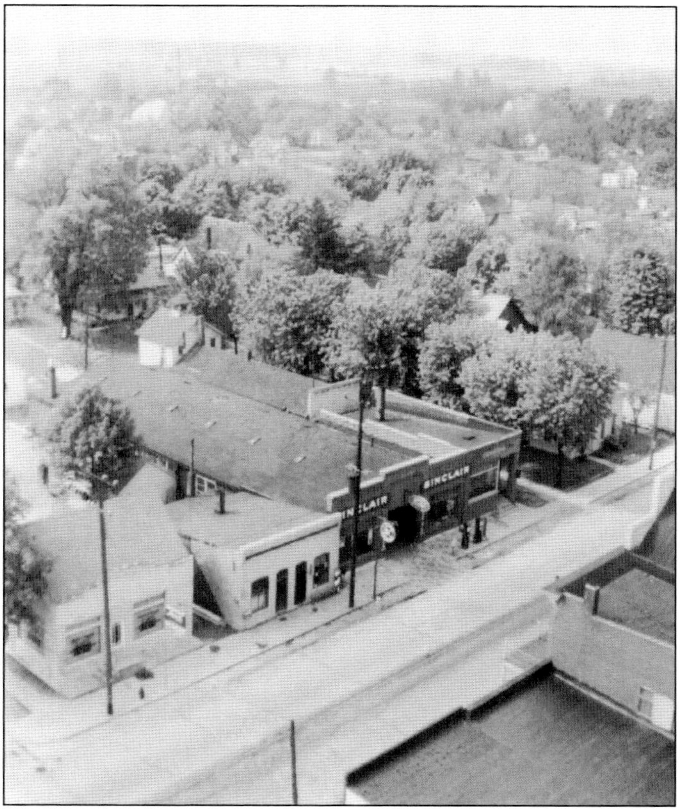

This c. 1938 photograph shows the Dickie Mouse on the corner. The large brick building in the center of the photograph is a Ford Auto Agency that also offered Sinclair Gas. The Yorktown Bank is next door, and behind the bank are a Duck Pin Alley and what was at one time a barbershop. The small building at the corner of the alley with the bell tower is the original fire station. (YMPTHA.)

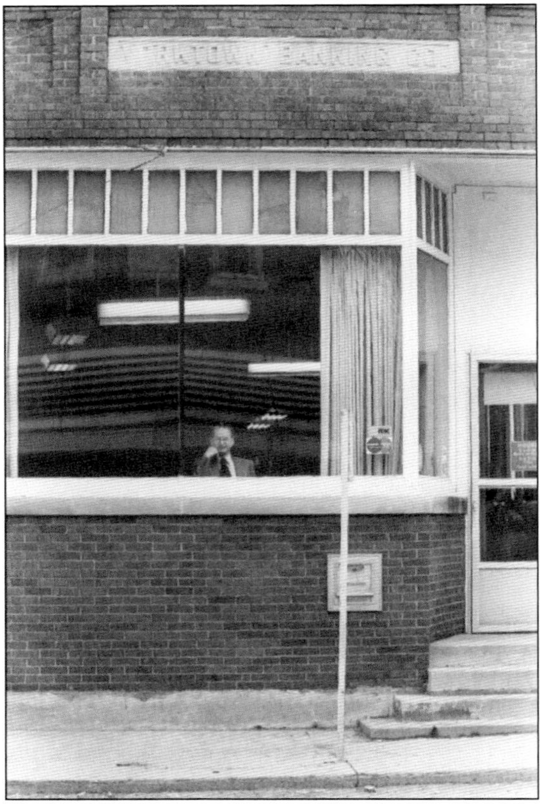

Yorktown Bank was started in 1908 and continued under this name until purchased by Industrial Trust. From that time forward, there have been several other bank mergers. Eventually, the business outgrew this building and a more modern facility was erected in the next block to the west. Here, Eddie Richcreek is looking out the front window. (Ronald Richcreek.)

Barber Wes Kidd is giving a haircut to Samuel Miller. Minnie Donovan (third from left) and a Mr. Pitzer are awaiting their turns or maybe just talking over the events of the day. This shop was located on the south side of Smith Street behind the Yorktown Bank. (YMPTHA.)

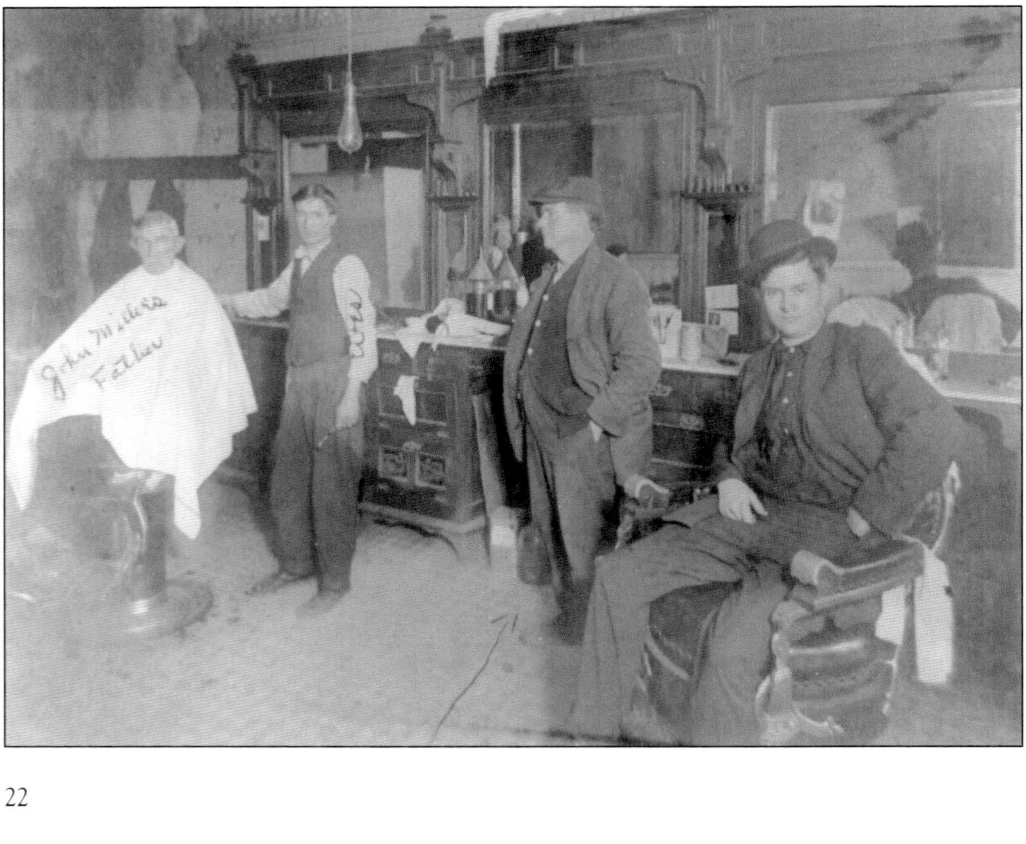

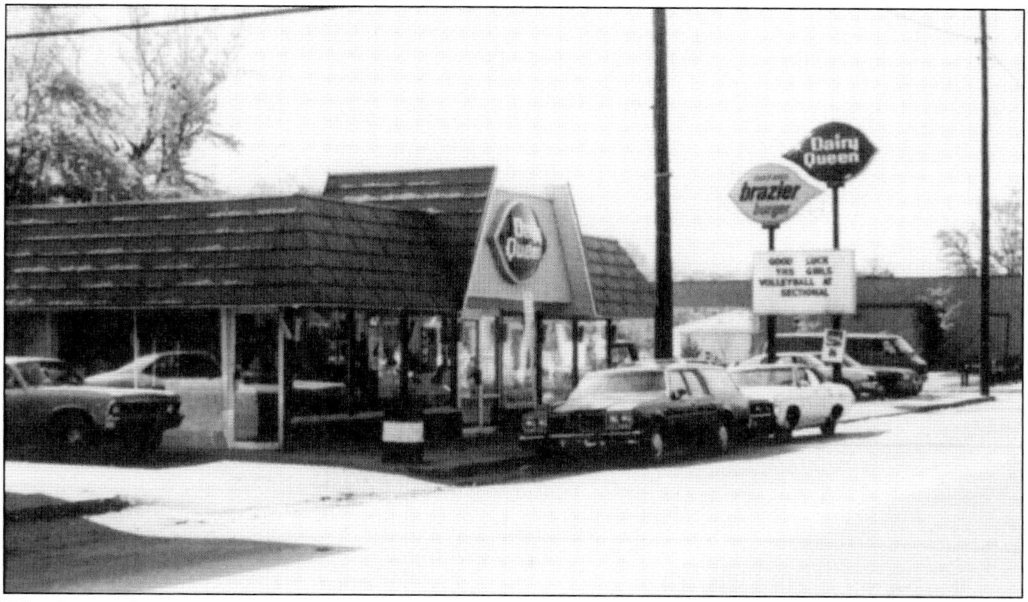

The Dairy Queen in Yorktown was in business for over 50 years. Originally, it was just a walk-up counter, but by 1965 an addition was added to the west of the building and added seating. However, it closed its doors in the early 2000s, and the building is now home to El Rancho Poblano Mexican Restaurant. (YMPTHA.)

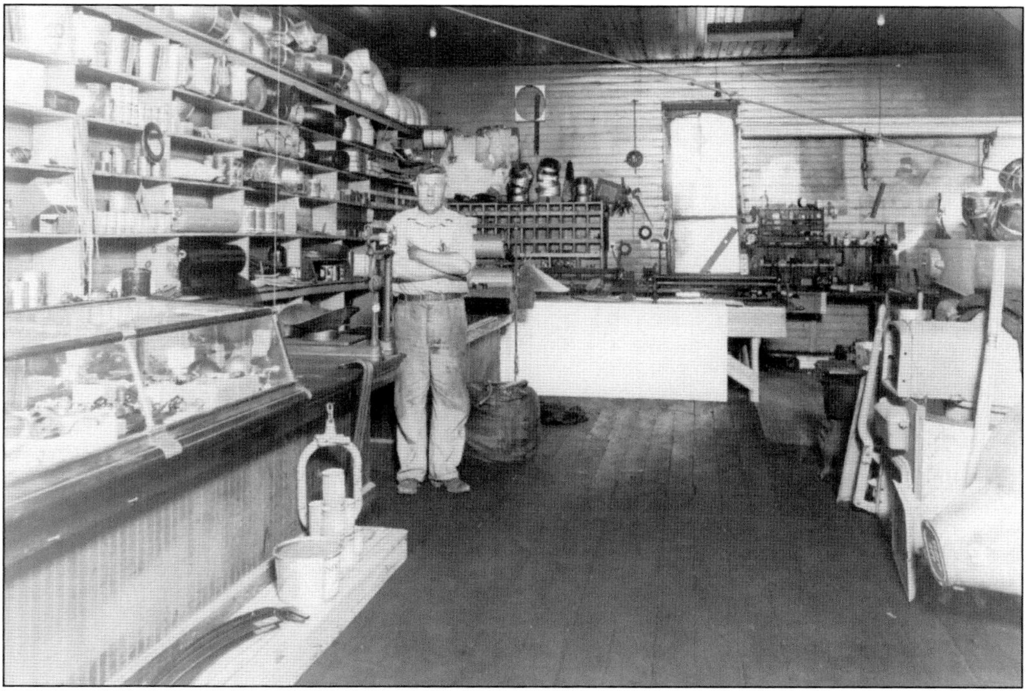

The original Child's Hardware sat on the south side of Smith Street, selling tools, farm equipment, and other necessities needed to function in a small town. Carl Childs was the proprietor for years before passing the store to his son Enoch Childs and moving to a new location across Smith Street. Carl is pictured here inside the original store around 1935; it appears to be well stocked with inventory. (Sheila Sheward.)

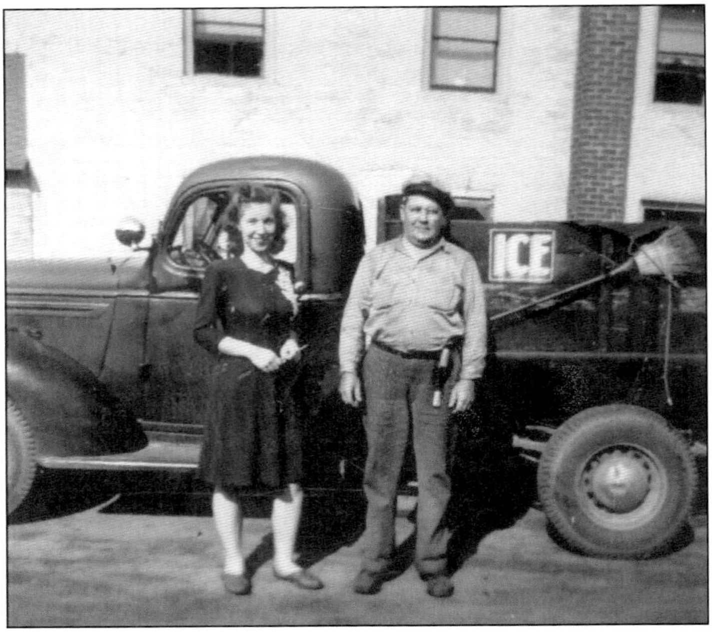

In 1945, Evelyn Warfel and her stepdad, Arthur "Duffy" Donovan, show off their delivery truck. Donovan's Ice started in a home on Market Street and later moved to Depot Street, where a larger building provided more storage. Customers placed their "ice cards" in their windows to tell Duffy how much ice they needed. He wore a piece of leather over the shoulder to protect his skin from the constant cold. (Evelyn Morrow.)

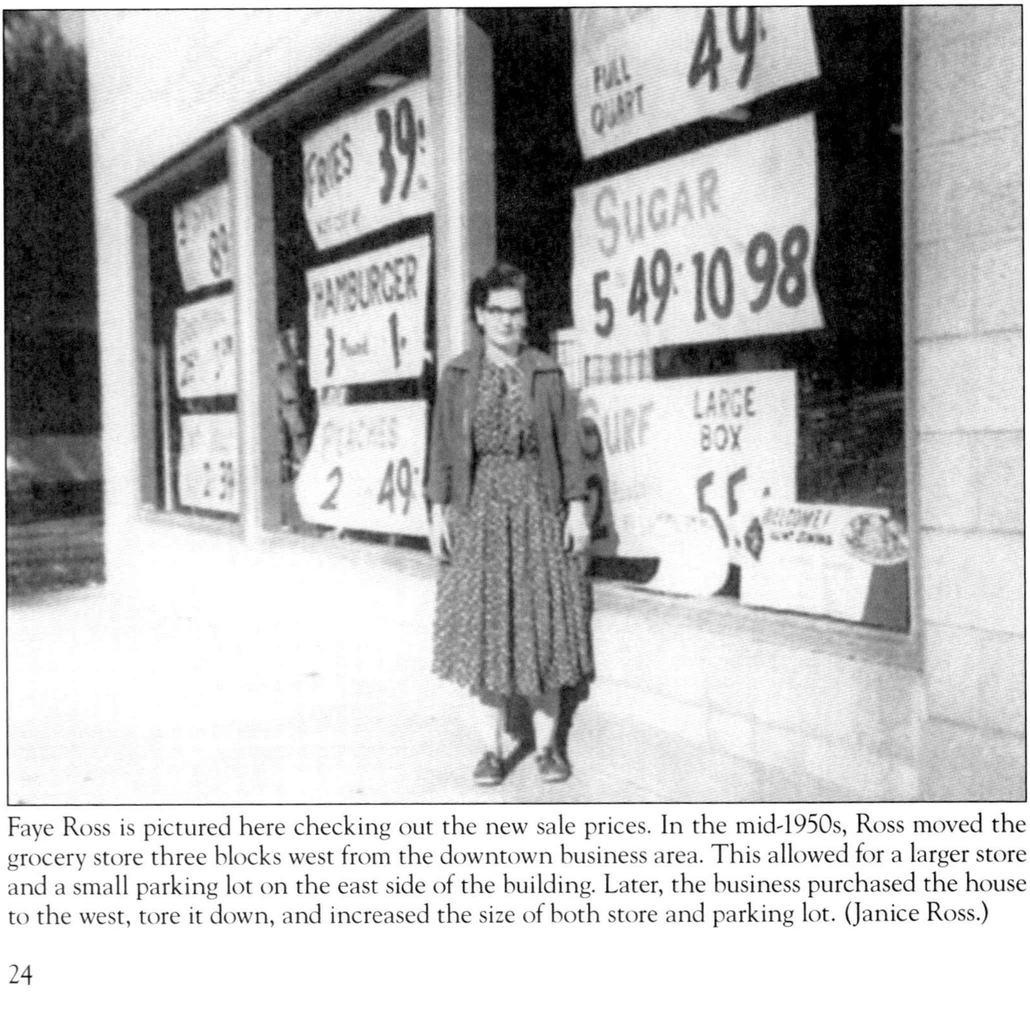

Faye Ross is pictured here checking out the new sale prices. In the mid-1950s, Ross moved the grocery store three blocks west from the downtown business area. This allowed for a larger store and a small parking lot on the east side of the building. Later, the business purchased the house to the west, tore it down, and increased the size of both store and parking lot. (Janice Ross.)

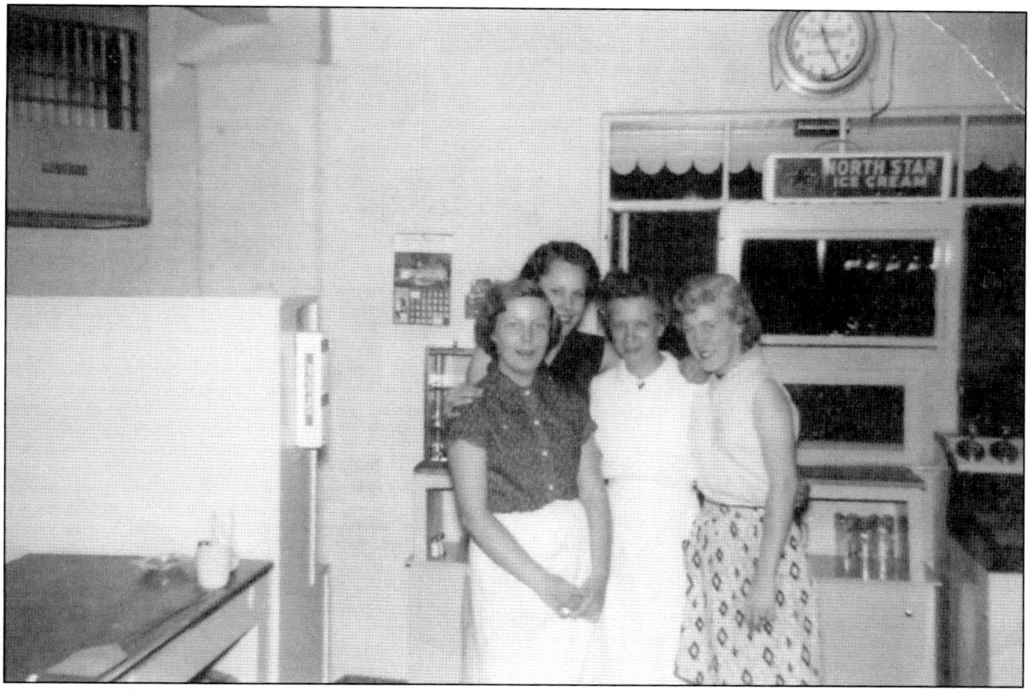

In 1949, Delray McKinley constructed a small brick building at the corner of Smith and Plum Streets. It was intended to be a variety store but soon converted to Delray's Diner, featuring home-cooked meals as well as the normal selection of sandwiches and french fries. Pictured are, from left to right, Linda and Marilyn Koontz, Jean McKinley, and Lavada Porter. This business changed hands frequently over the years and in the early 1960s was run by Edith Hall. One of Hall's menus featured daily specials for 85¢, which included an entrée, three sides, and drink. In 1979, Denny Monroe took over operations, running the business for eight years under the name Denny's Diner. After a leave of several years, Monroe again took over the operation and continued running Denny's Diner. (Both, Becky Monroe.)

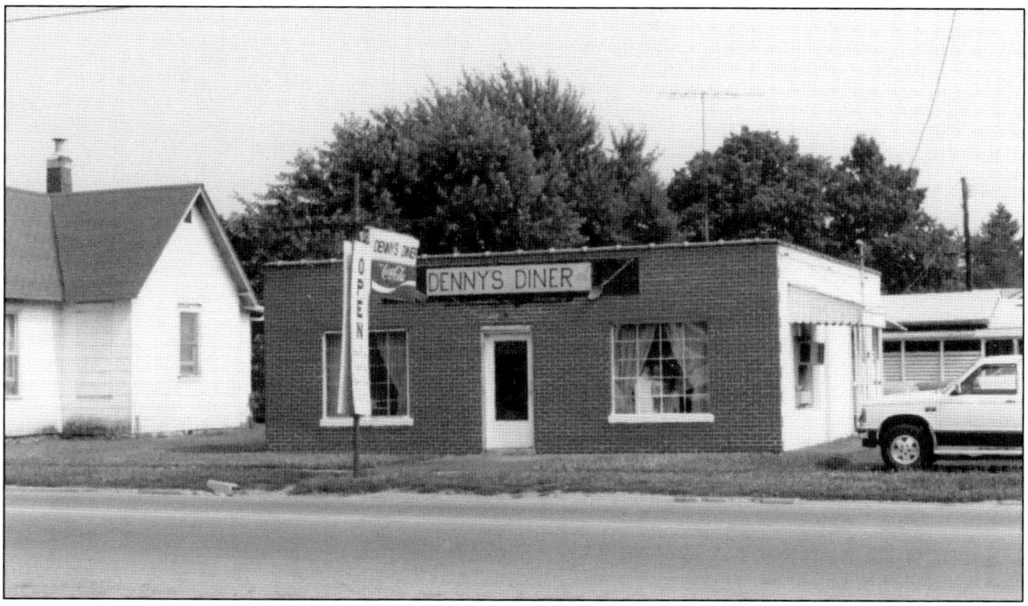

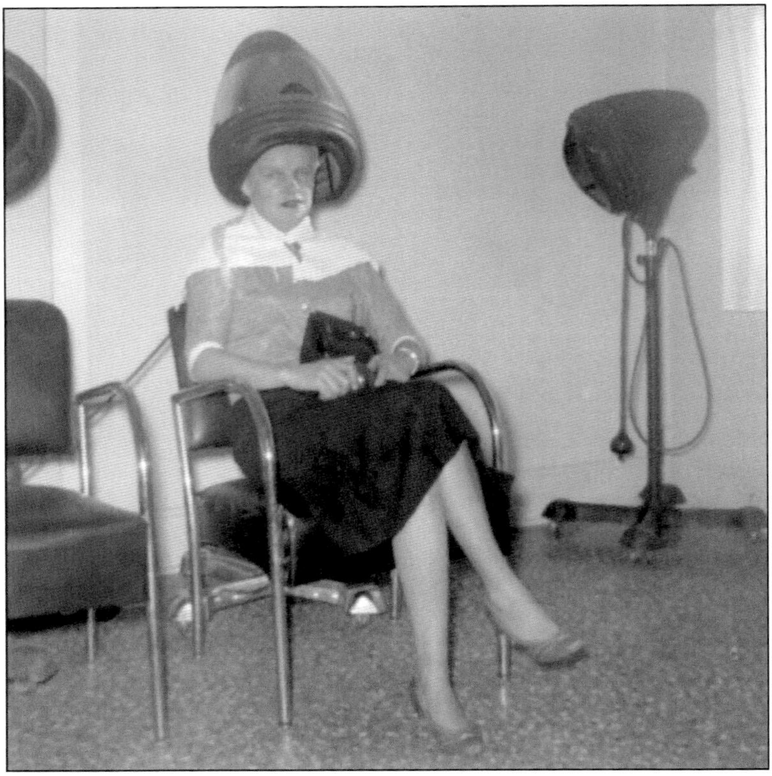

Erlene Pope and Dorthea Boyle, co-owners of Dorleen Beauty Shop on Smith Street, opened their business to patrons in 1959. The beehive-style hair dryers provided warmth and silence, making it easy for a woman to pamper herself while beautifying. Erlene takes time out to have her own hair done. (John Boyle.)

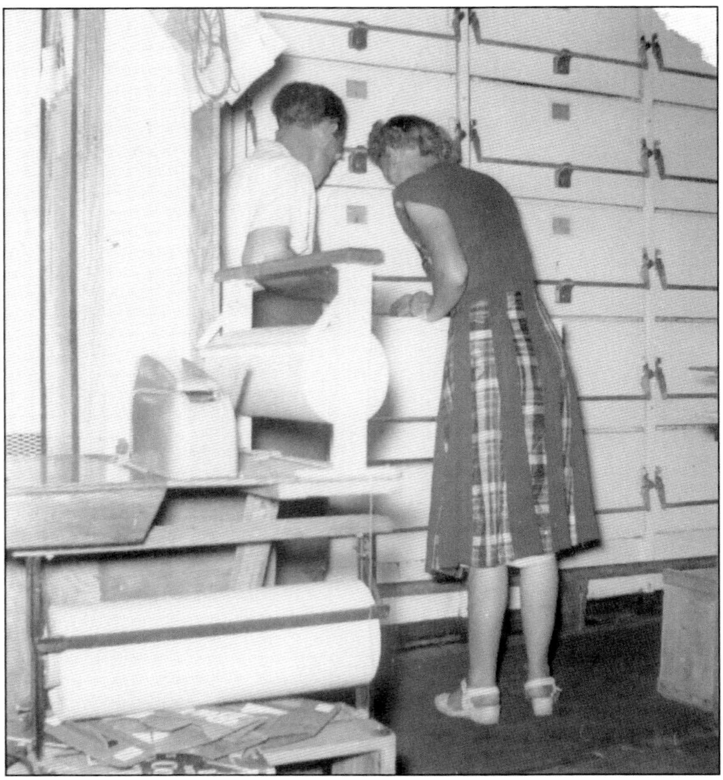

For many years, George and Maggie Newhouse owned a grocery in the downtown business area. They moved their operation to Mill Street near the railroad crossing. At the new location, the business was expanded to offer freezer lockers. This building also housed a grocery store, living quarters, and a factory where local residents could process fresh food in tin cans instead of glass jars. This photograph was made sometime around 1955. (Bea Porter estate.)

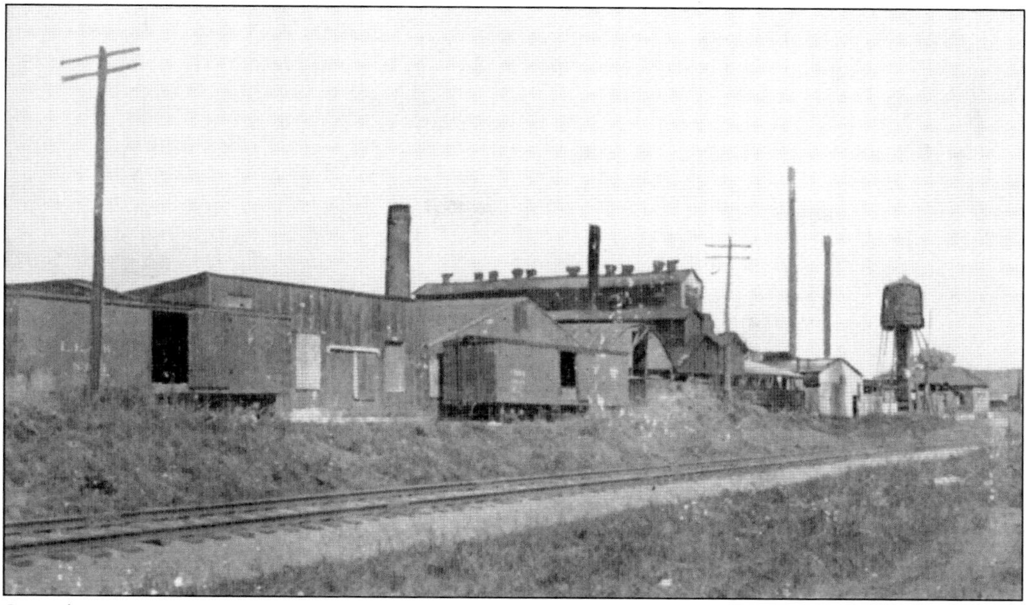

Seen here around 1915, the Skillen-Gooden Glass Factory, originally Patterson Glass Works (until 1894), was a competitor to the vast Ball Jar Company in Muncie. Despite producing several new types of jars, Skillen-Gooden's main product was bottles for drinks and medicine. In 1918, one of the glass-heating furnaces caught fire early in the morning and the entire factory burned down. (YMPTHA.)

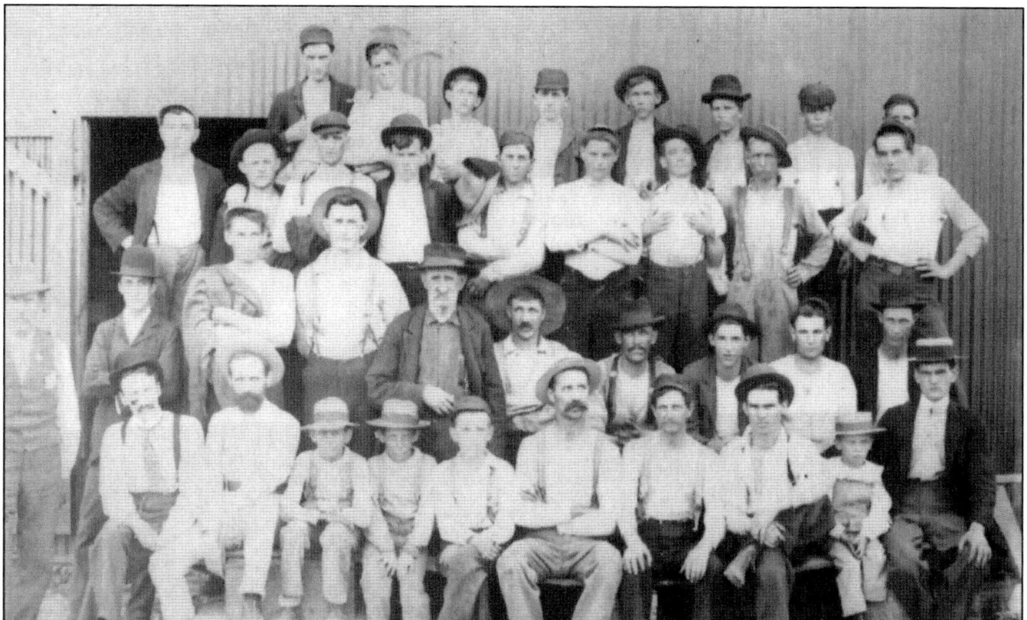

Employees of the glass factory pose in 1898 for this photograph, but only a few of the employees have been identified. On the first row are D.O. Skillen (third from the left), John Miller (fifth from left), and George Parkison (seventh from left). Earl Gooden, wearing a dark suit, is standing in the second row. (Dave Parkison.)

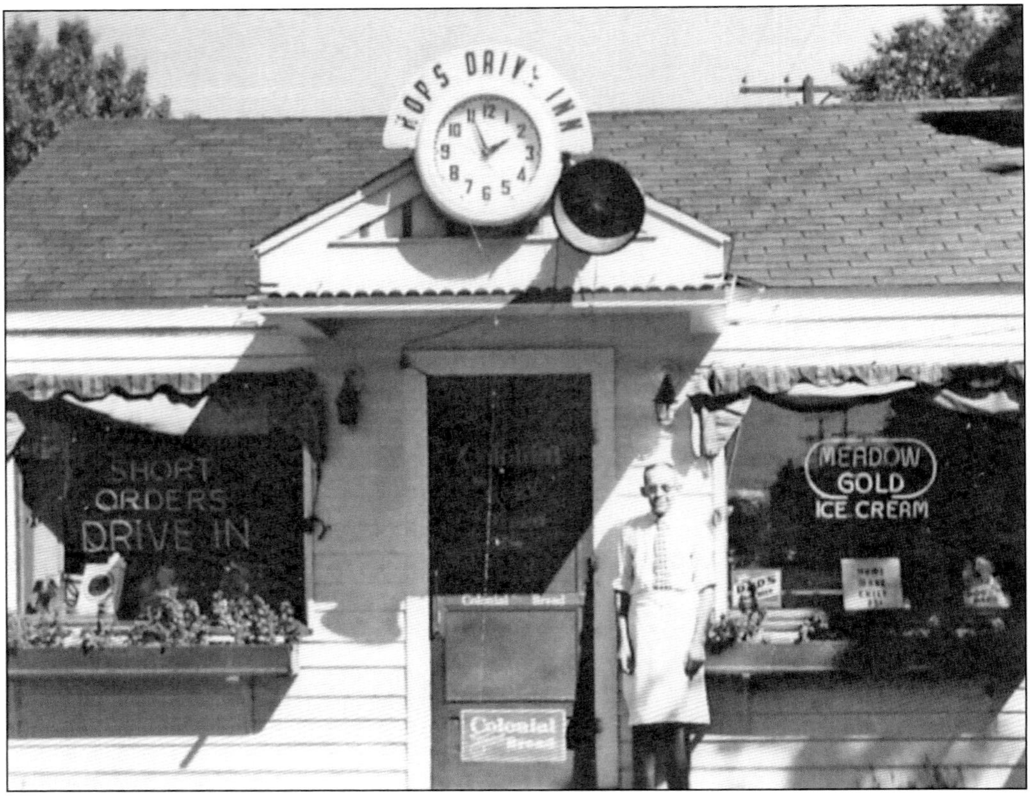

In the 1950s, Lewis Hopping ran Hop's Drive-In, located near the double bridges on the east end of town. Local teenagers loved to hang out there, eating hamburgers and drinking milk shakes or sodas after school. The drive-in later passed through the hands of several other owners before it was demolished to make way for the new bridge to be constructed over Buck Creek. (Paula Lennington.)

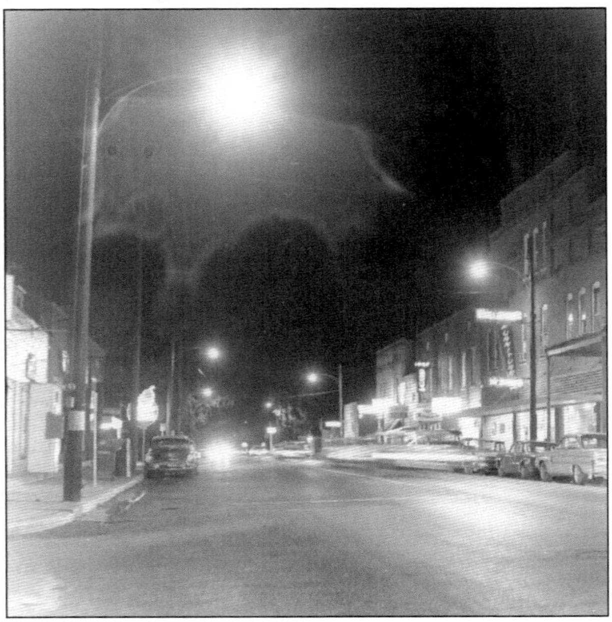

A rare nighttime view of Smith Street shows the neon signs of the businesses on the main street of Yorktown around 1965. On the left is the Dairy Queen sign with the swirled ice-cream logo, and on the right are Prillaman's Furniture and the Odd Fellows lodge. (YMPTHA.)

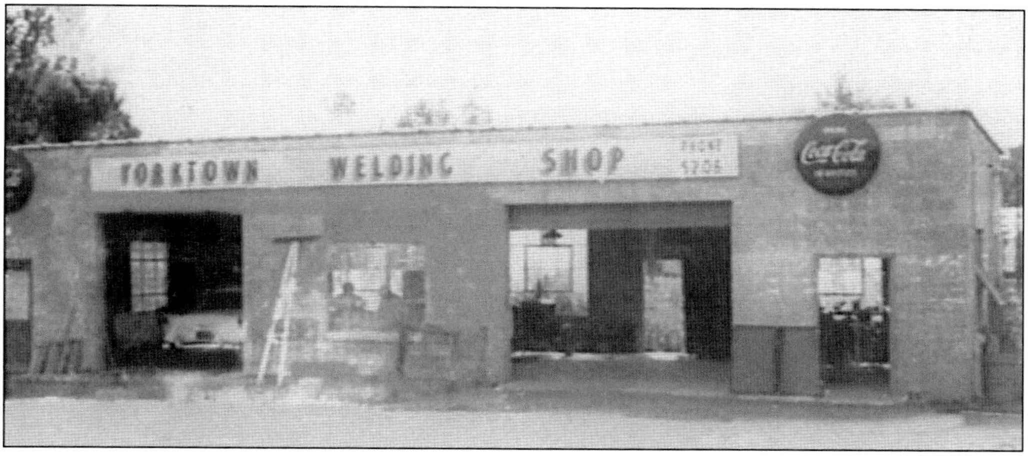

Pictured in 1956 is Cline Grimes's welding shop on Smith Street, east of Adaline. Grimes, a structural welder, worked for a union shop. In the photograph is his own welding shop, open only in the evenings and on weekends. When he could not be in town, his sons Dick and Benny ran the shop. Grimes retired and continued to work in his welding shop on automobiles and custom welding jobs. (Dick Grimes.)

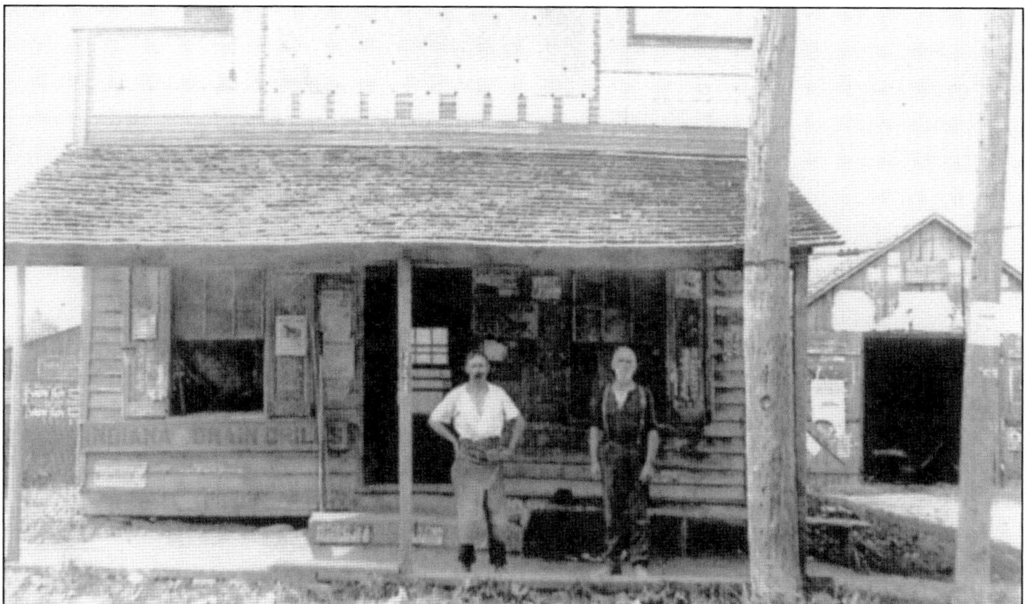

This feed store, co-owned by an Overmire and Jacob Erther, is believed to have been near the railroad and possibly close to where Mill Street crossed over the tracks. This c. 1915 photograph shows Erther and M. Lasill in front of the old building. (YMPTHA.)

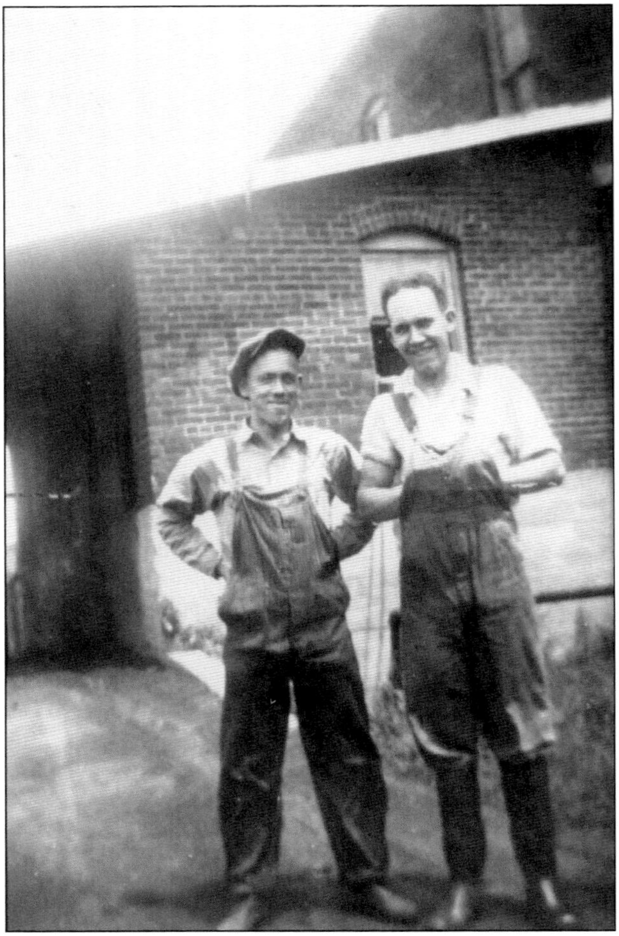

In the early 1920s, Paul Metzcar (left) and a coworker are pictured outside the Western Reserve Milk Company, located on the west end of Depot Street. Prior to the days of large tank trucks, fresh milk was picked up from local farmers in large aluminum cans. Each farmer would set the fresh milk in a cooled area, and the driver would pick it up and bring it to Western Reserve for processing. (Janice Ross.)

In the 1950s, the Marsh family's grocery business had expanded, and they were in need of warehouse facilities. In 1952, Ermal Marsh purchased the old Western Reserve plant and converted it to a warehouse. This enabled the Marsh Company to buy products in larger quantities and ship via its own trucks to its Marsh Foodliner stores. (Marsh Supermarkets.)

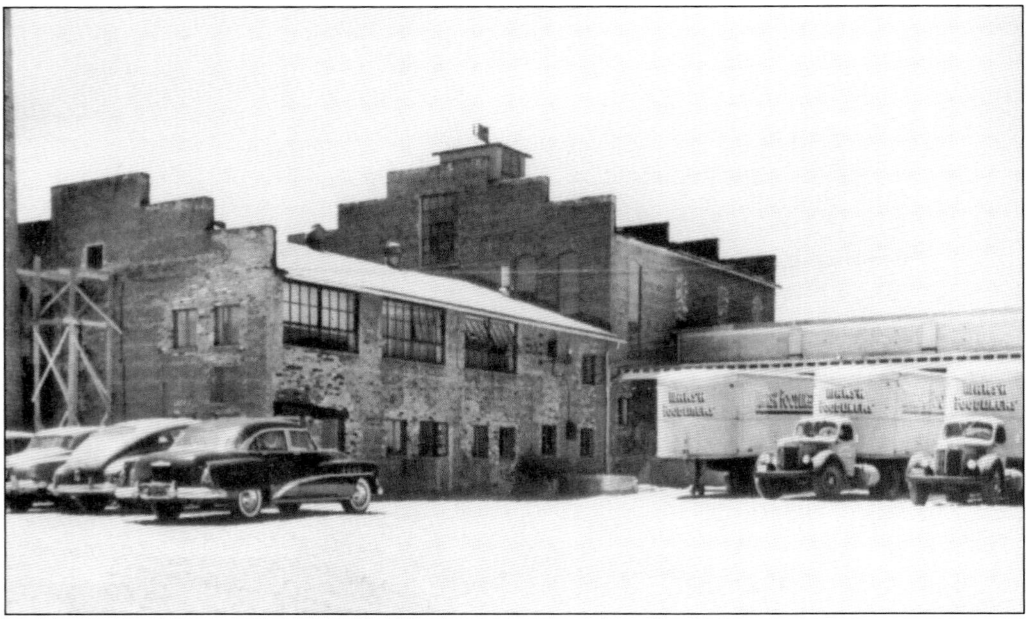

The production of Marsh ice cream began in the early 1950s in the basement of Foodliner No. 2 in Muncie. As the demand for this product grew, the operation was moved to the Yorktown facility. From here, it grew into a product that would receive national acclaim and was mentioned in industry journals, bringing in new accounts for years. Originally, the only flavor available was vanilla, but soon the company began to add chocolate, strawberry, and lemon ice cream in one-gallon containers. Below, Bob Ambrosetti, a longtime Marsh employee, is operating the highboy forklift. (Both, Marsh Supermarkets.)

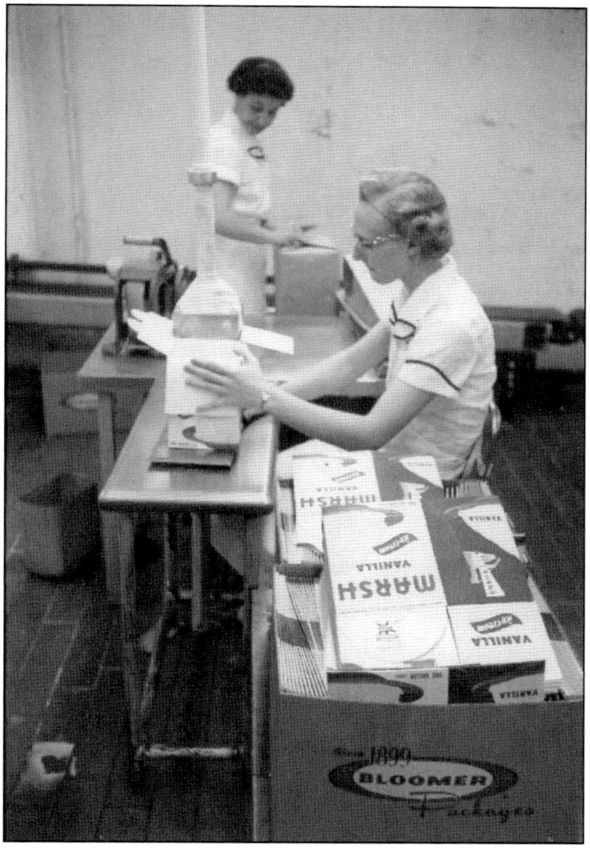

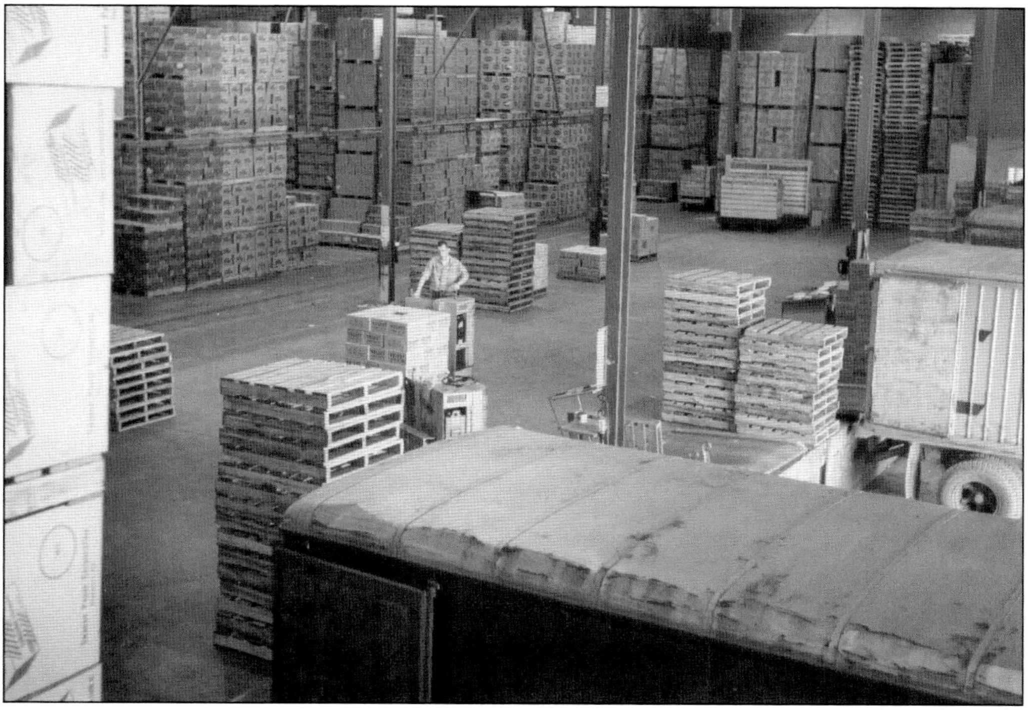

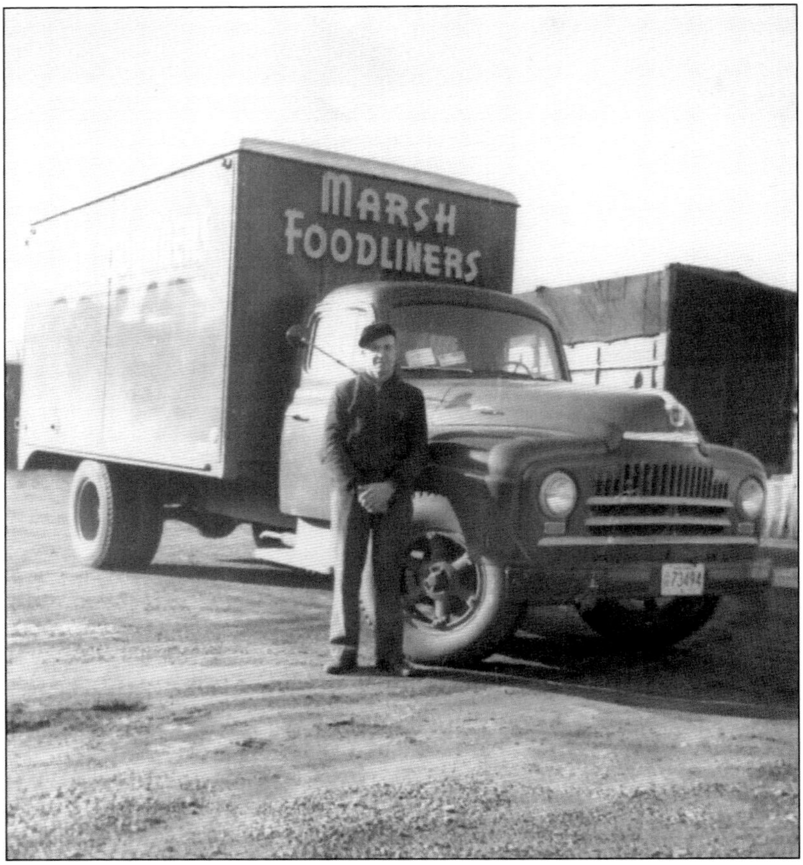

With a large warehouse, the Marsh Company expanded its truck fleet and shortly after began to further enlarge the size of its building. Dock areas were increased to three, and an indoor rail dock was added. Pictured is Jobe Clevenger standing next to some of the very early fleet. (Susan Clevenger.)

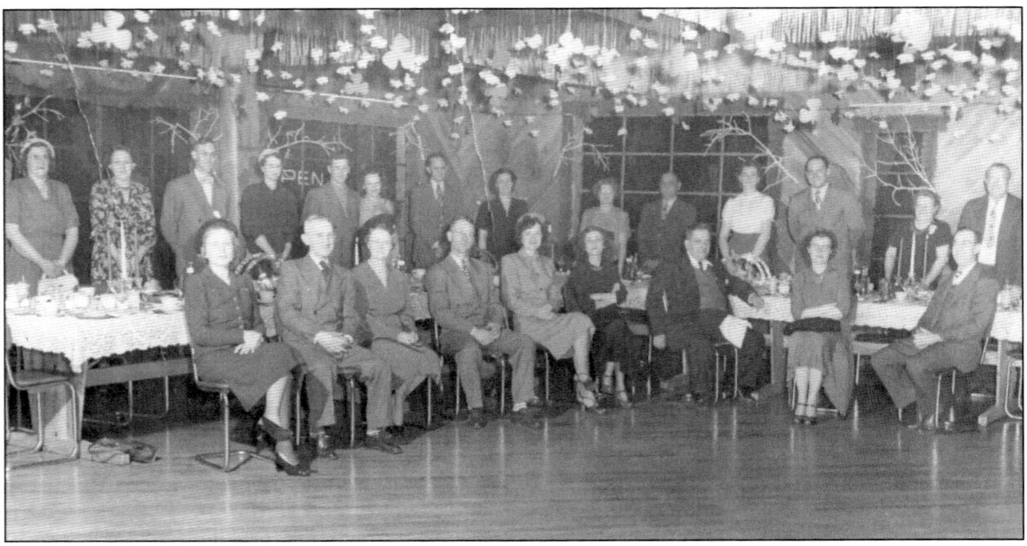

The Top Hat Restaurant, southwest of Yorktown, was originally the home of judge David Kilgore. Years later, an addition was made to the west side. The restaurant soon became a popular destination for community meetings, banquets, and dances. Here is one of the many groups that met for dinner and business meetings. In May 1974, the building caught fire and burned to the ground. (YMPTHA.)

Two

CHURCHES

The founder of Yorktown, Oliver Smith, recognized the importance of churches in the new community, so he set aside four lots for religious and educational purposes. The history of churches in Yorktown indicates there was once a Presbyterian church, but little is known about it. The Methodist Episcopal church, built in 1874, was probably the next-earliest. The following decades saw a rapid increase in the population of the town. The Methodists erected a new building in 1899 and constructed an addition in 1909. The Disciples of Christ, who shared the 1899 structure with the Methodist Episcopal congregation for a time, began their own building in 1907. Following World War I, a two-room addition was made. The Yorktown Nazarene Church formed as a group in 1926 and met in the home of John and Pearl Hodson. As the congregation grew, it met for a time in a large tent that was put up on a lot by the Yorktown Cemetery until the church began its first building in 1927. All of this growth of congregations and construction of buildings had occurred within just slightly more than half a century. In the first decade of the 21st century, within the town limits, the Old Fashion Baptist Church, formerly located in Muncie, purchased the Yorktown Christian Church and held services there. A new Yorktown Christian Church was built outside the original town limits. A new addition has already been built.

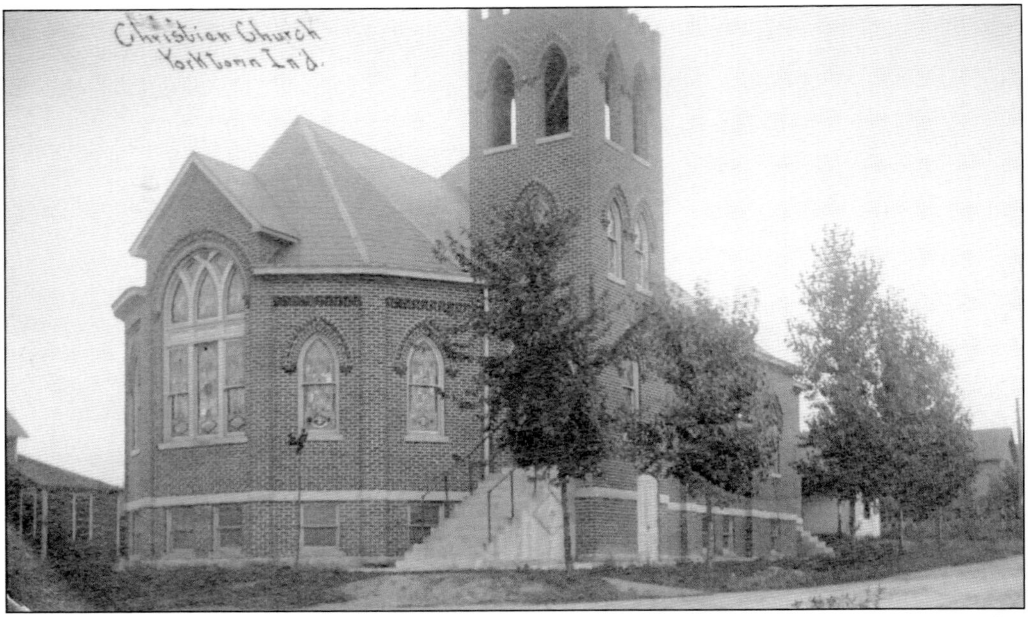

After sharing the Yorktown Methodist Episcopal Church building for several years, a separate structure for the Disciples of Christ was needed. In 1907, work began on a new building for the Yorktown Christian Church, and it was dedicated on April 18, 1909. In 1911, following a period of rapid growth, the church was able to pay off and burn the mortgage. During World War I, two rooms were added. (YMPTHA.)

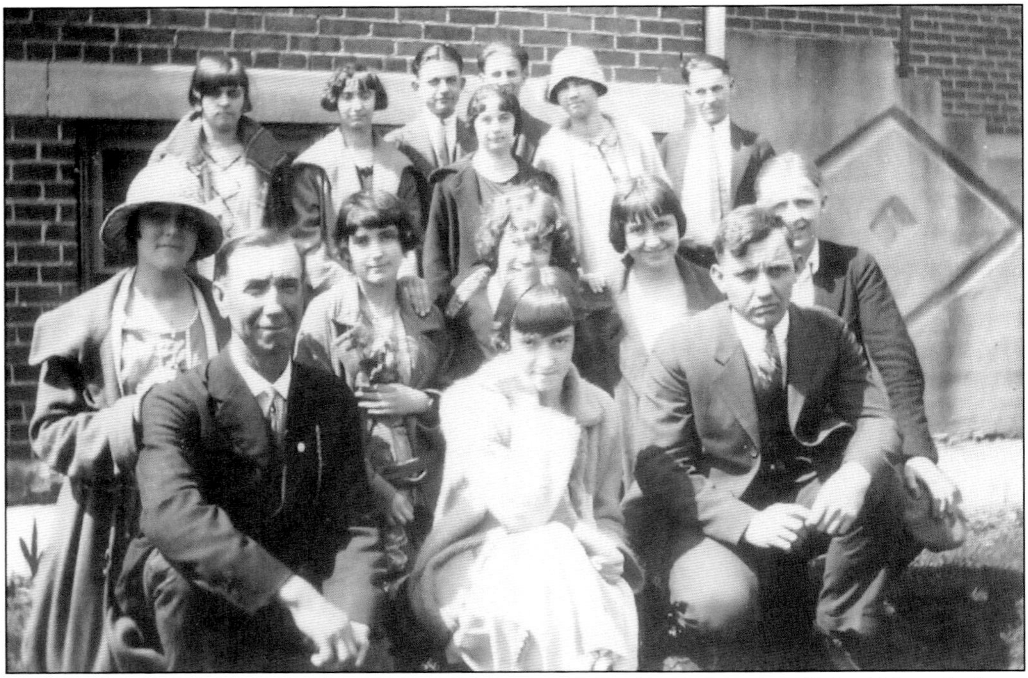

Pictured here around 1925 are members of the Christian Church Booster Club. Although there are several people in the photograph, only a few of them are named. In no particular order are P.J. Kautzman (trustee), Joneita Metzcar Downham, Glen ?, Faye Neff Ross, Ruth Gustin, Mary Snyder, Helen Brown, and Evelyn Miller. (YMPTHA.)

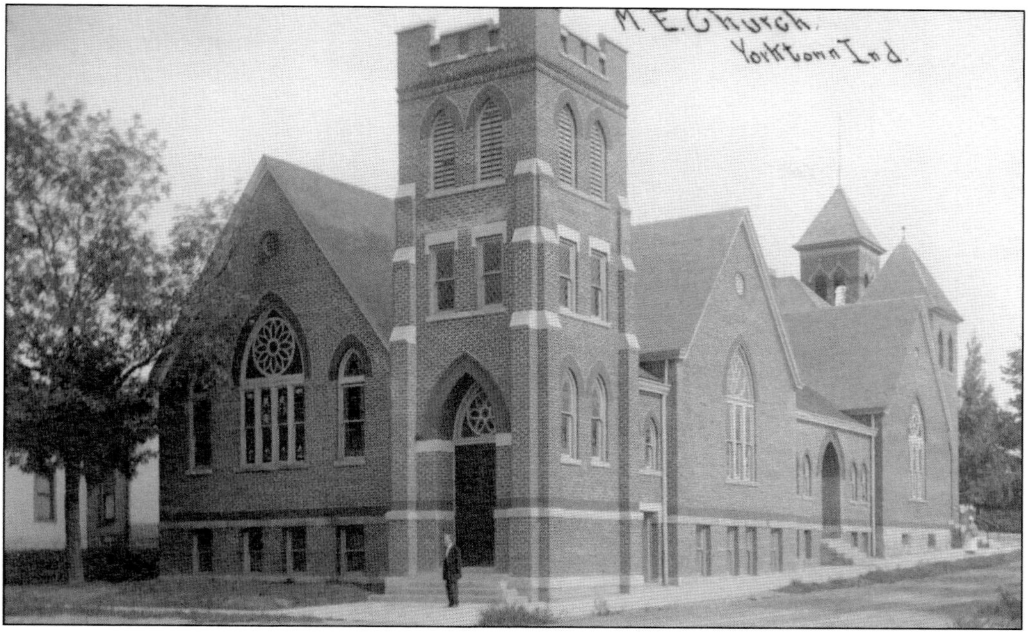

In 1874, David Sommers bought a lot on the southeast corner of High and Walnut Streets at a tax sale and sold it to the Methodists. In 1875, the contract for the new church building was written by trustees W.K. Helvie, James Burgess, Samuel Parkison, Joshua Dickover, and David Campbell. As Yorktown continued to grow, a new church was needed, and the building was completed in 1899. By 1909, more growth led to a new addition, which included a basement gymnasium and basketball court. (Both, YMPTHA.)

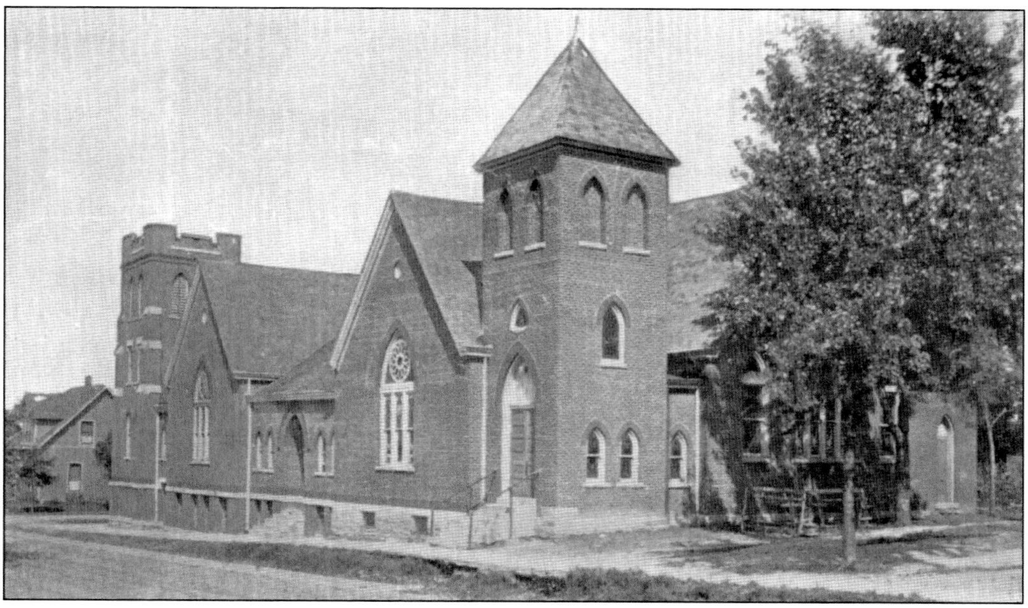

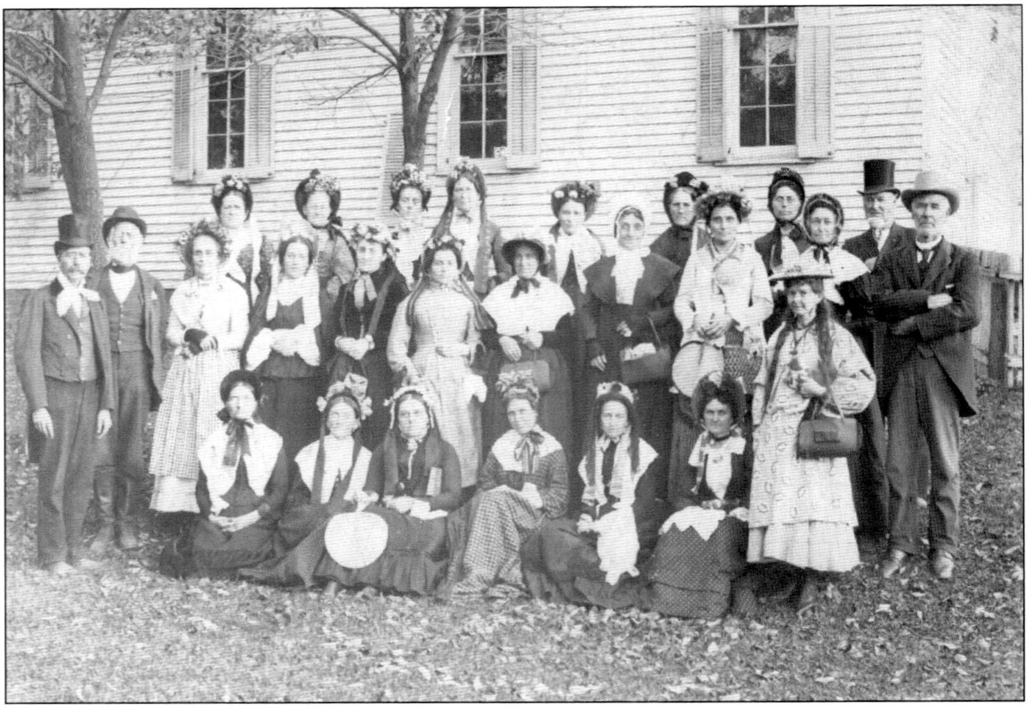

Pictured above around 1900 are men and women of the Yorktown Methodist Episcopal Church in front of the old frame building. They are, from left to right, (first row) ? McNary, ? Hohn, ? Warren, Belle Overmire, Louisa Donovan, Elizabeth Overmire, and Mame Warfel; (second row) Adam Warfel, L.W. Calvin, Mary Ann Marker, Kate Parkison, Dora Warfel, Emma Overmire, Ida Baum, Mary Williamson, Mattie Warfel, Mattie Flowers, and Harvey Koontz; and, in no particular order, (third row) ? Warfel, Daisy Calvin, Melissa Helvie, Mant Warfel, Susan Crouch, Elizabeth Matthe, William K. Helvie, and unidentified. Below is a group of men pictured on the front stairway of the Yorktown Methodist Episcopal Church in the 1920s. Those identified are in the back row: Elmer Ellis (far left) and J. Emil Sears (far right). (Both, YMPTHA.)

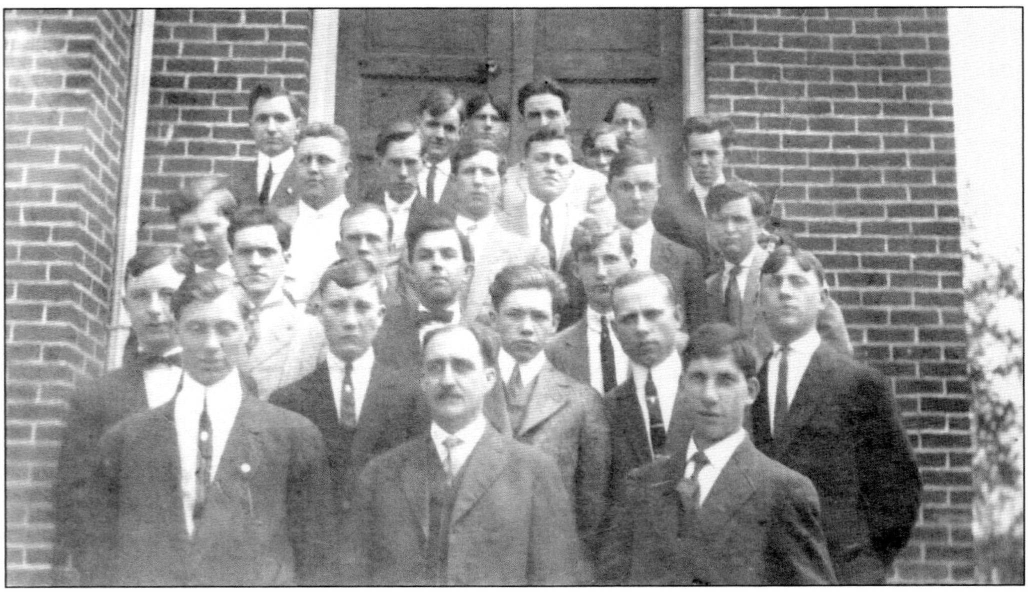

In 1948, Yorktown High School seniors pose on the steps to the side door of the Yorktown Methodist Episcopal Church. Pictured are, from left to right, (first row) Barbara Keller and Marilyn Mahoney; (second row) Barbara Troxler and Nancy Johnson; (third row) Jack Morrison and Opal Stewart; (fourth row) Dick Groves and Jim Ramsey. (YMPTHA.)

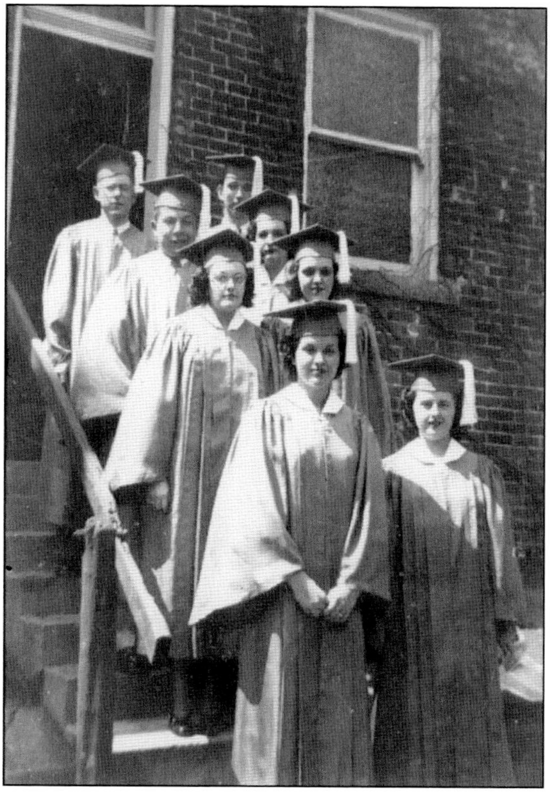

Pictured here is the aftermath of the Methodist church fire on Christmas Eve 1950. Despite the desperate efforts of several local fire departments and community members, little was saved of the church. This view of the south side of the building clearly shows the amount of devastation left behind. When the new church was erected at the same site, only a small portion of the original foundation was incorporated into the structure. (Marylou Schmidt.)

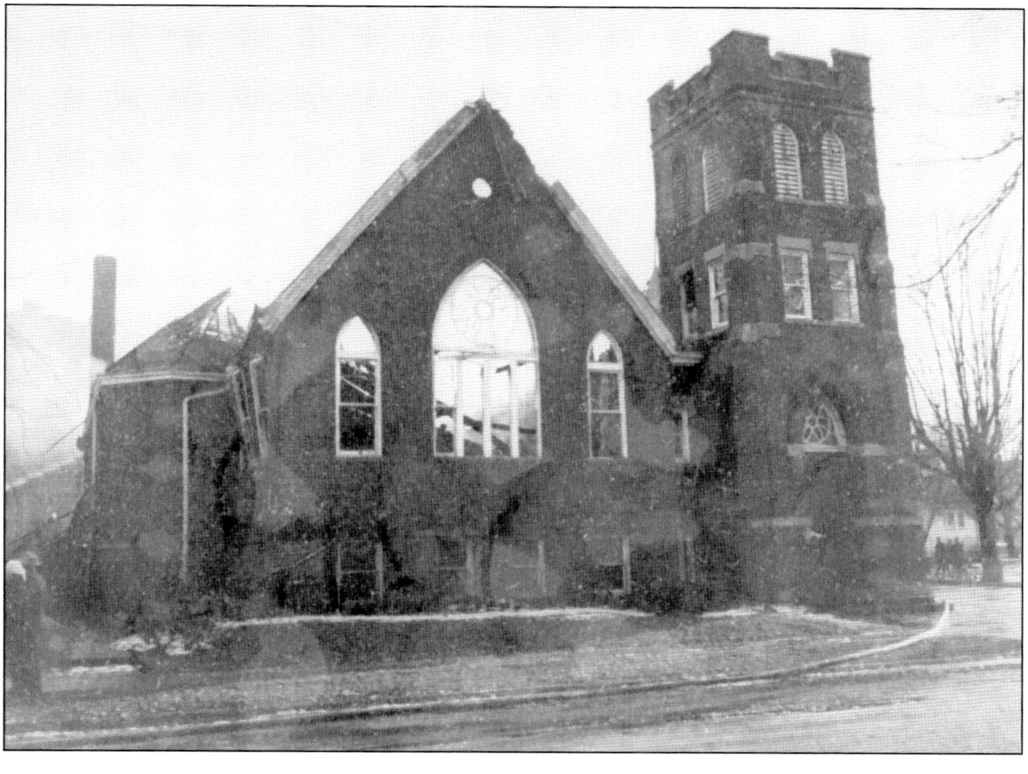

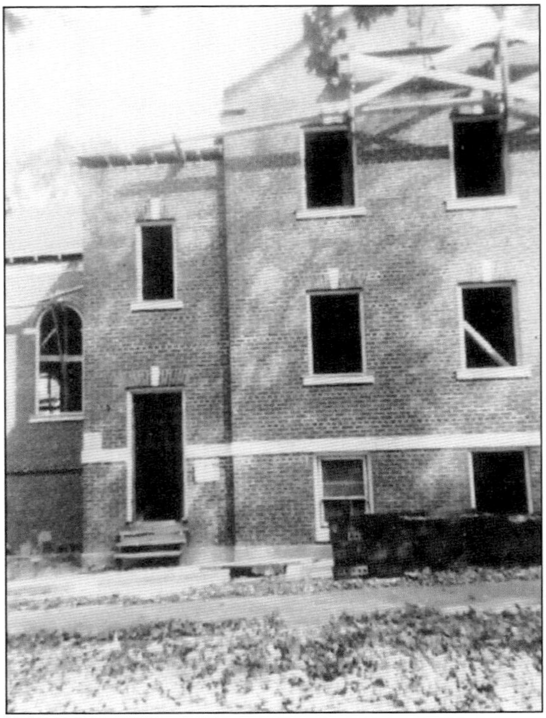

Once the smoke had settled, members of the Yorktown Methodist Church did not hesitate to begin plans for a new building. Fundraisers were held, community and church members alike pledged funds, and soon the plans for a new building were underway. Construction was led by James Anderson, and the facility was soon ready for church and Sunday school activities. This image was taken in 1951. (YMPTHA.)

Pictured in 1954 is the new Yorktown Methodist Church. The stairway leading to the sanctuary makes a perfect setting for photographs of a Bible school class or bride and groom following their wedding. The stairs have since been removed, and the main sanctuary has been added to the east end of the church. (YMPTHA.)

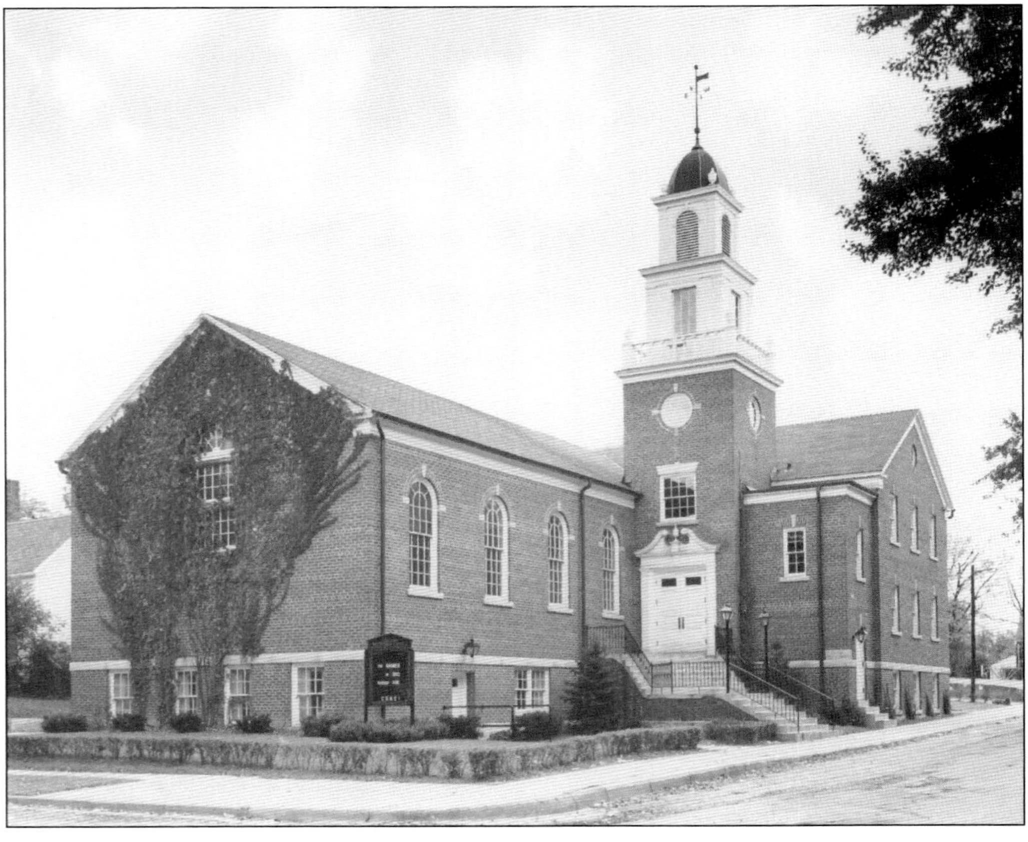

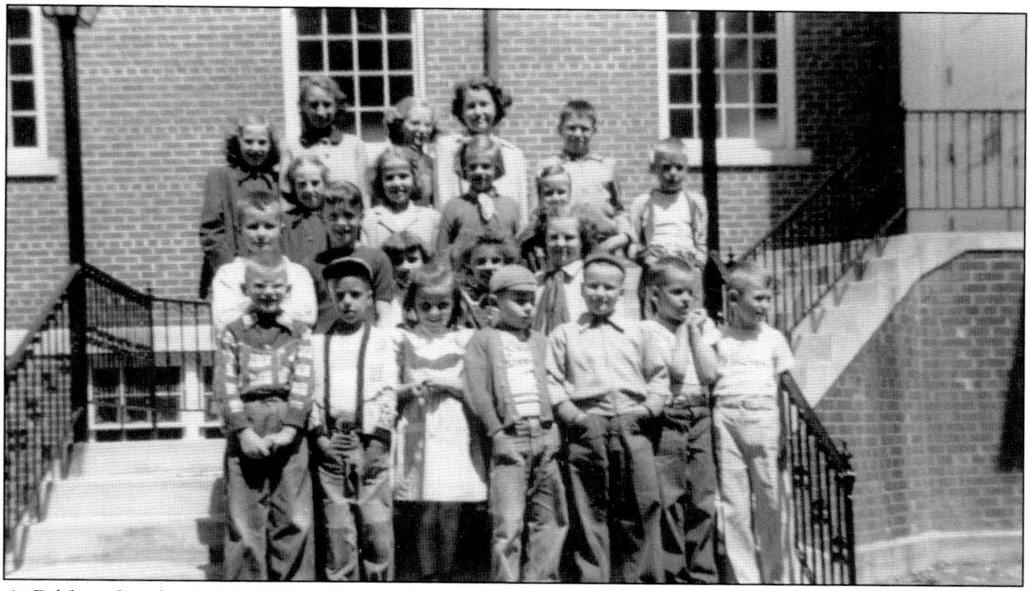

A Bible school group gathers on the steps of the Methodist church. Pictured are, from left to right, (first row) Jim Dwyer, Steve Bowers, Mary A. Hammersly, Sidney Mitchell, Joe Mann, Sam Miller, and Jack Hamilton; (second row) Bill Callahan, Anne Williamson, and three unidentified children; (third row) Joane Griffis, Carolyn Donovan, Barbara Boyle, Barbara Gibbs, and two unidentified children; (fourth row) Melanie Griffis, Katy Hamilton, Judy Masterson, Carolyn Parkinson, and Tom Parkinson. (Becky Monroe.)

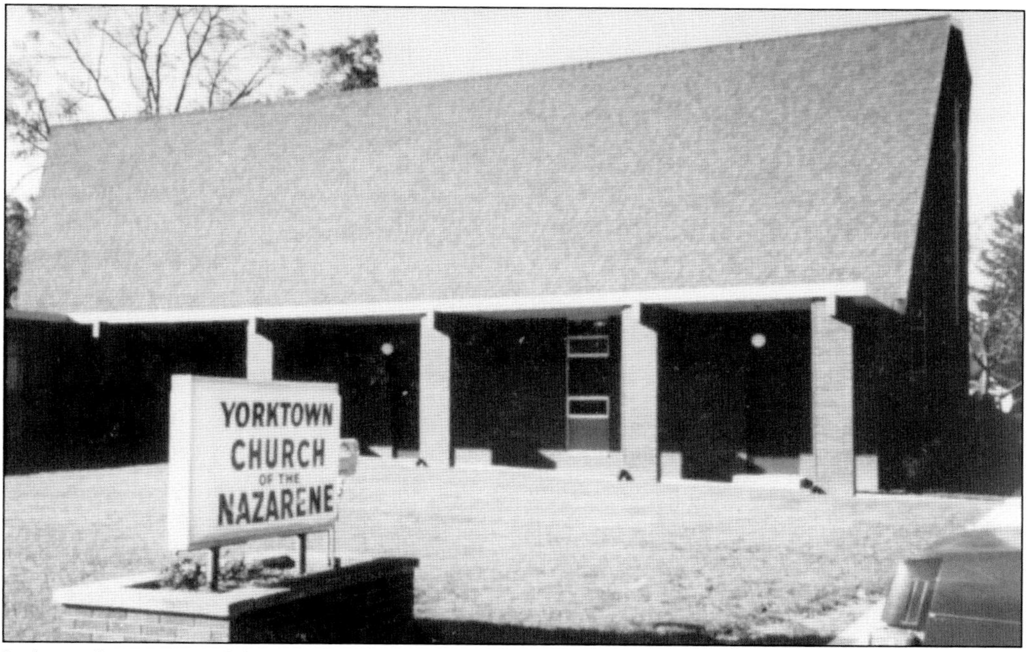

In lieu of an image of the original building, pictured here is the current Yorktown Church of the Nazarene. In 1926, the first 18 congregants met at the home of John and Pearl Hodson, attending Sunday church services and Wednesday evening prayer service. A small frame building was constructed in the 1940s. Under the leadership of pastors Chester Pasko and A.F. Hayes, the congregation grew, and a new building was erected in 1973. (YMPTHA.)

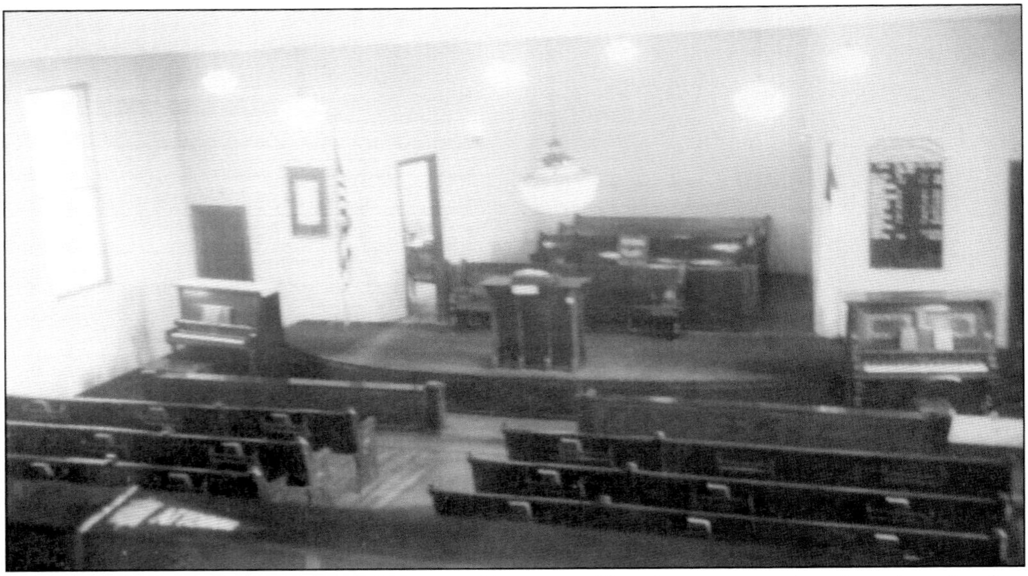

The wood-frame structure of the Yorktown Nazarene Church appears to be of modest size, but the view from the balcony indicates there was ample seating available. The sanctuary occupied most of the main floor, while the balcony and basement areas held additional rooms for Sunday school classes. (Phyllis Myer.)

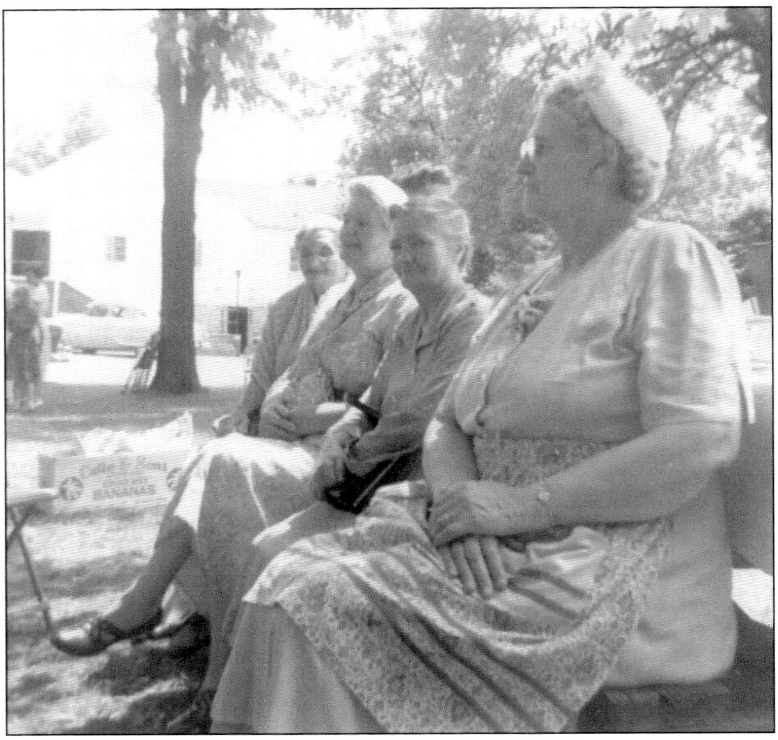

Nazarene women, from left to right, Mrs. ? Baker, Pearl Hodson, Anna Barlow, and Rachel Terrell enjoy an outing across the street from the church. In the background, with the stairway leading to the front, is the original wood-frame 1940s Yorktown Nazarene Church. (Brian Couch.)

Three

Homes, Friends, and Families

When it came to housing, the Yorktown area was no different than other communities. The town had everything from typical bungalows to large Victorians. Several of the homes that sat along Smith Street have been torn down or moved and most often replaced with businesses. At least two sections featured a row of houses that were very similar in construction. One was located on Mill Street, consisting of five brick houses and called Brick Row. Those houses belonged to the glass factory and were home to some of its employees. Three or four of those residences still stand. The other area is on Cornbread Road. Several houses on the south side of the road are of a very similar construction—two stories with the door on the side and most often a porch.

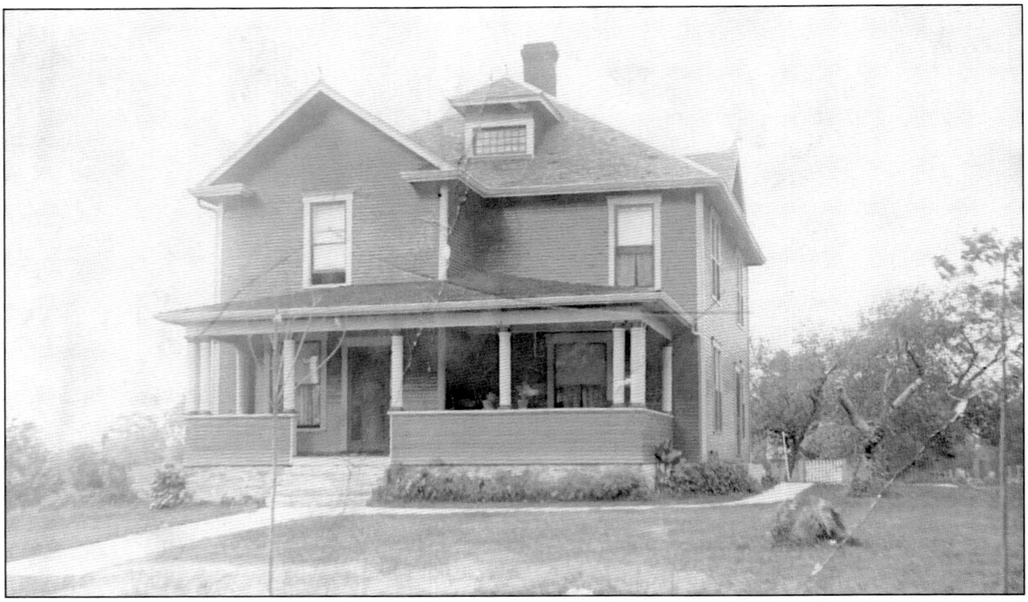

This house located at the west end of town and on the north side of Smith Street is pictured around 1900 as a stately two-story residence. Jim and Helen Hudgel called this home for many years. Since this photograph was taken, the top story has been removed, and the structure is currently a one-story duplex. The residence is owned by Marguarite Badders and serves as a rental. (Rhonda Williams.)

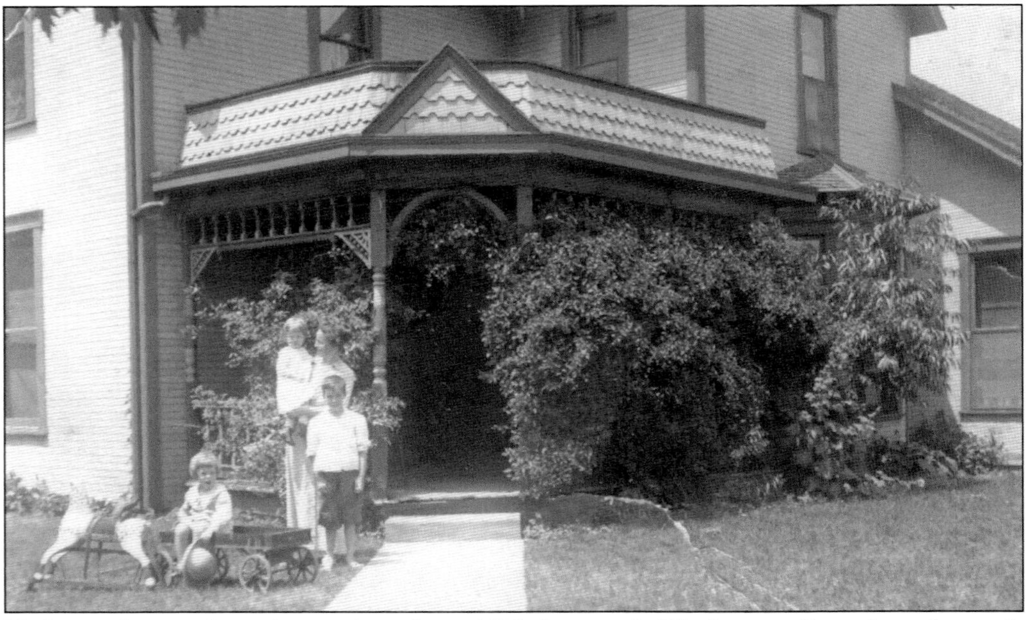

Nothing is known about the people in this c. 1920 photograph. The house still stands on the north side of Arch Street, next to the Baptist church parking lot. The ornate covering over the porch has been removed. In the past, there was an apartment on the second floor. Ed and Patsy Luzader raised their family here and stayed until after the children had moved on. (YMPTHA.)

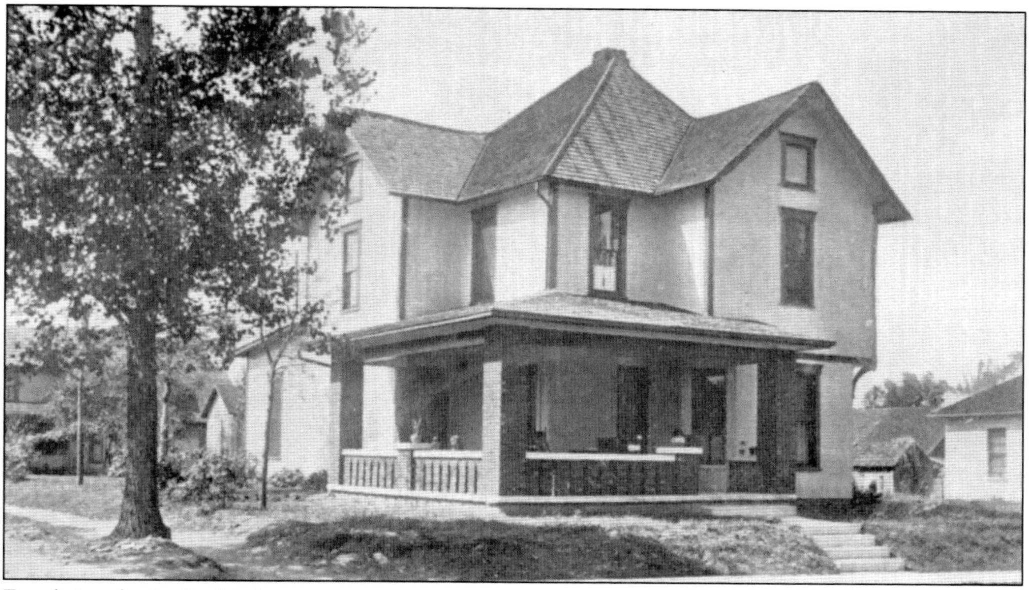

Frank Leader built this house pictured around 1910 at the corner of Arch and Market Streets. Leader was involved with the Patterson Glass Works and later worked for Warner Machine. The next occupants were a very young Lucille Fenwick and her mother. Lucille married Walter Luke. They raised their family and remained in this house until their deaths. At right, Lucille Luke (left) and Lillian Ward admire the flowers in the Lukes' garden around 1955. For years, the garden featured a fishpond and train tracks that ran all the way around the yard. Walter Luke worked for the railroad and built a small train for his entertainment and that of the neighborhood children. (Above, YMPTHA; right, Bob Ellis.)

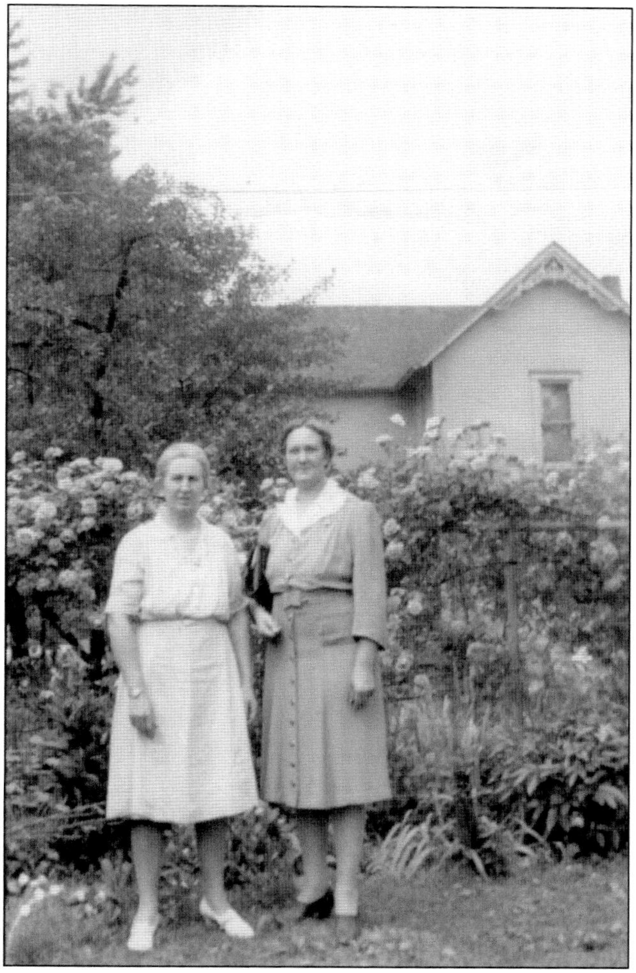

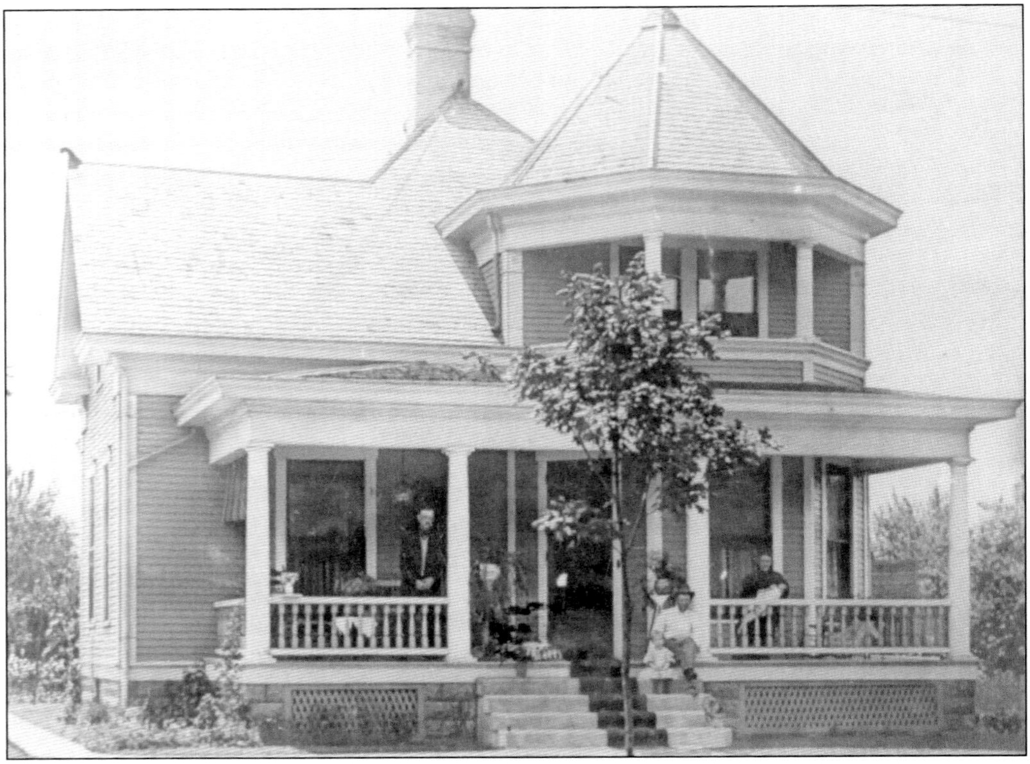

This house is on the south side of Smith Street and a half block west of Vine Street. Early occupants were part of the Yingling family. Bill and Gladys Wilhoit and their son Bill were residents for many years. The house changed hands many times before being purchased by Phil and Beverly White, who did a complete renovation and enjoy the use of the newly created porches. (YMPTHA.)

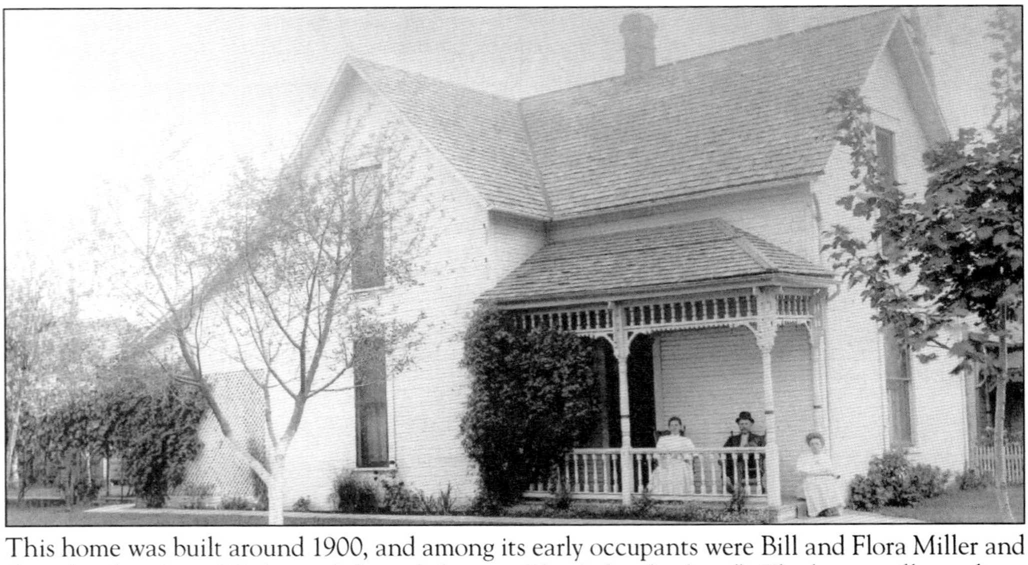

This home was built around 1900, and among its early occupants were Bill and Flora Miller and their daughter Jean Workman (whose father was Flora's first husband). The home still stands on High Street. Several modifications have been made, but the basic structure remains and it is still a lovely home. Nothing much is known about any owners between the original and the current owners. (Barbara Young.)

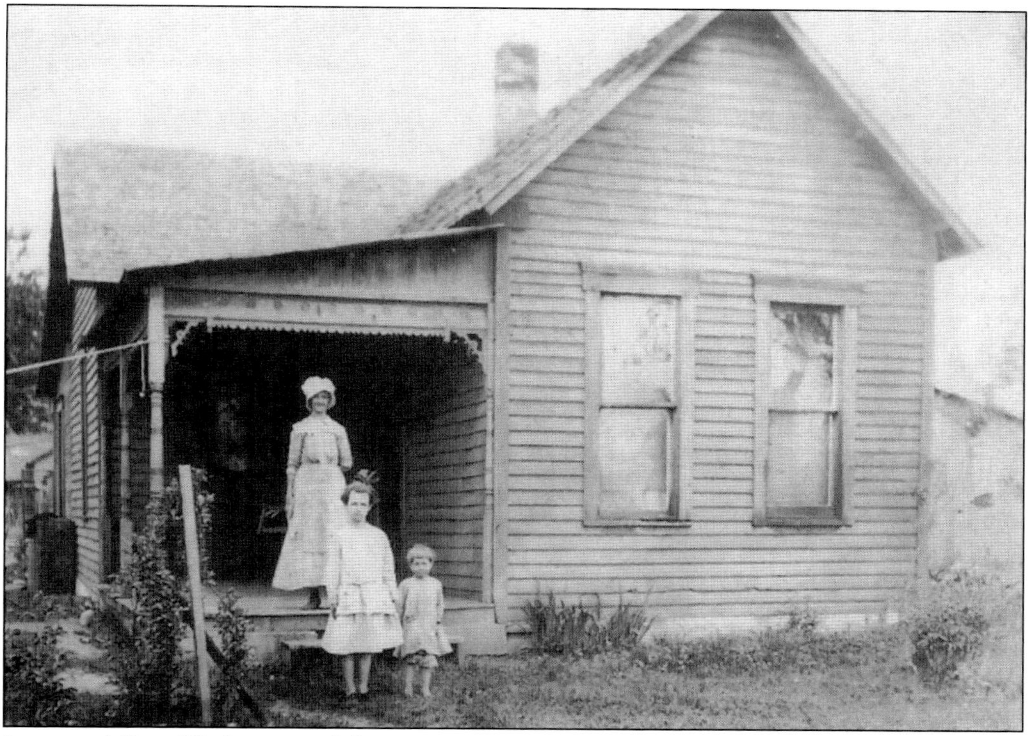

James and Cora Watkins raised their family in this quaint cottage located on Canal Street, pictured around 1910. One of their children was Ora "Tete" Watkins, who married Elizabeth "Betty" Kendelburger. They raised their two sons, Jim and Don, in the home and remained residents until their deaths. Except for the enclosed porch, the house looks very much the same today. At right, Tete and Betty Watkins pose with their eldest son, Jim, in the side yard of that home in the early 1930s. The house is no longer in the Watkins family. (Both, Shawn Gray.)

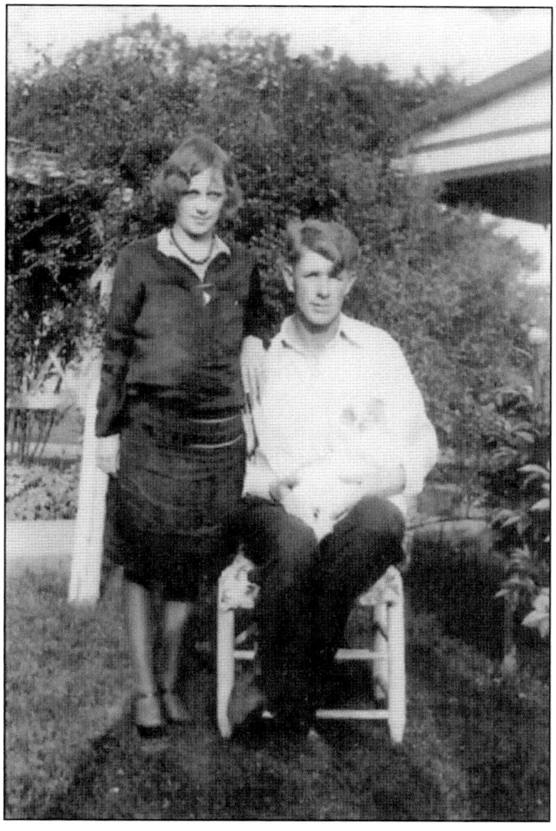

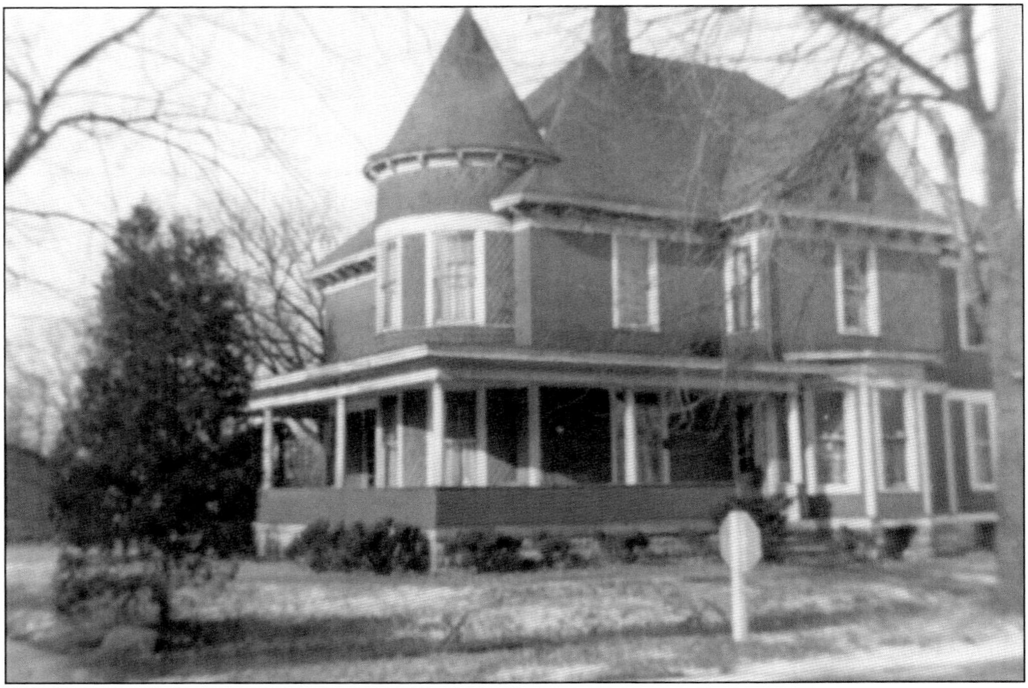

Solomon and Louisa Howell Donovan built their Victorian home around 1900. It stood at the northwest corner of Smith and Vine Streets and featured five bedrooms and a bath with indoor plumbing. A dumbwaiter that ran from the basement to the attic often provided entertainment for some of the many children who lived there over the years. The 1910 census indicates there were 11 family members (three generations) occupying the home. The paneled stairway in the entry featured a built-in bench, and pocket doors allowed the adjacent parlor to be shut off from the remainder of the house. By 1957, the house had fallen into disrepair and was torn down. Lumber from the demolished structure was used to build a new home for O. Love Donovan Sears. The photographs were taken in 1954. (Both, Becky Monroe.)

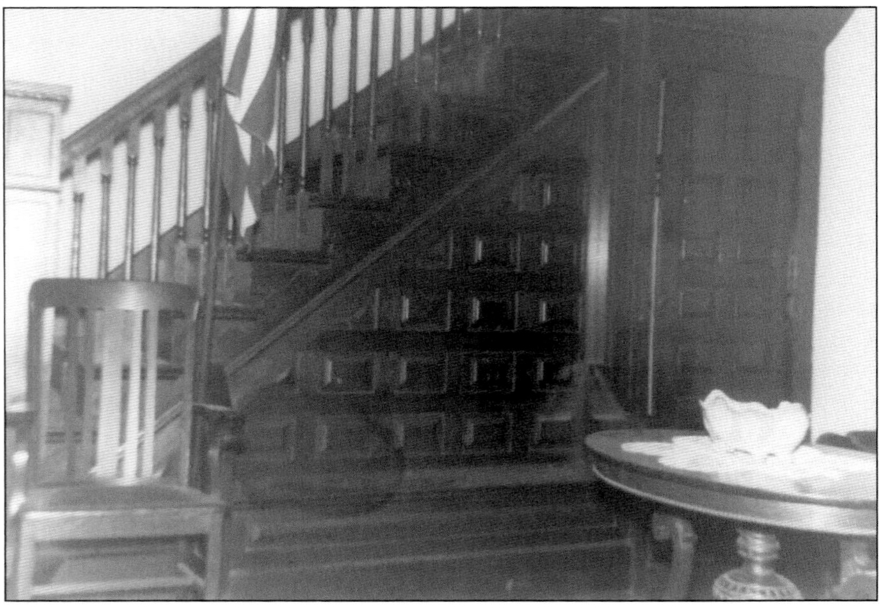

Four of the five children belonging to J. Emil and Love Donovan Sears are pictured here looking like they would never cause a bit of trouble. Jane and John are seated, and standing are Tom and Maria Louise. The youngest daughter, Patricia, had not yet been born at the time. (Becky Monroe.)

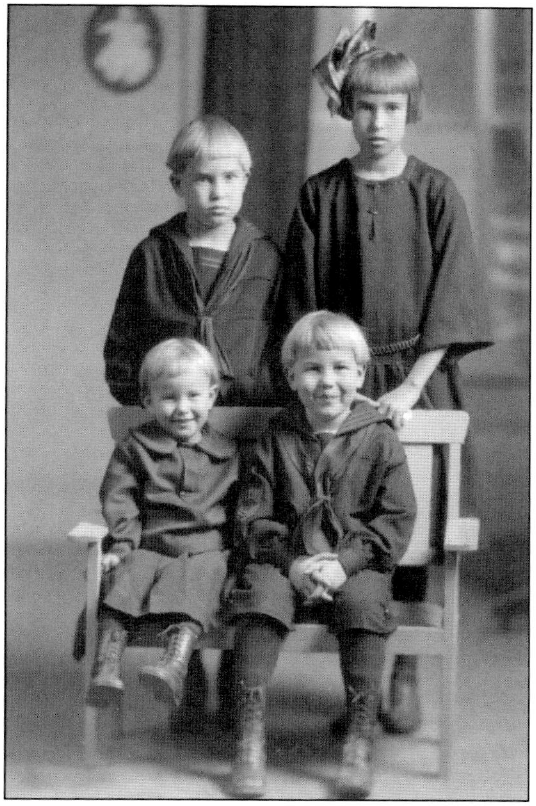

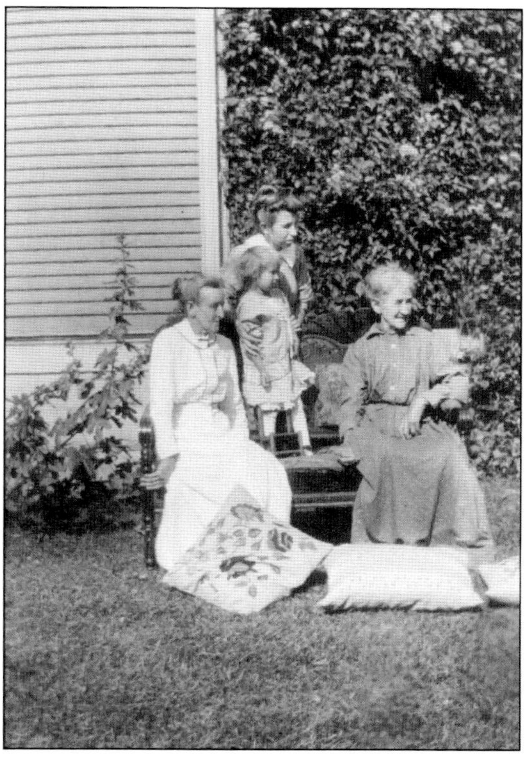

A young Maria Louise Sears joins her mother, O. Love Donovan Sears, grandmother Louisa Howell Donovan, and great-grandmother Mariah Staggs Howell in the side yard of the home built by Solomon and Louisa Donovan. The ladies appear to be displaying their needlework. At the time of this photograph, the three younger generations occupied the same house. (Becky Monroe.)

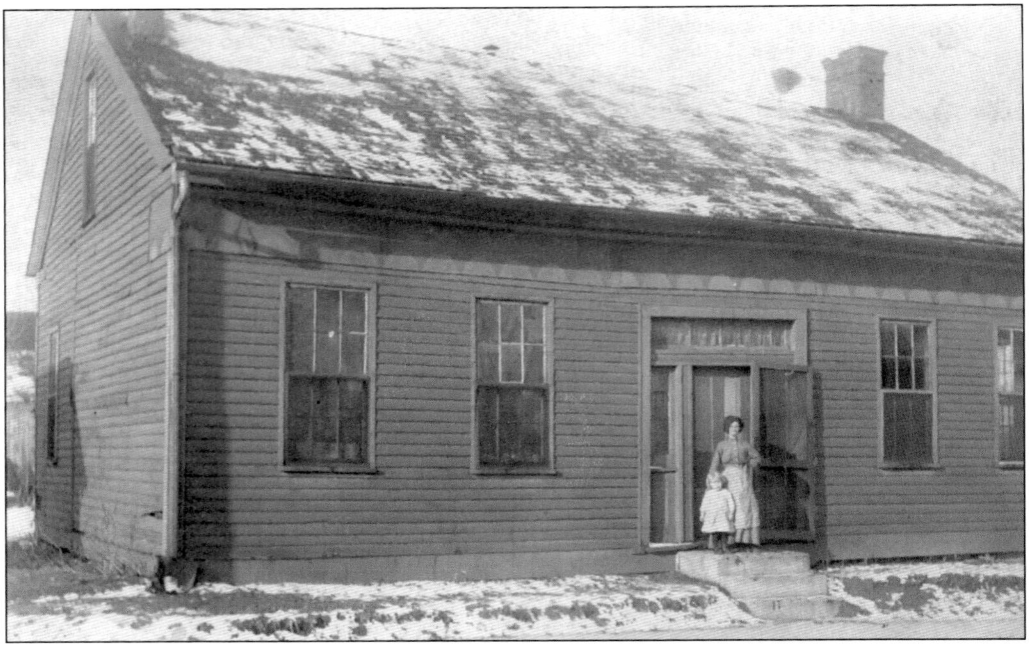

West and across the alley from the Sears-Donovan house sat this cozy home on the south side of Smith Street. Dolly Yingling and a child appear to be waiting for company. Later, the house belonged to the Koontz family and then remained uninhabited for many years. The lot was usually filled with weeds and flowers gone wild, mostly bleeding hearts and violets. (Shawn Gray.)

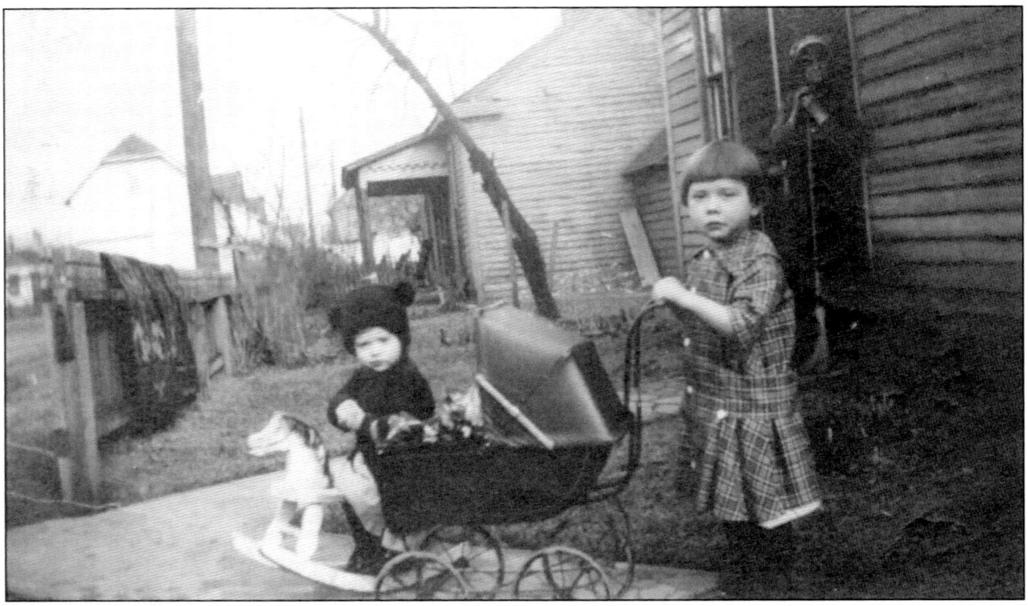

Edwin and Hertha Donovan, children of William and Fanny Donovan, appear to be having a good time with the hobby horse and doll buggy while Grandma watches from the front door. (Becky Monroe.)

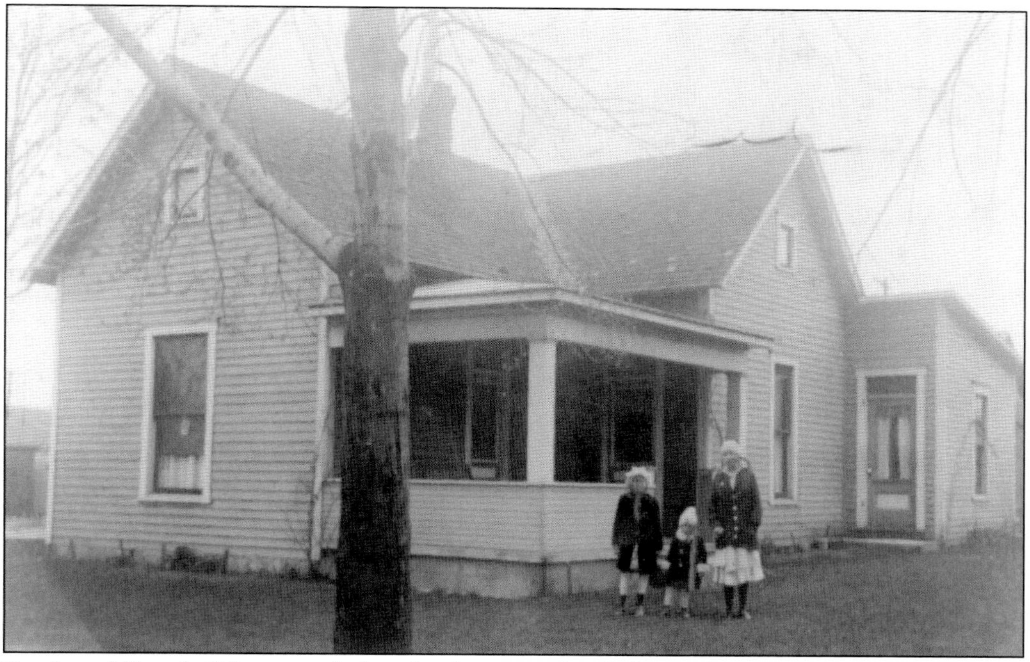

Frank and Blanch Kilgore resided in this home on Smith Street for many years. Three of their four children are pictured here. The house was later torn down to make way for parking at Ross Market. A small hole appeared in the asphalt years later where a well had been in the side yard, exposing the brick-lined well. It was quickly filled in. (YMPTHA.)

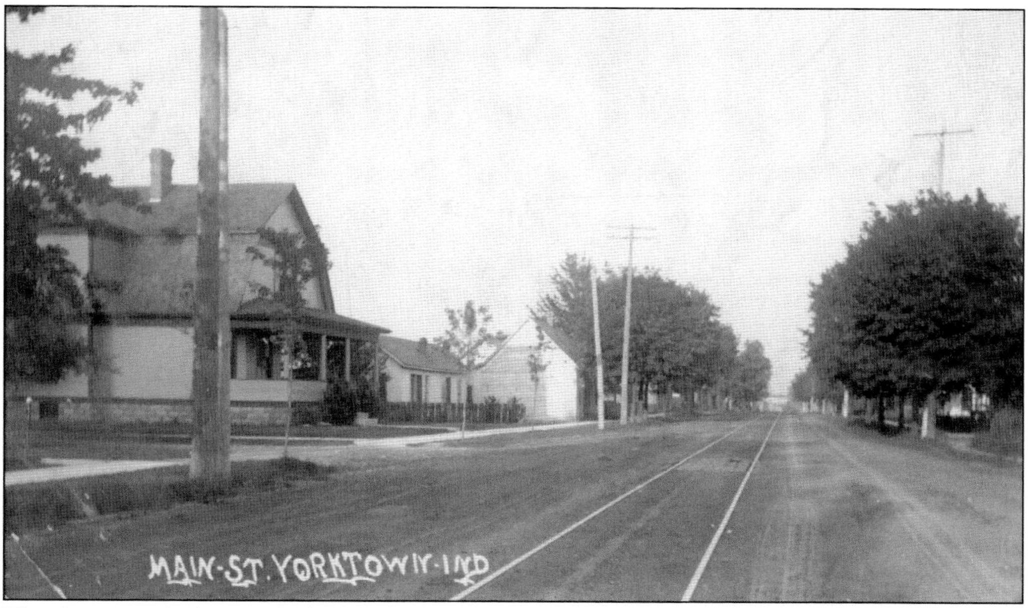

This home with the gambrel roof, located at the northeast corner of Smith and Vine Streets, was owned by Clyde and Cora Byerly. The house remains standing, minus the front porch. Dick and Virginia Pugsley and their children lived here for several years before the entire home was converted to apartments. (Rhonda Williams.)

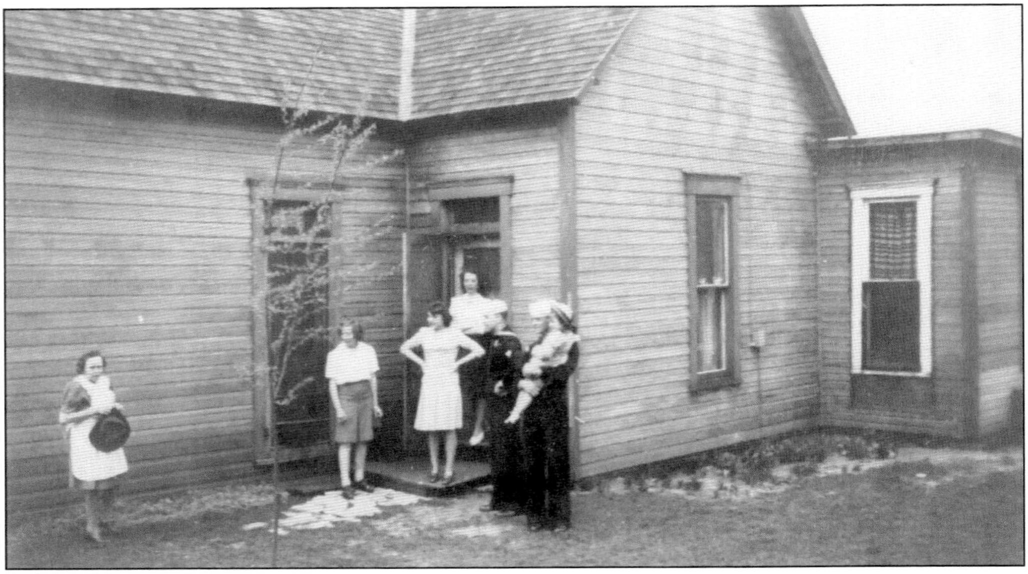

Mae (Sears) Richman (left) and Betty May Richman pause in front of the home of May and Guy Richman while they visit with, from left to right, Martha Bragg, Virginia Richman, Bob Evans, Forrest "Dort" Richman, and Jennifer Carpenter. After this photograph was taken around 1942, a covered porch was added to the front of the house. (Betty Mae Fisher.)

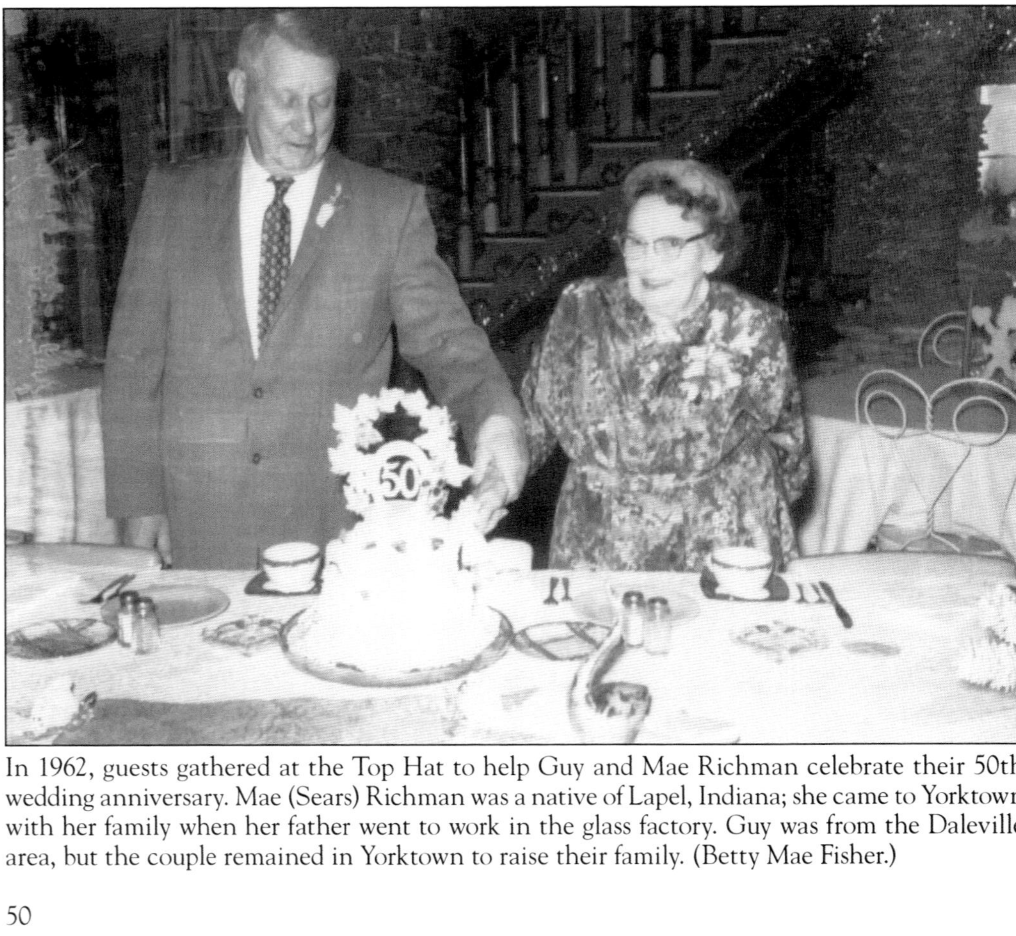

In 1962, guests gathered at the Top Hat to help Guy and Mae Richman celebrate their 50th wedding anniversary. Mae (Sears) Richman was a native of Lapel, Indiana; she came to Yorktown with her family when her father went to work in the glass factory. Guy was from the Daleville area, but the couple remained in Yorktown to raise their family. (Betty Mae Fisher.)

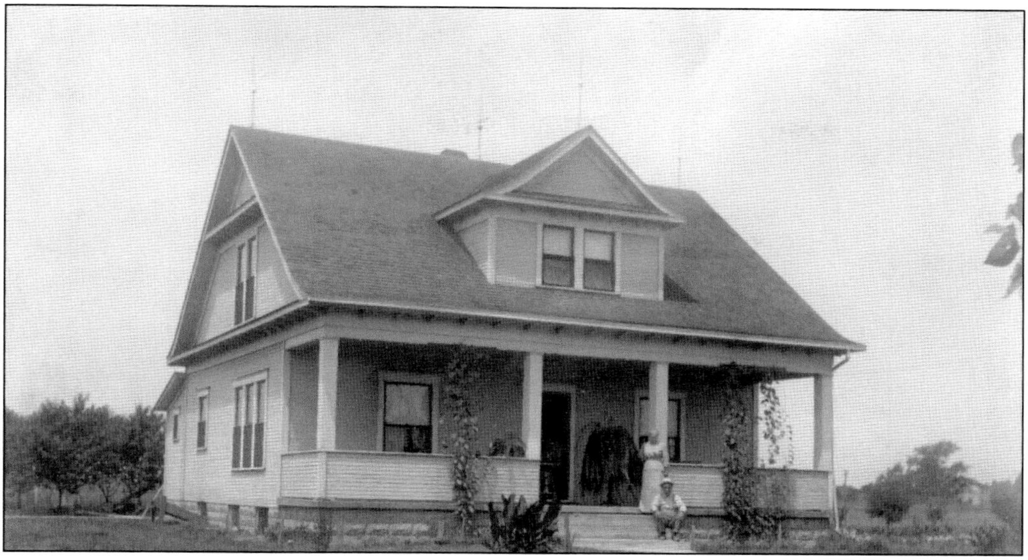

The back of this postcard is simply labeled "Campbell Family Home, Yorktown." The house still stands about half a mile south of the railroad crossing on the west side of Broadway. Ray and Denise Booher are the current residents. They have done extensive renovation during the last few years. (YMPTHA.)

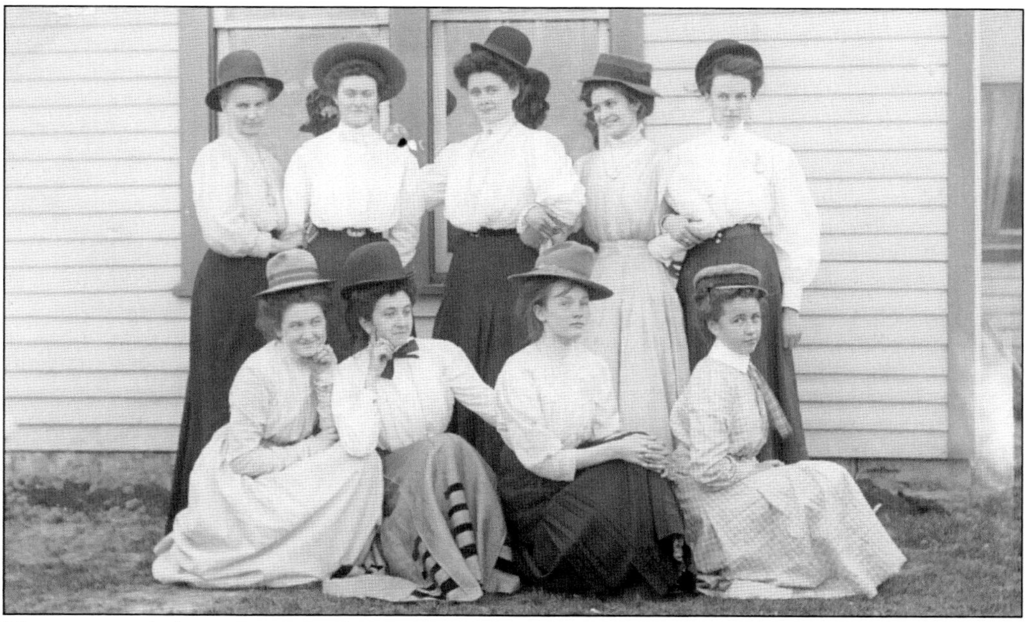

These young ladies pose around 1910 next to Lewis Stewart's home in what appear to be their fathers' hats. Nine ladies are pictured, but only eight names are provided. Identified in the first row are, from left to right, Alma Stewart, Dessie Walker, Nora Haney, and Muriel Cunningham; those in the second row include, in no particular order, Mae McCollister, Molly Walker, Edith Cunningham, Alta Shellabarger, and one unidentified woman. (YMPTHA.)

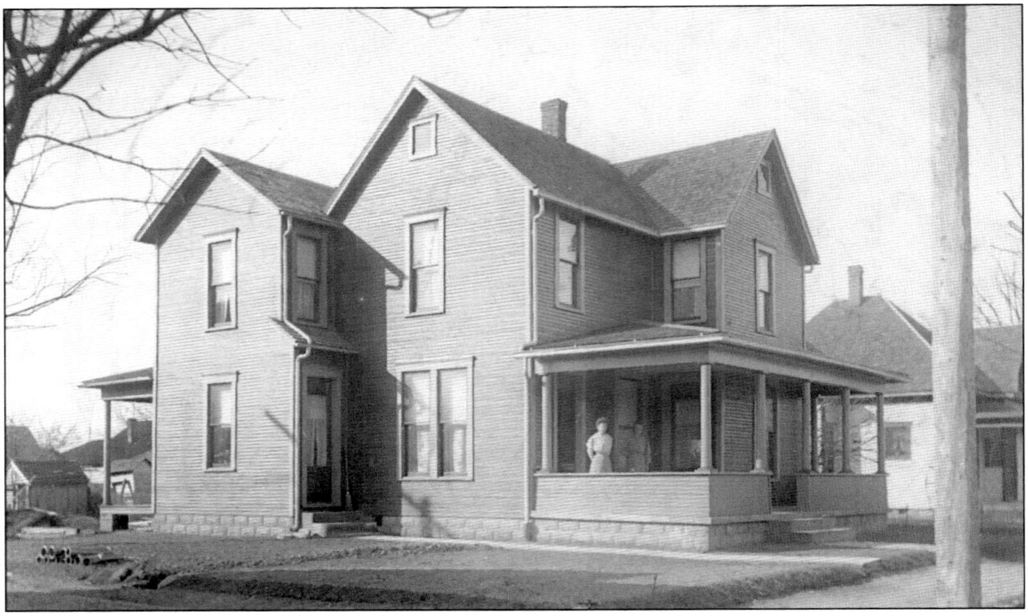

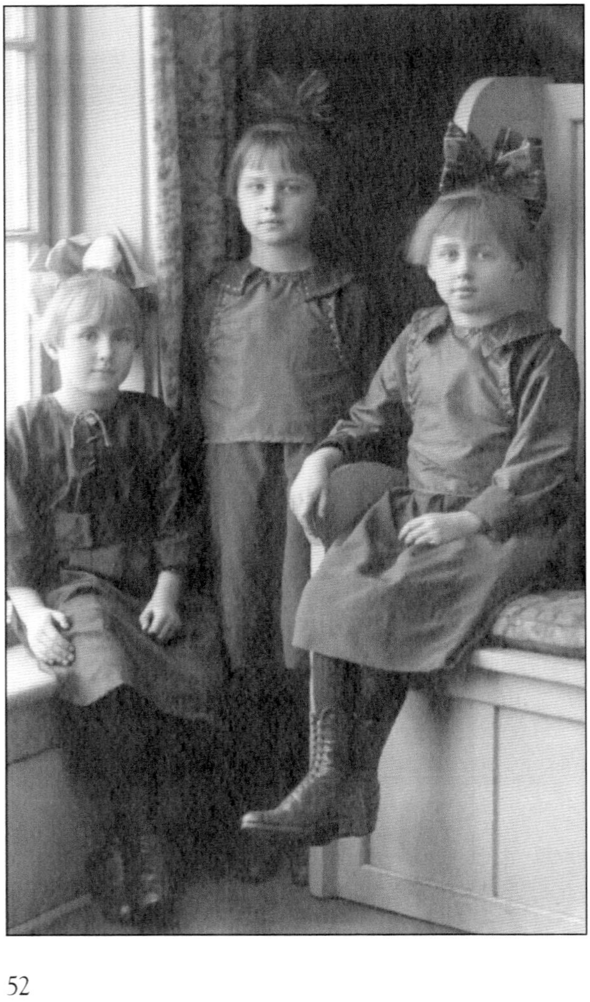

Pictured around 1918, this classic farm home sat on south side of Smith Street in the center of Yorktown. Chester and Hattie Walker lived here for a time with their daughters—Margaret, Leona, and Vera. The upstairs was turned into an apartment and often served as a first home for many young couples. The house was torn down several years ago to make way for a bank. At left, Margaret, Leona, and Vera Walker pose for a photograph; the girls are not specifically identified. (Both, Rhonda Williams.)

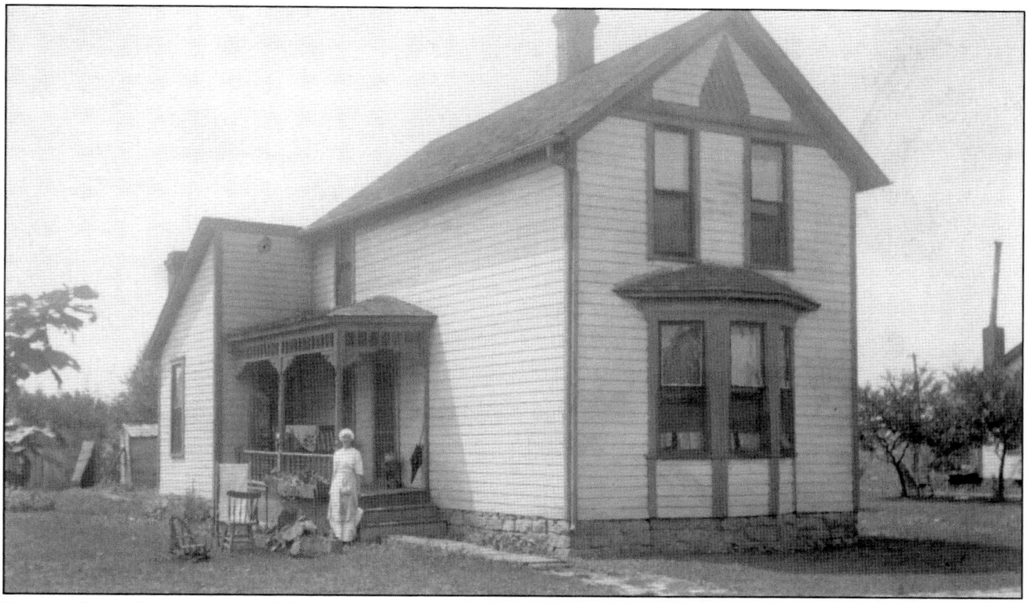

Located one house east of Broadway, on Cornbread Road, this house has undergone a good deal of remodeling but still has a lot of the original character and charm. There were at least three houses of similar design along this section of Cornbread Road. The woman in the photograph is unidentified. (Jeff Koenker.)

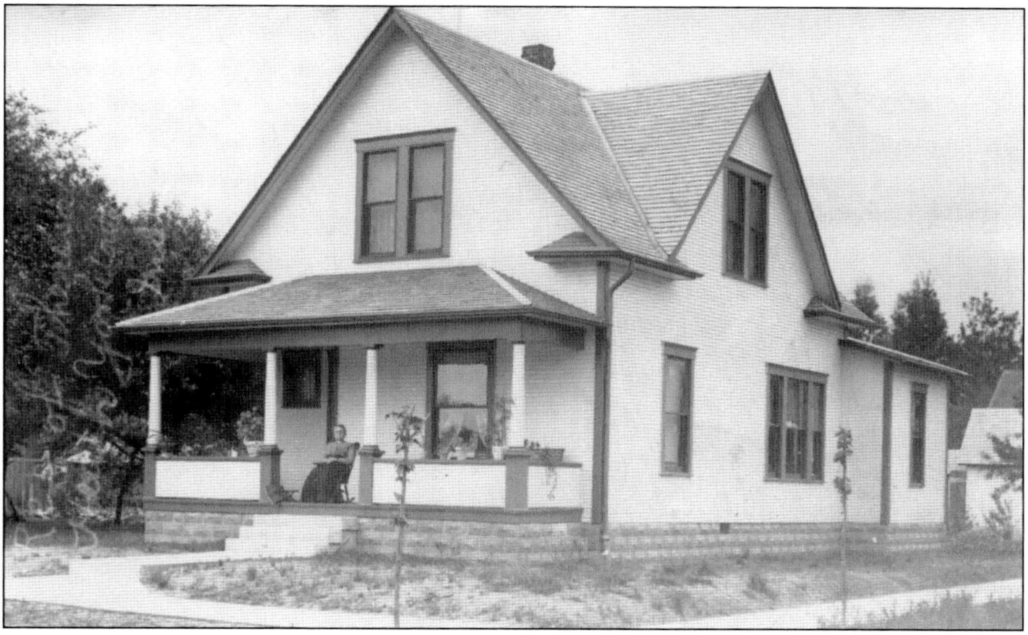

According to information written along the front edge of this postcard, this house was the residence of Thressa Heath. Several years later, an addition was built onto the back and served as the sales and display room for Barr Appliances. After the Barrs moved to the west end of town, the property was purchased by Mike and Carolyn Grieves and turned into Printing Creations. (Jeff Koenker.)

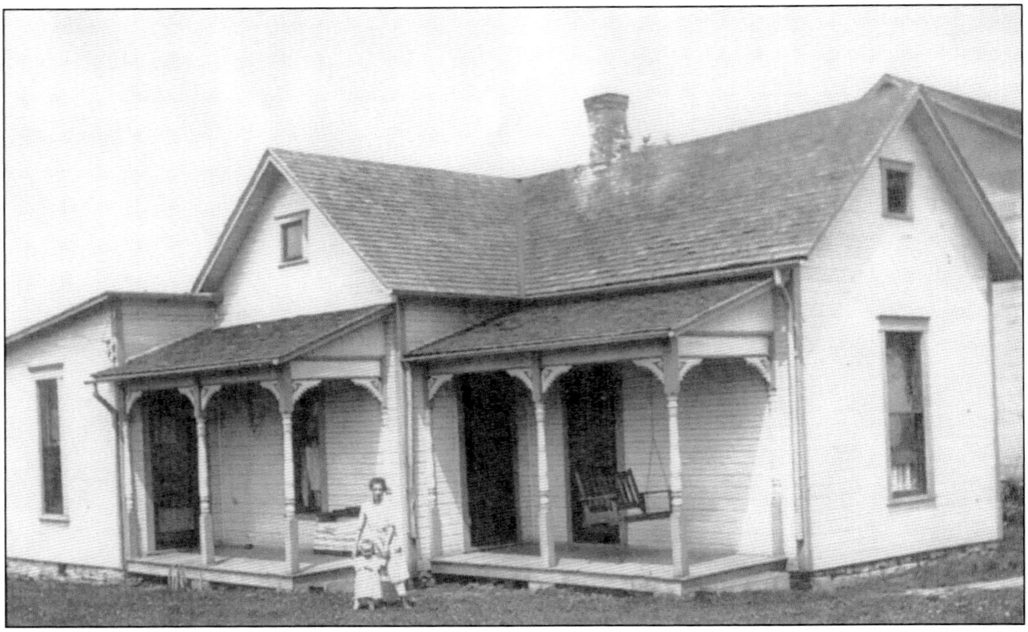

Located at the northwest corner of Depot and Walnut Streets, this house was home to the Neff family for many years. Amanda Neff and her granddaughter Jane Smith play in the yard. In more recent years, part of the home was turned into a beauty shop known as Mable's. (Janice Ross.)

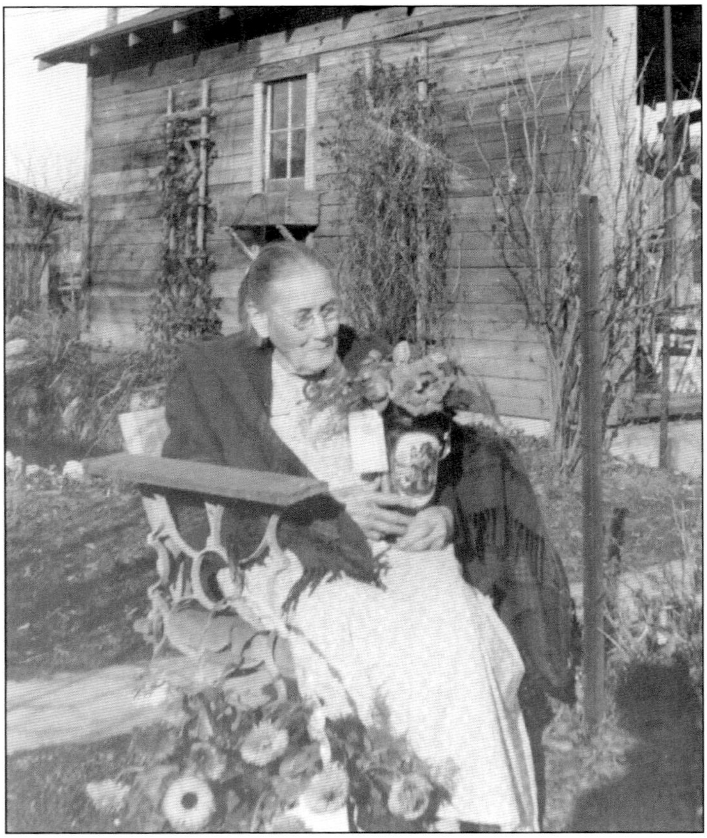

Leona Figel, or "Grandma," as the neighborhood children referred to her, sits in her backyard surrounded by gifts. The quaint building behind Leona looks like it has served the family well. (Shawn Gray.)

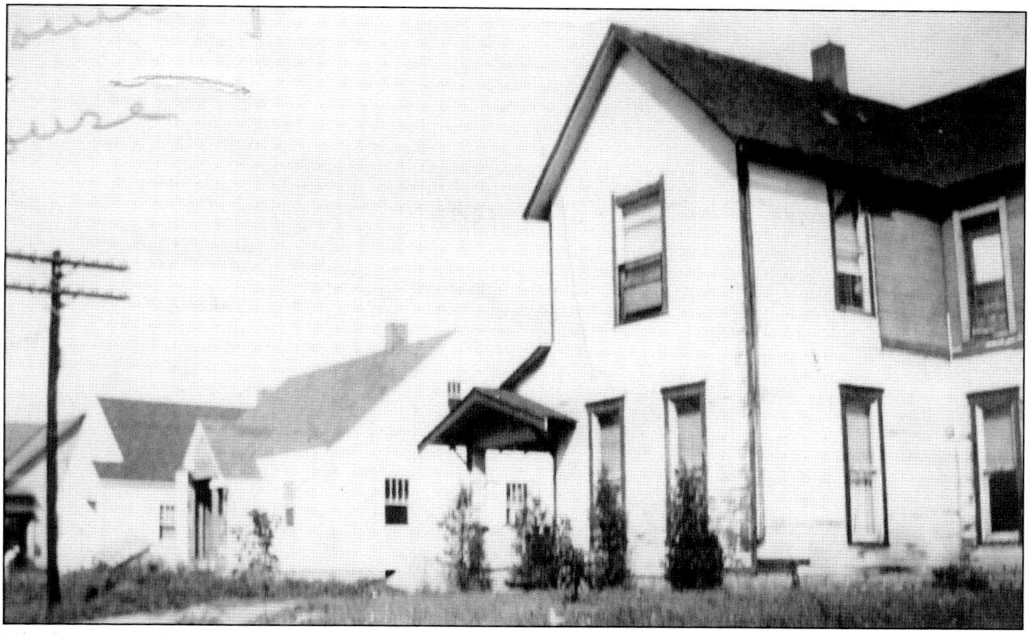

The house on the right was moved in the 1930s from the southwest corner of Broadway and Smith Streets to the north side of Cornbread Road and just west of the bridge spanning Buck Creek. Before being moved, the house had an apartment upstairs. The door to that apartment can still be seen in this photograph, but the steps have been removed. Elmer and Lillian Ellis raised their family in this home. (Bob Ellis.)

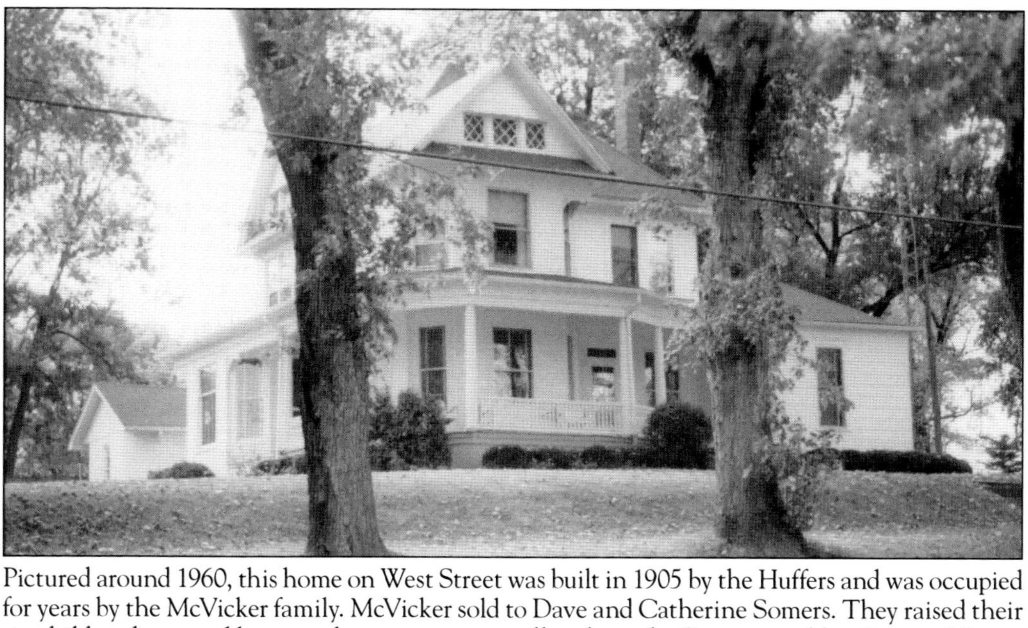

Pictured around 1960, this home on West Street was built in 1905 by the Huffers and was occupied for years by the McVicker family. McVicker sold to Dave and Catherine Somers. They raised their six children here; and later, ready to move to a smaller place, the Somerses sold to Don and Susan Clevenger. Marta Guinn is the present owner, and the pool area provides an excellent source of exercise and entertainment for the children. (Susan Clevenger.)

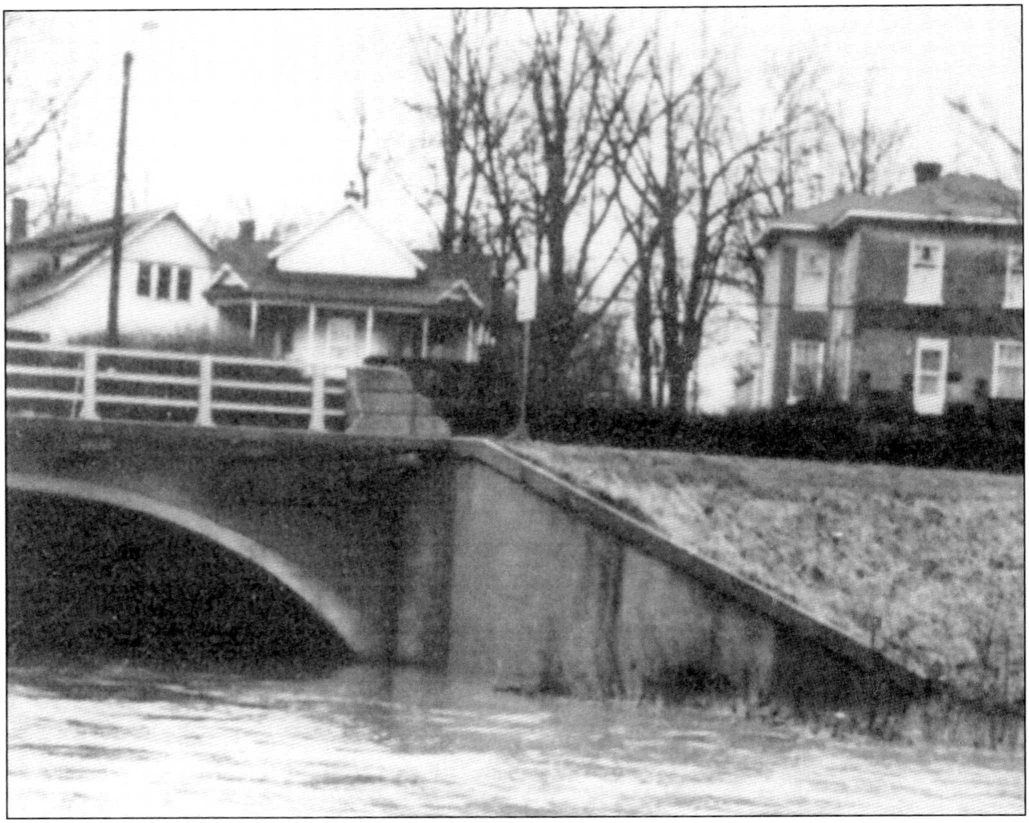

Serving as a gateway at the east end of Yorktown, the three houses pictured above in the mid-20th century sat on a hill overlooking the bridge where Smith Street crosses Buck Creek. The house on the left has been torn down, but the others remain. It is believed the original owners of these two properties on the left were part of the Overmire family. The home on the right now has a porch across the front and was originally owned by R.S. Cummins. The early-1900s photograph below provides a close-up of the residence in the center of the above photograph. For many years, this house was occupied by Paul Estes. The couple is unidentified. (Both, YMPTHA.)

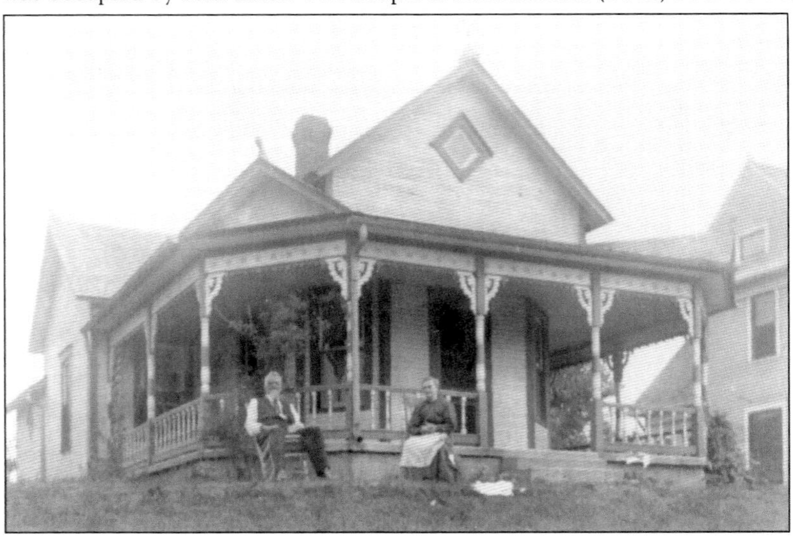

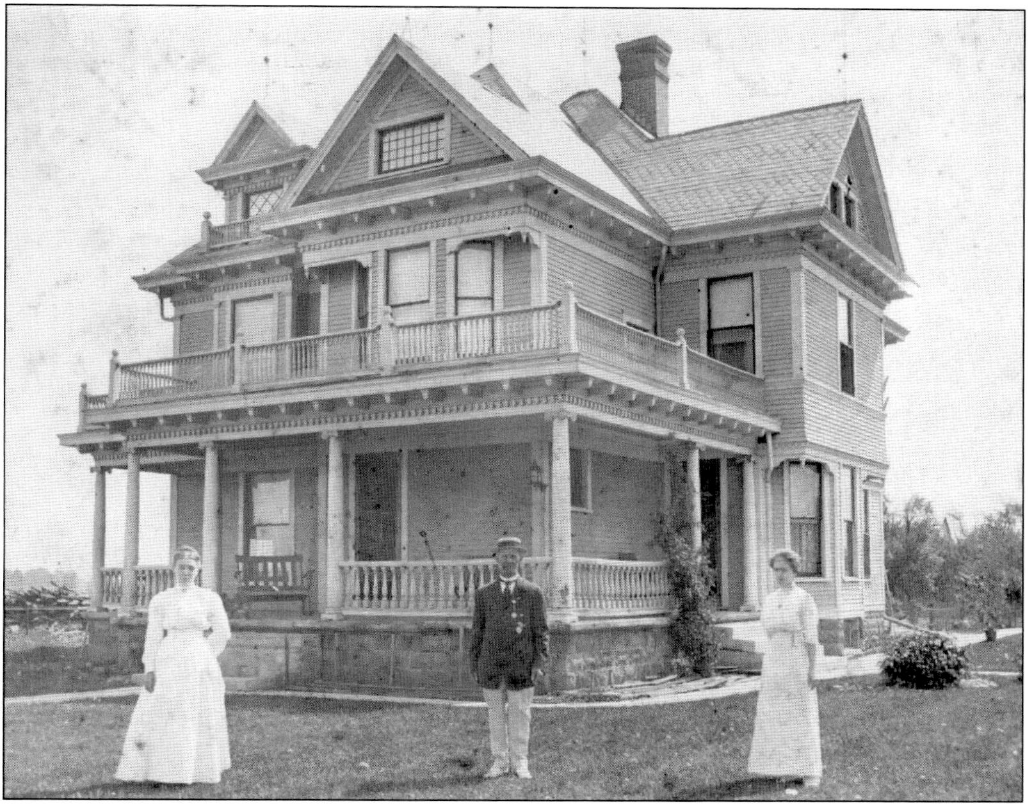

Seen in the c. 1910 photograph above, this Queen Anne house was built around 1905 by Martin and Mary Hofherr. The home features wide woodwork, an open stairway at the front of the structure, and an enclosed one from the kitchen area. A large front porch and a smaller one at the back both sit ready to welcome guests. The house features several dormers and a stairway leading to the attic. Pictured below in the 1950s, two barns still sat behind the house. The larger one was a round bank barn built into the side of the hill. Due to neglect, the round barn collapsed a few years ago. The smaller barn is of the English style and still stands on the property, currently owned by Scott and Julia Jordan. (Both, YMPTHA.)

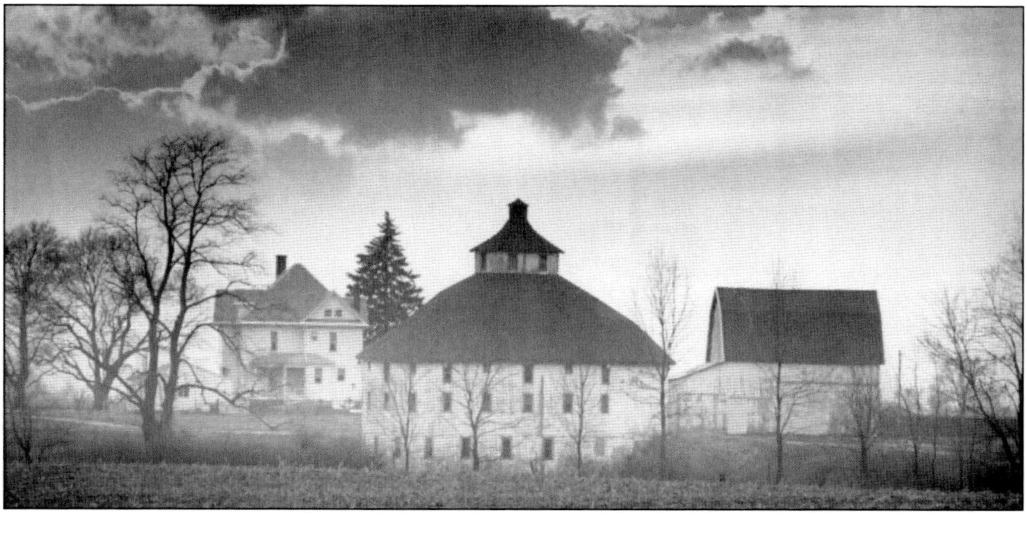

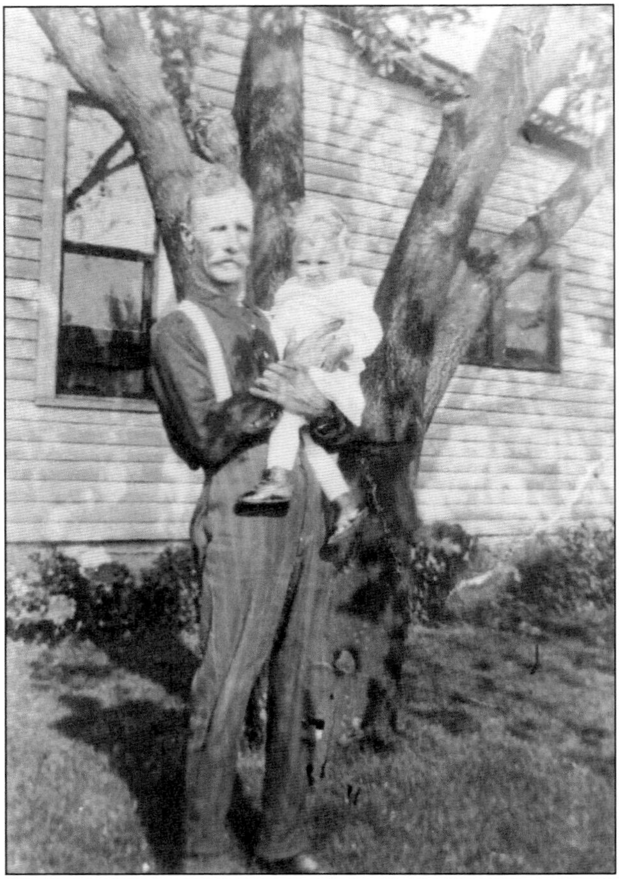

Around 1910, George Parkison pauses to show his granddaughter Evelyn Miller around the yard of their small home, located at the intersection of Plum and High Streets. George and his wife, Susan, lived in this house from 1892 until his passing in 1930. This house was later occupied for many years by the Applegate family. (David Parkison.)

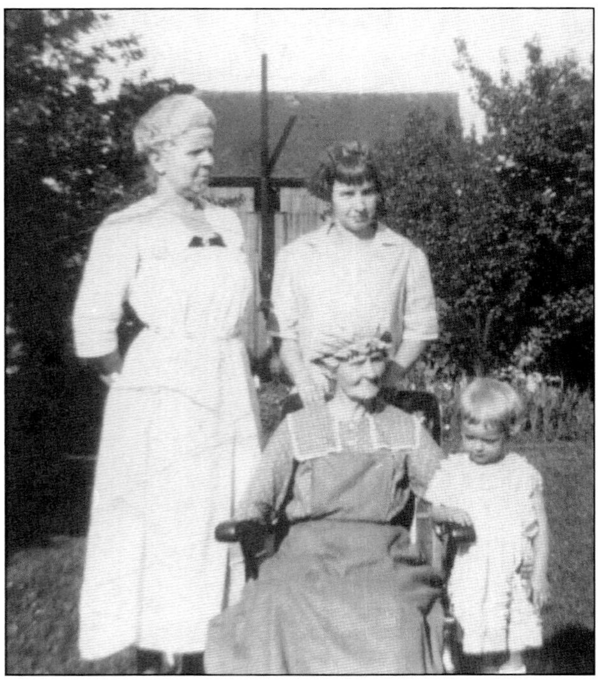

This four-generation photograph shows family enjoying time together. Seated is Susan Parkison with her great-granddaughter Lois Byerly. Standing are Minnie Parkison Miller and Viola Byerly Miller. This image was taken in the backyard of George and Susan Parkison's home on the corner of High and Plum Streets. (David Parkison.)

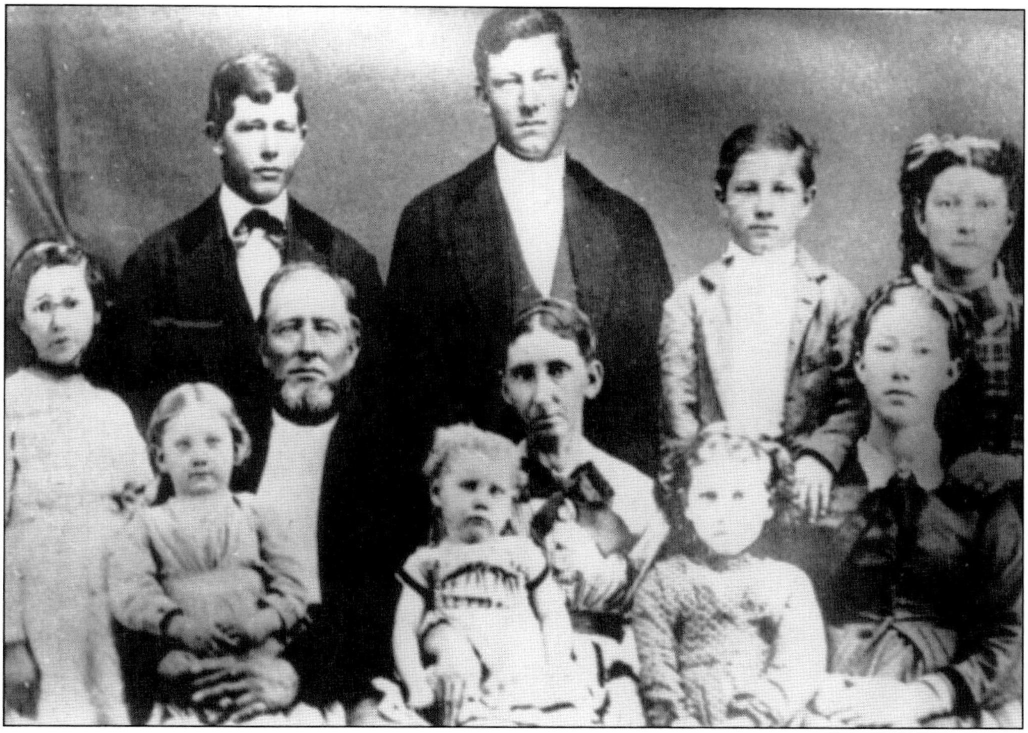

In the mid-1870s, the Lorenzo Koontz family has gathered for a family portrait. Pictured are, from left to right, (first row) Amanda Viletta, Indonia Josephine, and Urilla Bell; (second row) Martha Ellen, Lorenzo, his wife, Matilda, and Mary Ellen; (third row) William, Jacob, Albert, and Deborah. Below, and several years later, Jacob Koontz and his family are shown in front of their large brick home on Andrews Road. Many years later, this house burned and was then torn down. (Both, YMPTHA.)

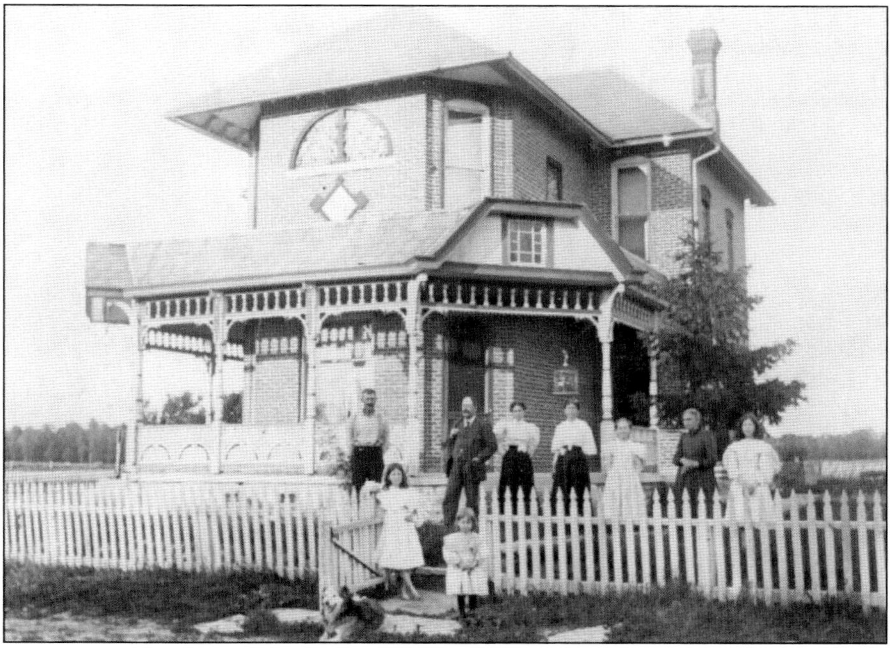

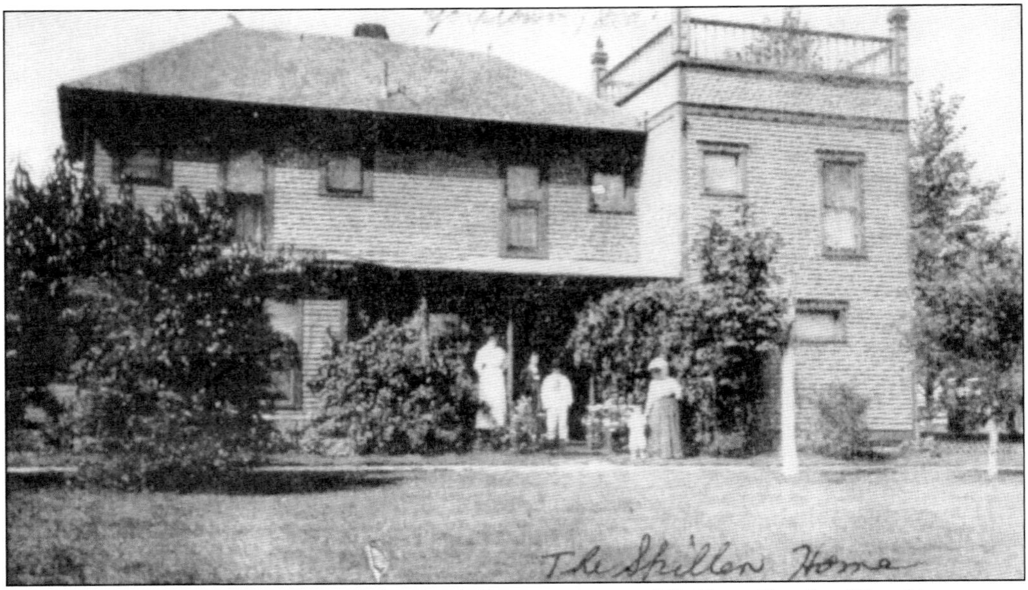

Seen here around 1915, the home of D.O. Skillen, co-owner of Skillen–Gooden Glass Factory, sat on Cornbread Road just west of Buck Creek. The house is still standing, but the second story has been removed. There are several older homes in the area that have had the second story removed because of the expense of heating such large areas. The young girls pictured in the electric car are members of the Skillen and Gooden families and seem to be a little young to be driving; however, it is probable there was no age limit for driving or requirement for a driver's license in those days. (Both, YMPTHA.)

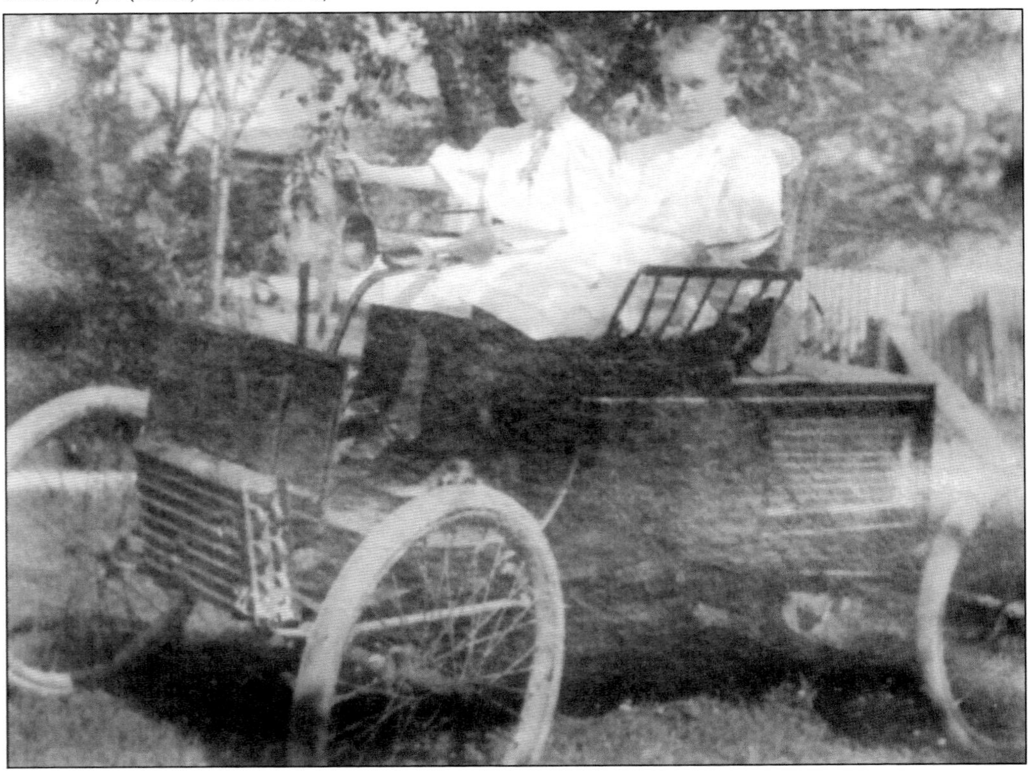

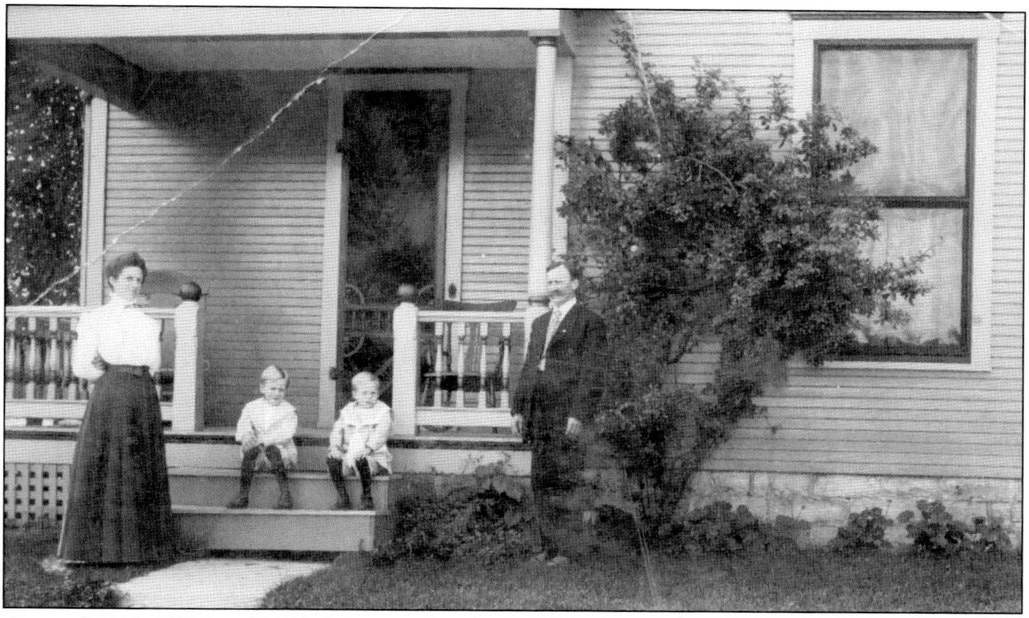

Around 1910, William T. Warfel, a teacher for several Mount Pleasant Township schools, poses with his wife, Hester, and sons, Hubert and Richard. The house at the southwest corner of Smith and Elm Streets was remodeled to apartments with a shared bathroom and kitchen. Later, the house was torn down and replaced with a warehouse-type structure. (YMPTHA.)

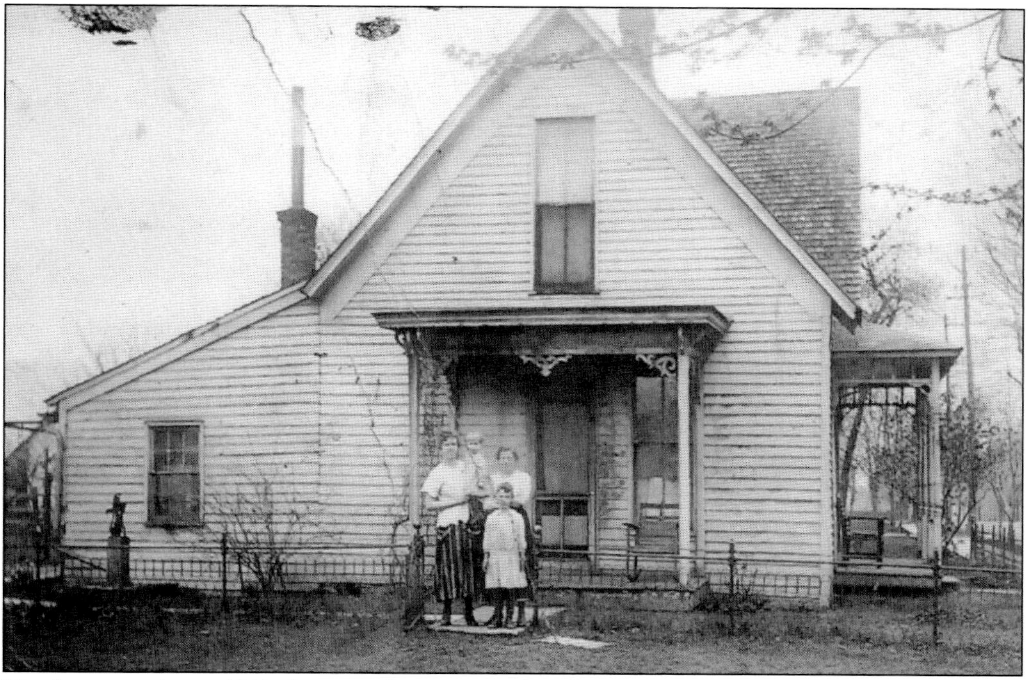

The house in this c. 1910 photograph sat across the alley from the current post office and to the west. There is a different home at this location now, but the 1911 Fire and Insurance map shows a change of structures. There is no indication as to what happened to the original structure shown in the photograph. Standing alongside the house are members of the Watkins family. (Shawn Gray.)

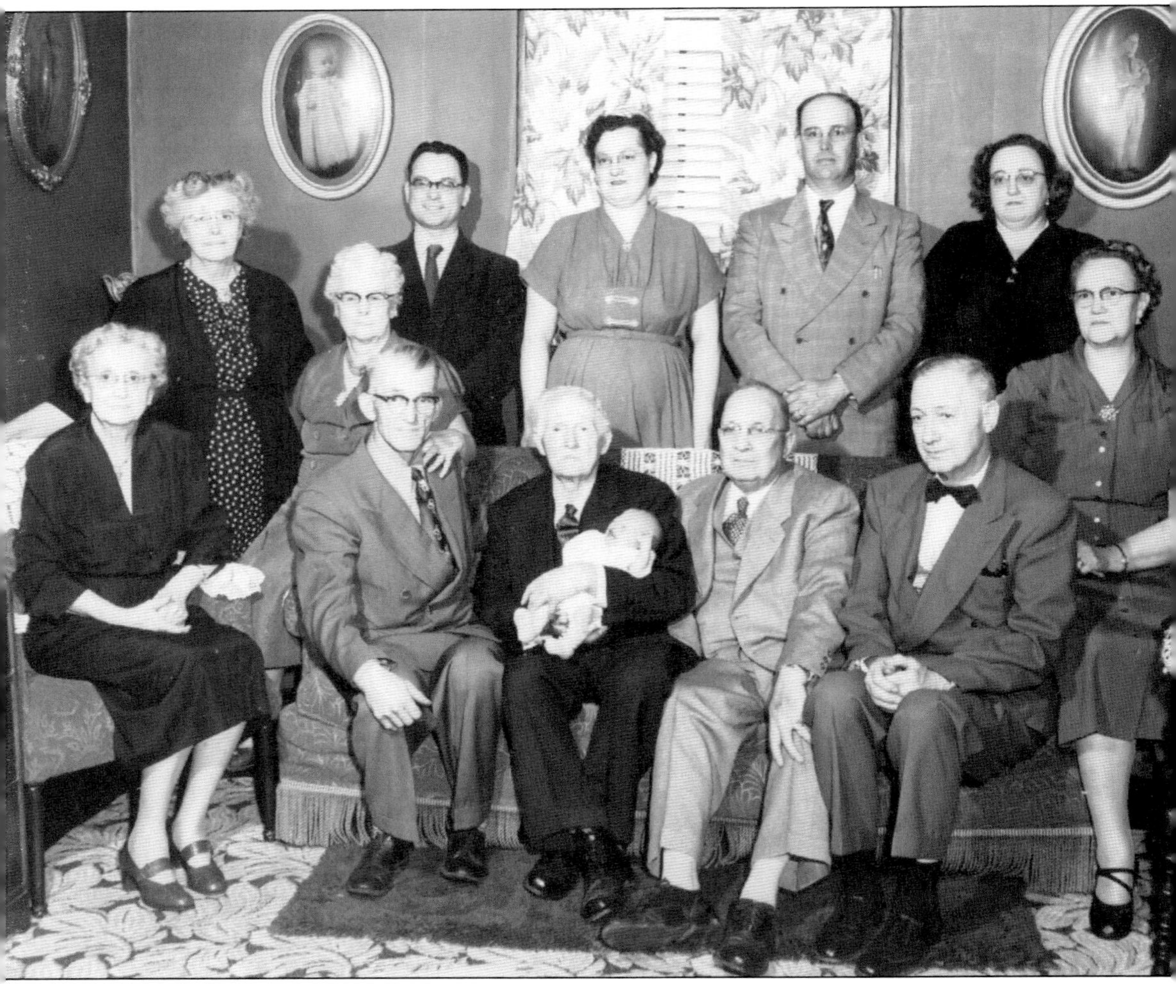

Pictured in March 1954, Rick Swift, 10-day-old son of Richard and Janet Swift, is being held by his great-great-grandfather William West. Others shown are, from left to right, (first row) great-grandmother Anna Funkhouser, great-grandfather Loren West, great-grandfather Glen Funkhouser, and great-grandparents Elmer and Lillian Ellis; (back row) great-great-grandmother Stella Swift, great-grandmother Rose West, grandparents Elmer and Buna Mae (Ellis) West, grandfather Lafe Swift, and grandmother Mary Funkhouser. (Bob Ellis.)

Four

Nearby Neighbors

Outside the original boundaries of Yorktown, three other settlements and a commercial area developed. In 1876, William Reed settled in the northern portion of the township, which became known as Reed Station. It was home to two grocery stores, which sat across the street from one another. When electricity was extended from Muncie to Cammack, Earl Hensley filed a petition to run it on to Reed Station. Monthly bills ran about $1. A small shanty next to the railroad allowed passengers to raise a flag so the train would stop. During inclement weather, passengers waited in the shanty.

Cammack, also to the north, is just east of Reed Station. Many of the older homes are gone, but a few small businesses remain along the main street. In recent years, many of the remaining buildings have undergone revival. Carpenter Hardware houses businesses on the lower level and apartments upstairs. The old gas station is now Cammack Station, a popular dining spot filled with memorabilia from the oil and gas industry.

West Muncie is east of Buck Creek and slightly to the south of the original plat. It was developed by a group of New York investors and several area residents. A dam near Cornbread Road was constructed to form a lake and a large resort hotel was built in 1893. Heavy rains in 1894 broke the dam, and expense prohibited repair. No other main attraction remained, the hotel was no longer needed, and all but a small portion was demolished. The remaining structure was used as a home, which has also been torn down.

The Werts Properties, east on State Road 32, consisted of approximately 500 acres. It was originally a farm, and businesses were soon built along the highway. The area was best known for Silver Fox Farm, the Silver Fox School of Aviation, Werts Novelty, a rodeo area, and a boxing arena. There was also a section called Werts Tourist City. Small cottages, constructed of flagstone mined from the property, dotted the area. There were gravel pits, too, one of which, when no longer active, was stocked with fish and became known as In-law Lake.

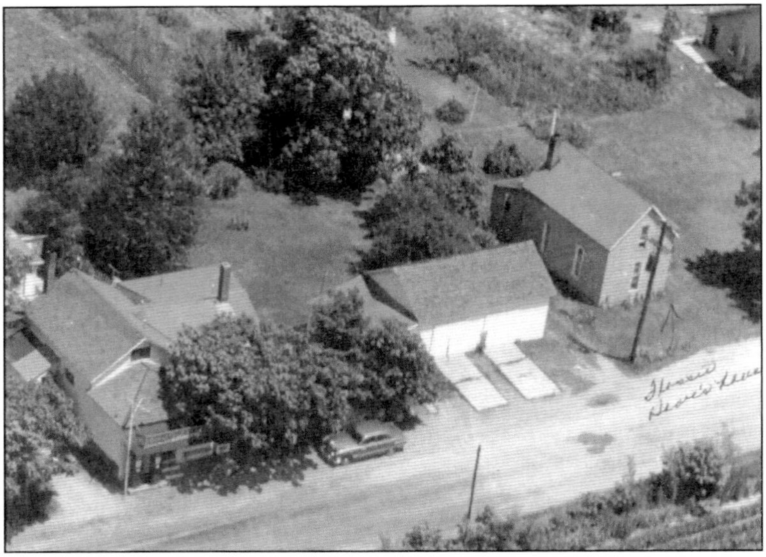

This aerial view shows the grocery store at Reed's Station. The house belonged to Flossie Howe, who is the grandmother of Dick Howe, the owner of the present-day Cammack Station. The garage located between the store and house was used as a warehouse for the store. (YMPTHA.)

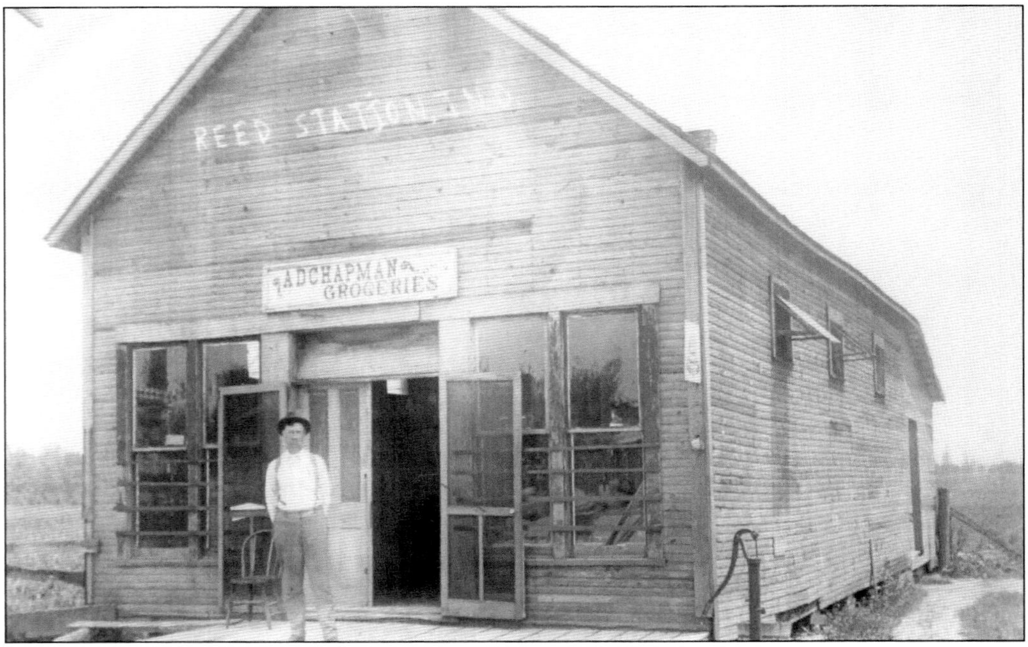

A.D. Chapman stands in front of his grocery in Reed Station. An iron pump stands in front of the store. In addition to running the store, Chapman drove a huckster wagon throughout the countryside. He sold groceries and various sundries to outlying farmers. He would also trade goods for chickens, eggs, and produce. (Don Guinn.)

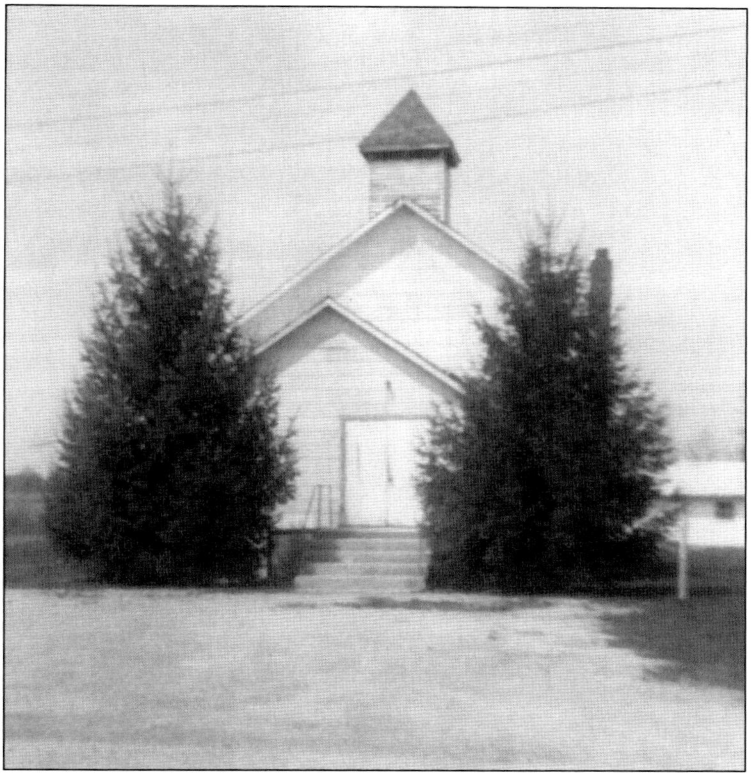

In 1886, John and Sarah Tuttle deeded property to the trustees of the Reed Station Christian Church. Records have been lost, so it is uncertain when the first building was erected. The first records found are dated 1914 and indicate the church was in the era of kerosene lamps and coal stoves. In May 1974, ground was broken for the modern building currently there. (Betty Thurman.)

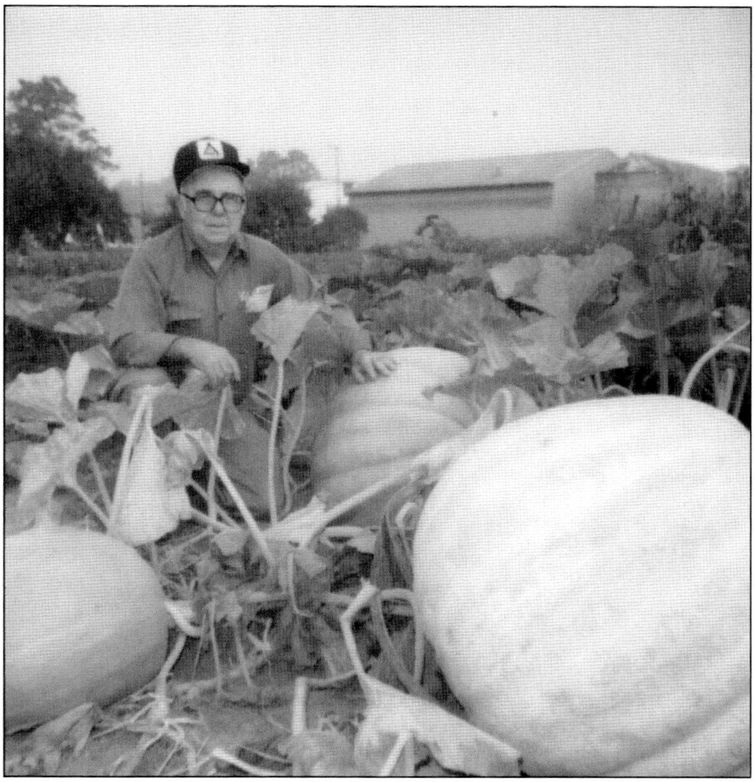

Just east of Reed Station and across the tracks from Cammack, Charlie Fuson, one of the area farmers, hugs one of his giant pumpkins in the late 1950s. In addition to farming, Fuson owned Fuson Farm Implement, where local farmers could buy their equipment. He also carried a line of miniature farm equipment for children. Fuson was well known by many of the Mount Pleasant Township children as their school bus driver. (YMPTHA.)

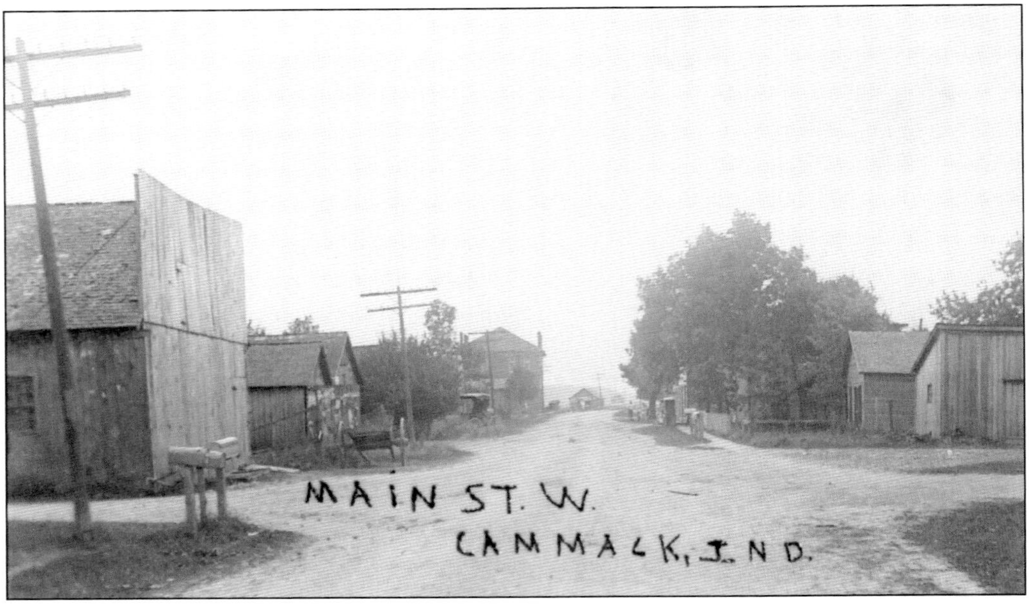

In the c. 1900 image above, with a view looking west down the main street of Cammack, a variety of businesses, homes, and barns can be seen along the way. Very few of these structures remain today. The large building in the background was the Red Men's Lodge. Pictured below around 1910, the upper level was often used as a gymnasium by the boys of the neighborhood. The Improved Order of Red Men is a patriotic fraternity chartered by Congress. It is a nonprofit organization devoted to inspiring a greater love for the United States of America and the principles of American liberty. (Above, Dale Stephenson; below, Jeff Koenker.)

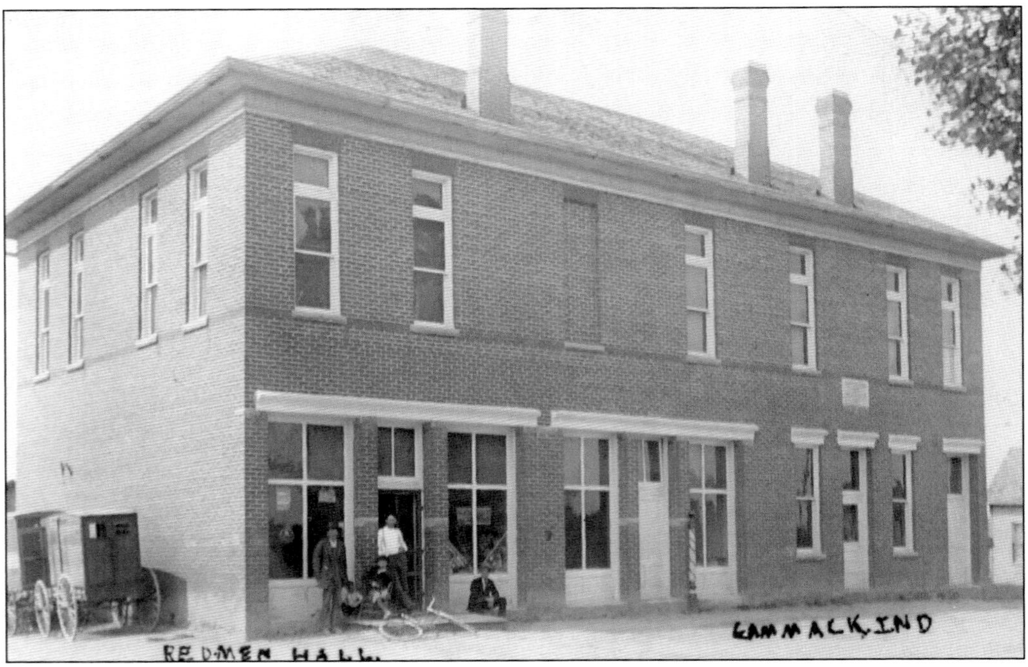

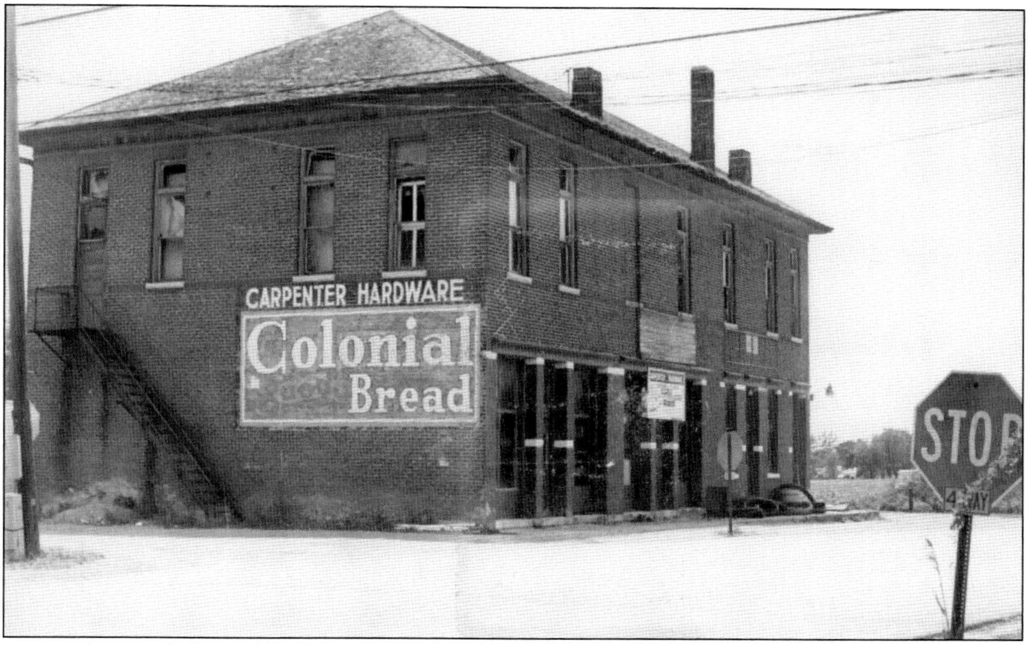

Pictured around the mid-20th century, the Red Men's Lodge property was purchased by Herman "Carpy" Carpenter and converted to a hardware store. Carpy's featured old-fashioned floor-to-ceiling shelving. If a desired item was not on display, there was a good possibility it was upstairs. Once the item was found, Carpenter sold it for the price marked, which may have been from 20 years earlier. (YMPTHA.)

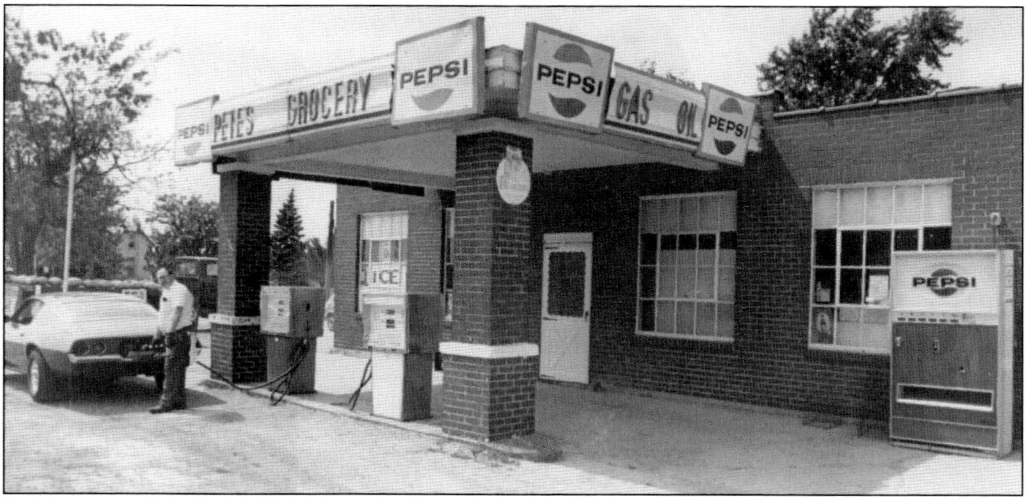

Before Pete Davis took over the operation of a small grocery and service station in Cammack, it was owned by Russell and Ada Lavonne Donovan. The inside of the building that is seen here around 1955 looked much like it would have in the 1930s, with an old Coca-Cola cooler, some benches, and a meat case. Davis would sell meat for customers to take home or make a sandwich for them to eat while visiting with friends. (YMPTHA.)

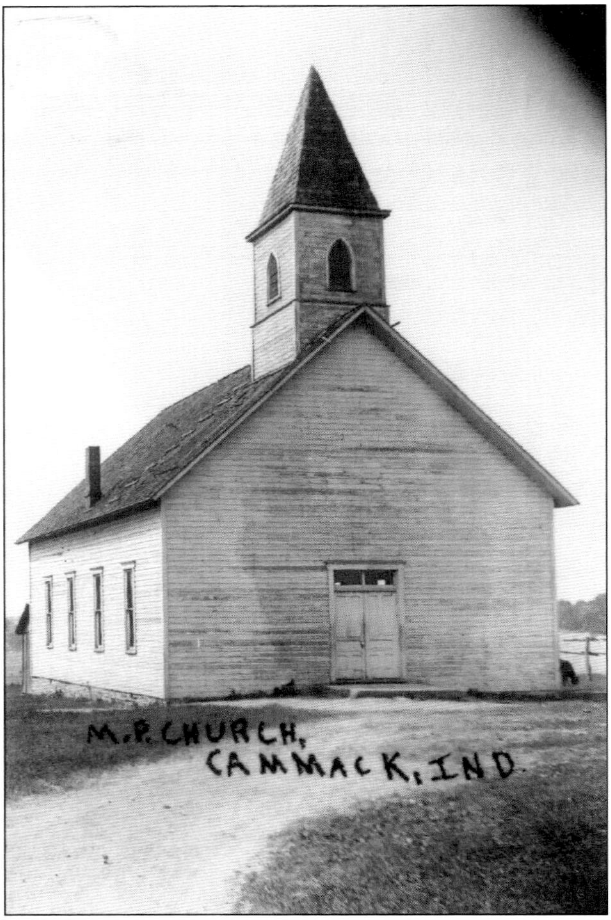

The original Methodist church built at Cammack in 1893 was constructed of wood with a pitched roof and belfry. Later, an addition was added to the back of the building for classroom purposes. This entire structure was torn down in 1984 and replaced with a modern brick building. (YMPTHA.)

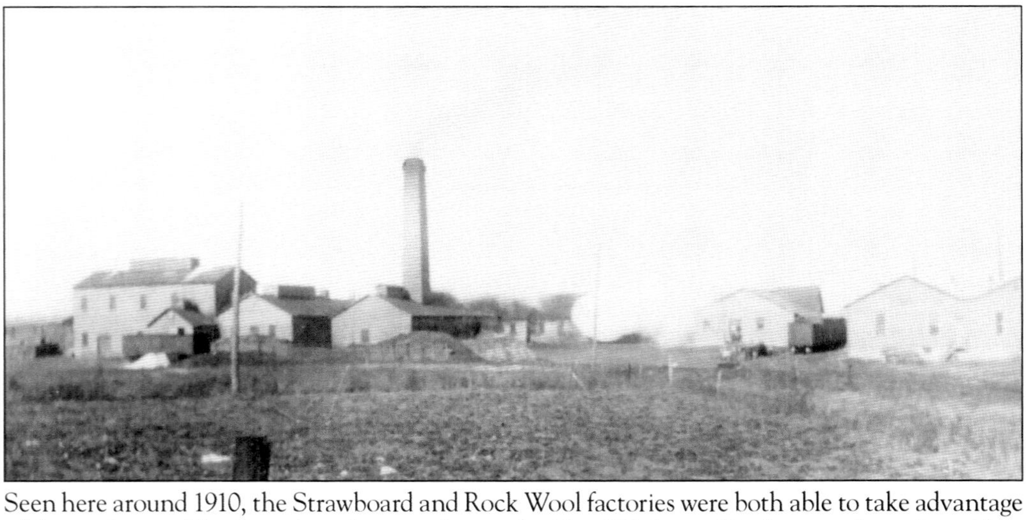

Seen here around 1910, the Strawboard and Rock Wool factories were both able to take advantage of the gas boom. The Strawboard sat on the north side of Highway 32, close to where the middle school is now, and manufactured a type of cardboard made from straw. One item it manufactured was inserts for egg buckets. They were round with egg-shaped indentions, allowing for eggs to be stacked within the buckets. (YMPTHA.)

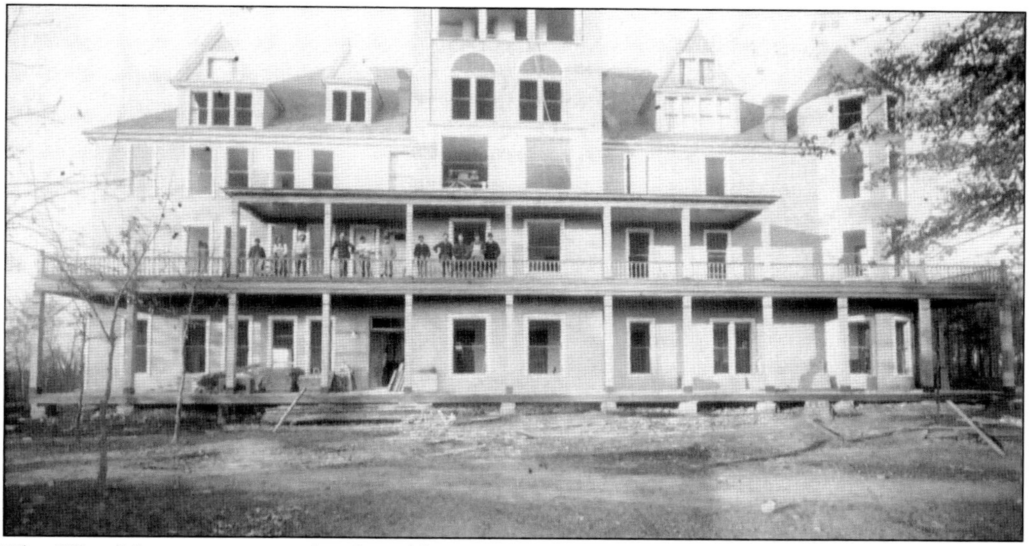

The West Muncie area was developed by a group of men from New York as well as some local residents. A large area was platted, streets were named, and work began on a lake that would run south of Cornbread Road. The 150-acre lake was opened to the public in August 1892. The first event held at the Lake View Hotel was a grand ball, and carriages pulled up in front, allowing guests to spill into the new hotel. In 1894, heavy rains caused the dam to break, draining the lake. Investors chose not to rebuild the dam, which brought hardship to the hotel. Since it was no longer needed, the hotel was razed around 1915—except for a small portion that remained as a house, which has since been torn down. (Both, YMPTHA.)

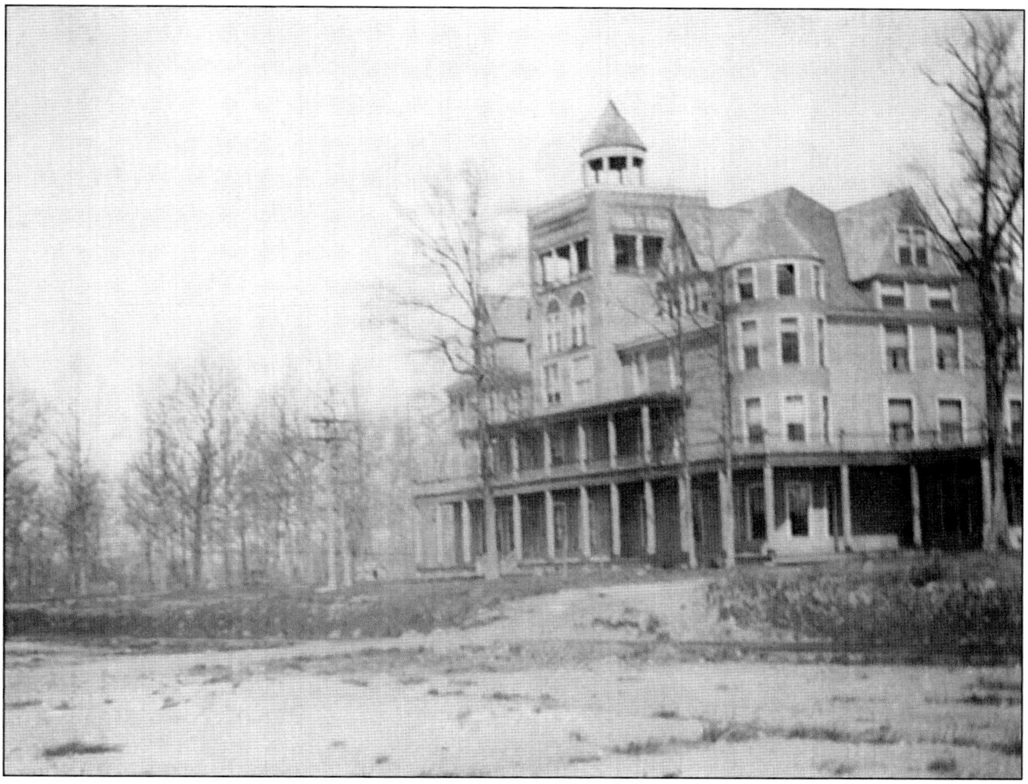

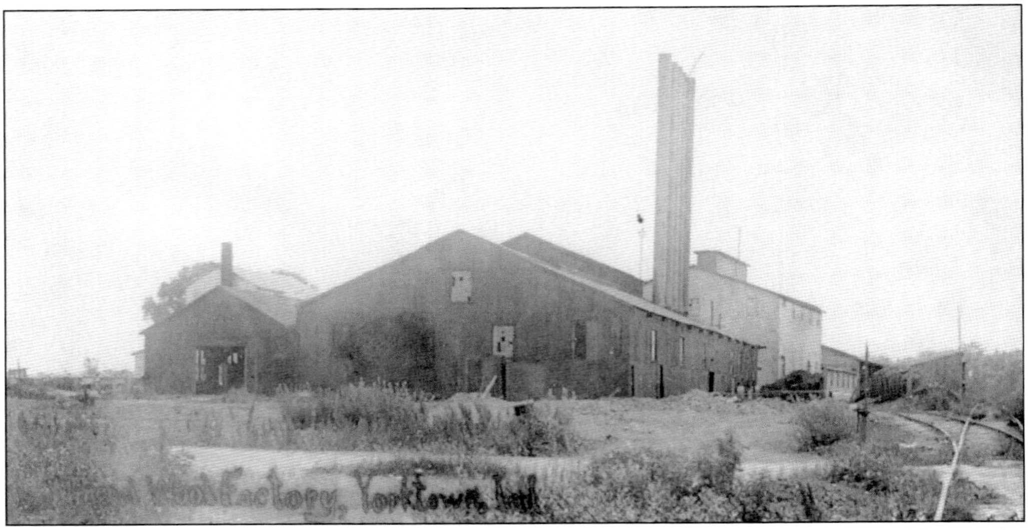

The Rockwool factory was located east of Yorktown between Highway 32 and Adaline. The Rockwool factory manufactured insulation to be used in the attic areas of homes and other buildings. This insulation was made from basalt rock and chalk; company employees complained about the constant itch it caused to their skin. (YMPTHA.)

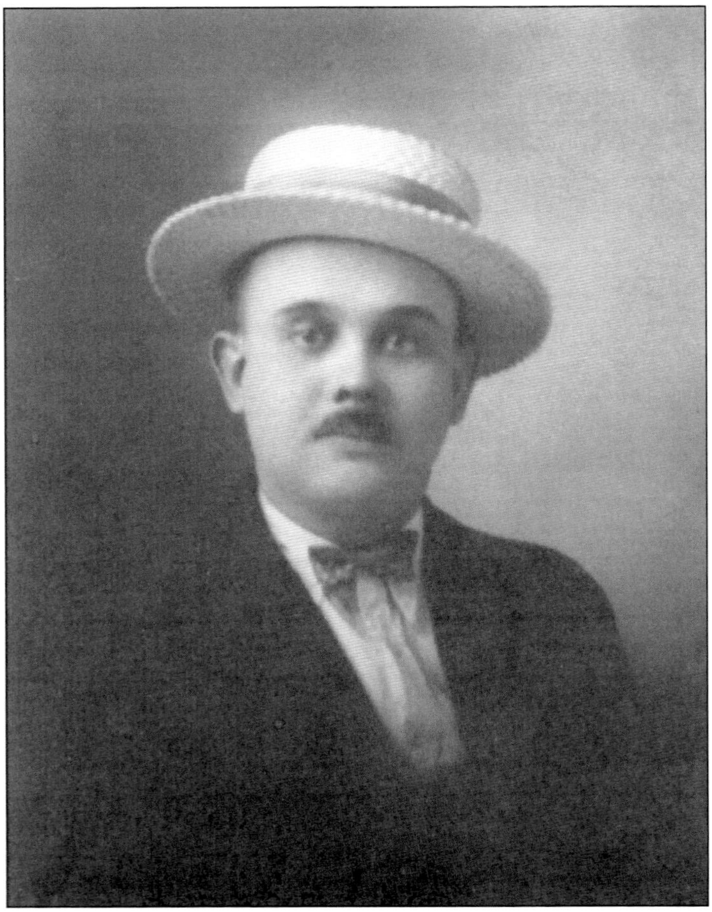

In 1920, Fred Werts purchased 500 acres east of town that he used for farming and commercial enterprises. Among these were the Silver Fox Farm, a rodeo, and several other business ventures. Under the name Werts Novelty, he manufactured pull tabs, punchboards, and other gambling devices. He also hosted boxing matches with several noted boxers of the time. Werts turned his businesses over to family members and ended his career as an evangelist. (YMPTHA.)

One of the first areas to be developed by Fred Werts was his Silver Fox Farm. Utilizing this name, he opened an airport in the fall of 1929. According to a scorecard from yet another business known as Baby Golf, the actual name was the Silver Fox School of Aviation Golf Course. The airport offered flying lessons and a small commercial service. (YMPTHA.)

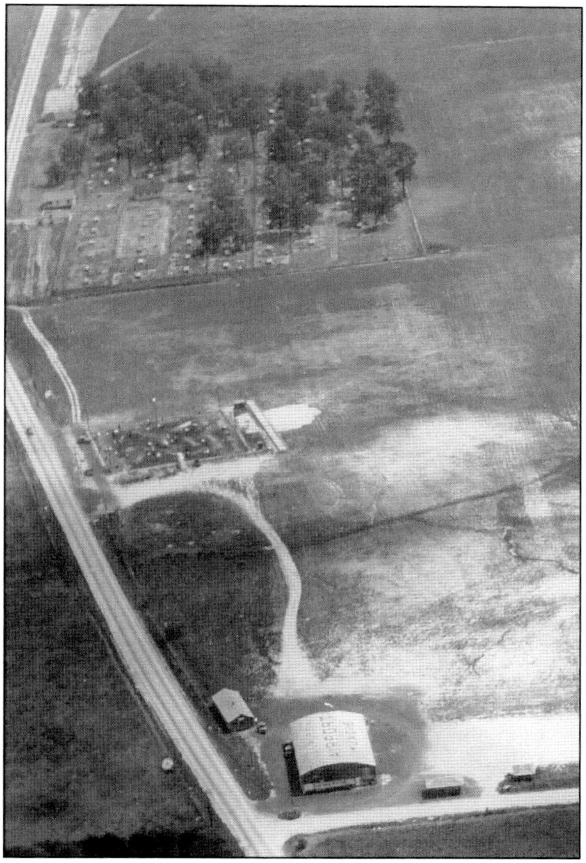

At a later date, a building replaced the Baby Golf Course and was originally used as an area where big bands performed. It was later used as a skating rink, which operated under two names—the Roller Bug (Marietta and Curly Downing) and Kahler's (Fred and Martha Kahler). After the skating rink ran its course, the building was turned into a warehouse for Morrow Machinery Movers. (YMPTHA.)

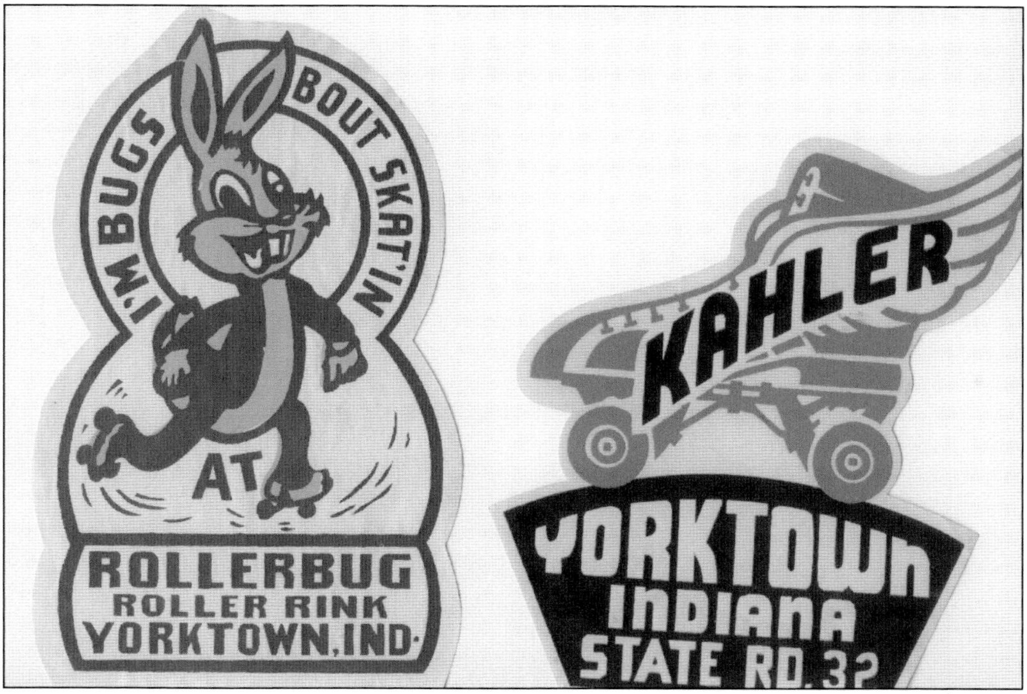

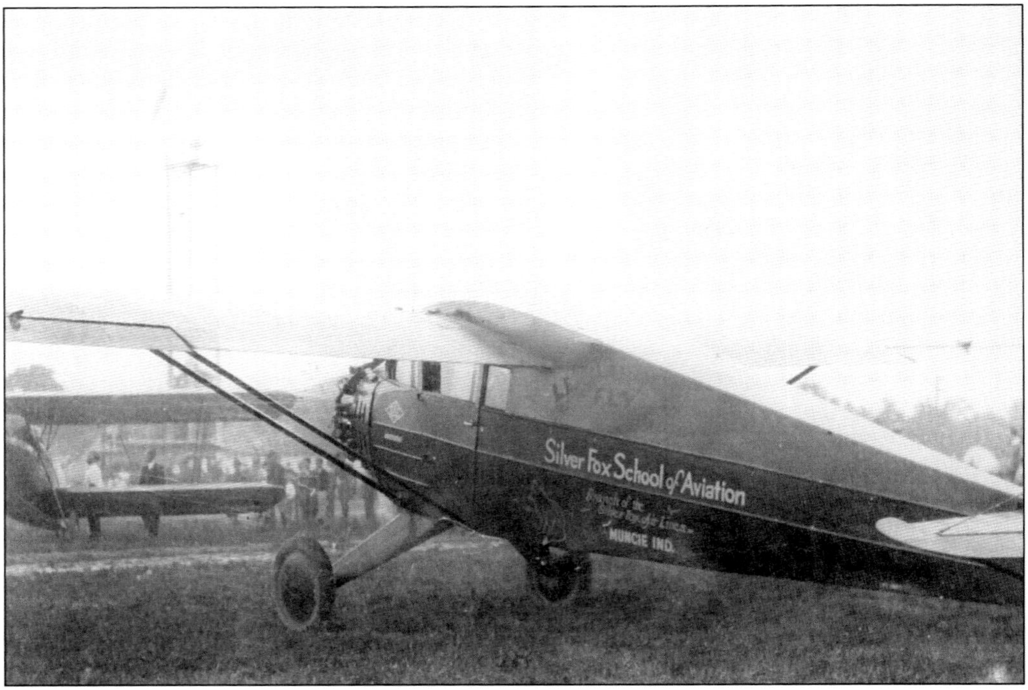

An airplane belonging to the Silver Fox School of Aviation advertises that it is a branch of the Silver Fox Air Lines of Muncie, Indiana. Even though Werts owned a good deal of property in the Yorktown area, his home was in Muncie. A flyer advertising an open house in 1929 indicates that the airport is located on State Road 67. Prior to updating Middletown Pike, Highway 32 was also Highway 67. (YMPTHA.)

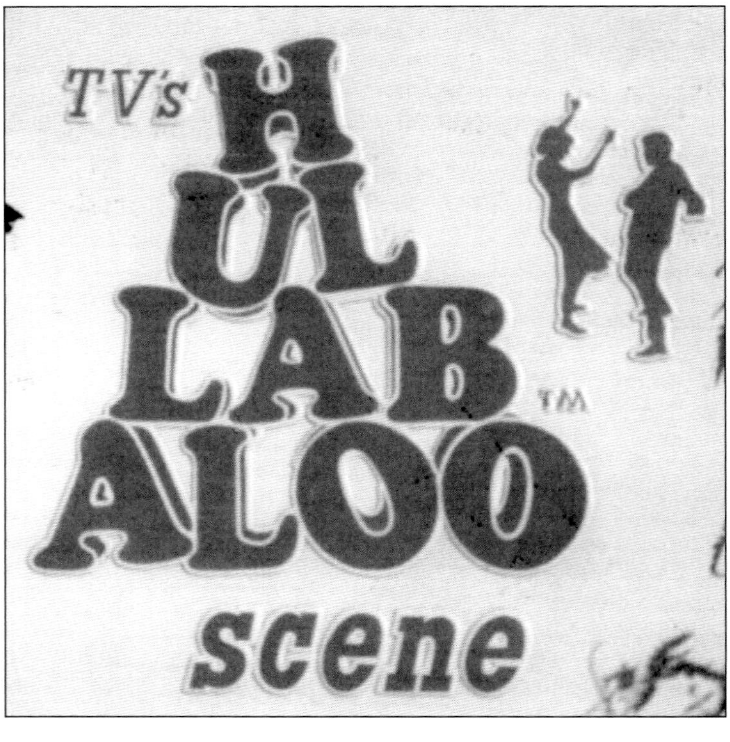

In November 1967, a vacant building owned by Junior Morrow and sitting on the old Werts property was opened as a dance spot for teenagers called the Hullabaloo Scene, part of a national chain of 64 similar dance spots. Some of those appeared on national television and featured live bands such as the Chosen Few and Faith along with a disc jockey and go-go girls. (YMPTHA.)

Five

Local Heroes

Due to the disastrous fire that destroyed a portion of the business district on the corner of Smith and Walnut Streets, the town of Yorktown established its first town government in late May 1913. The officers elected were as follows: Harry Gardner (First Ward), Peyten Keyes (Second Ward), John S. Huffer (Third Ward), John Brady (clerk), Jonas Warfel (treasurer), and Arthur Jones (constable). The original fire station was located behind the Yorktown Bank. The alarm system consisted of a bell. Volunteers knew to drop whatever they were doing and bring their buckets. A second location was built on Broadway in 1929. A wooden addition was made to the north end of the building and became the town hall. Yorktown police operated out of this part of the building. The third fire department home was built on Broadway just east of the Methodist church parking lot and also housed the Mount Pleasant Township and assessors' offices. The current fire department is on Smith Street and has 35 members, six vehicles, and mobile units. The police department has 10 members and 13 vehicles.

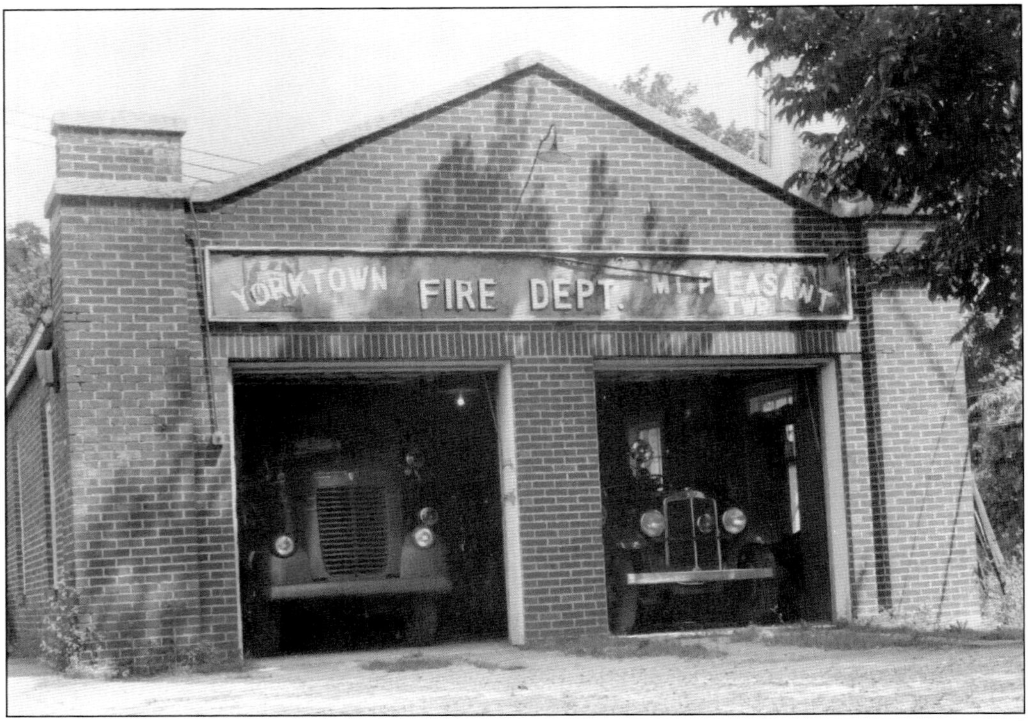

When the amount of firefighting equipment outgrew the first station, a larger facility was erected on Broadway, north of Smith Street. Constructed in 1929, this building served the department until 1963, when additional equipment and a larger facility were once again needed. A tanker was being housed in the garage of one of the members of the fire department and was several blocks away. (YMPTHA.)

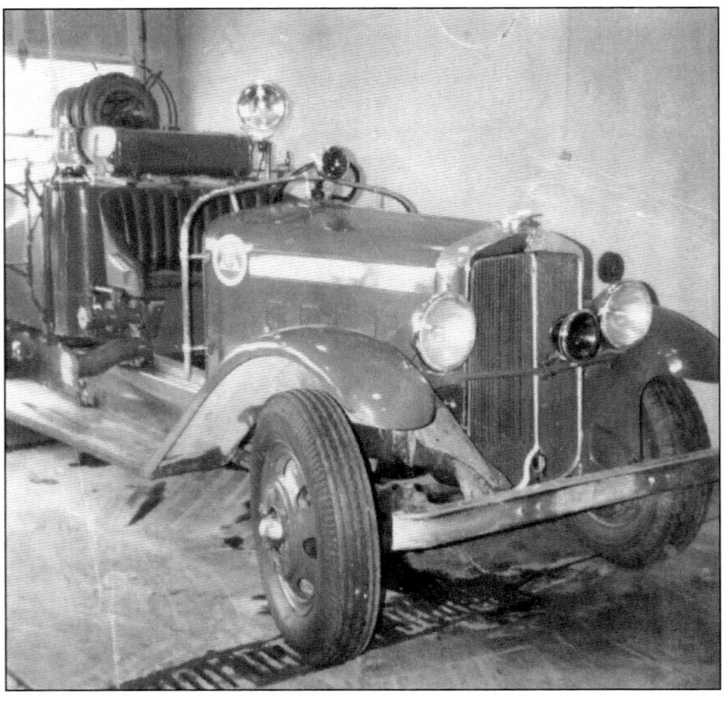

This 1933 Stutz fire truck was the pride of the service for years. Even after it became obsolete, the fire department still shined it up and brought it out for parades and festivals. When the truck was retired, it was purchased by a lifelong member of the community, and upon his death, his family returned the truck to the department. This truck is currently being restored. (YMPTHA.)

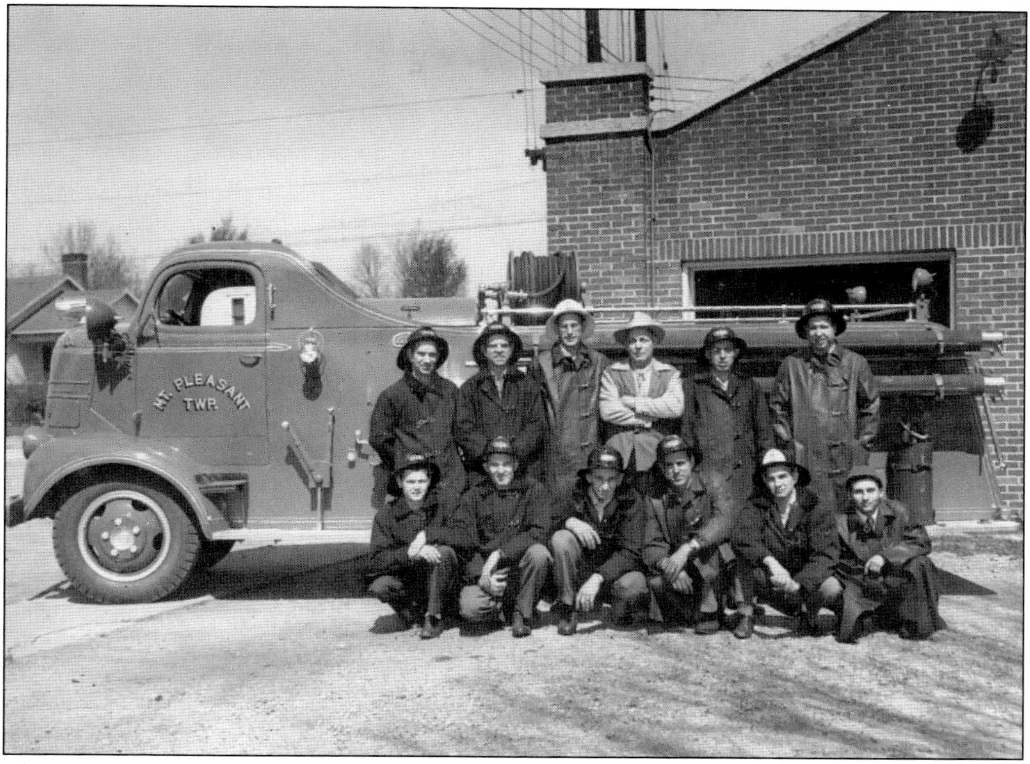

This 1945 Dodge truck was acquired from Army surplus and transformed into a pumper by Howe Fire in Anderson, Indiana. It served the community for many years before being retired and sold. Pictured are, from left to right, (first row) unidentified, Raymond Childs, Lowell Morrow, Gib Fuller, unidentified, and Pat Weaver; (second row) Bill Martin, Tom Lennis, Ralph Garrison, trustee Ray Miller, Mort Everett, and Vaughn Ellis. (YMPTHA.)

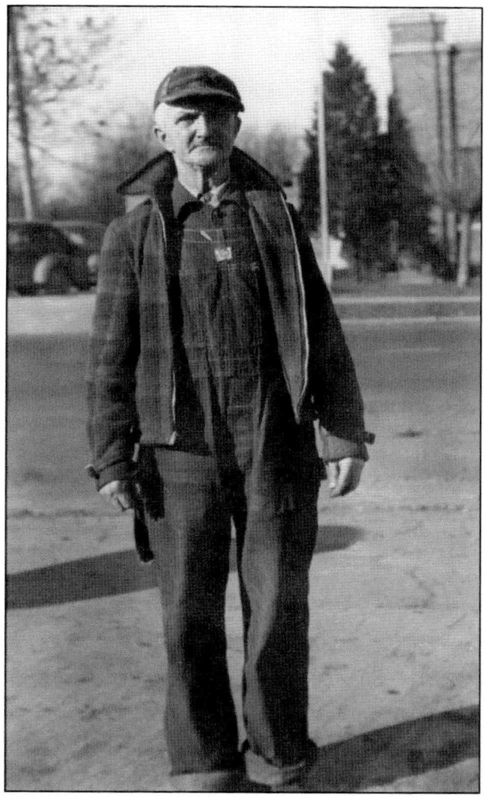

Buford "Midge" Barlow was for many years a member of the volunteer fire department. When the station north of Smith Street was closed and a larger one built two blocks to the south, transportation became an issue for Midge because he stood less than five feet tall. Since he did not drive, he never hesitated to jump into a car in front of his business and tell the driver to take him to the station. (Sara Applegate estate.)

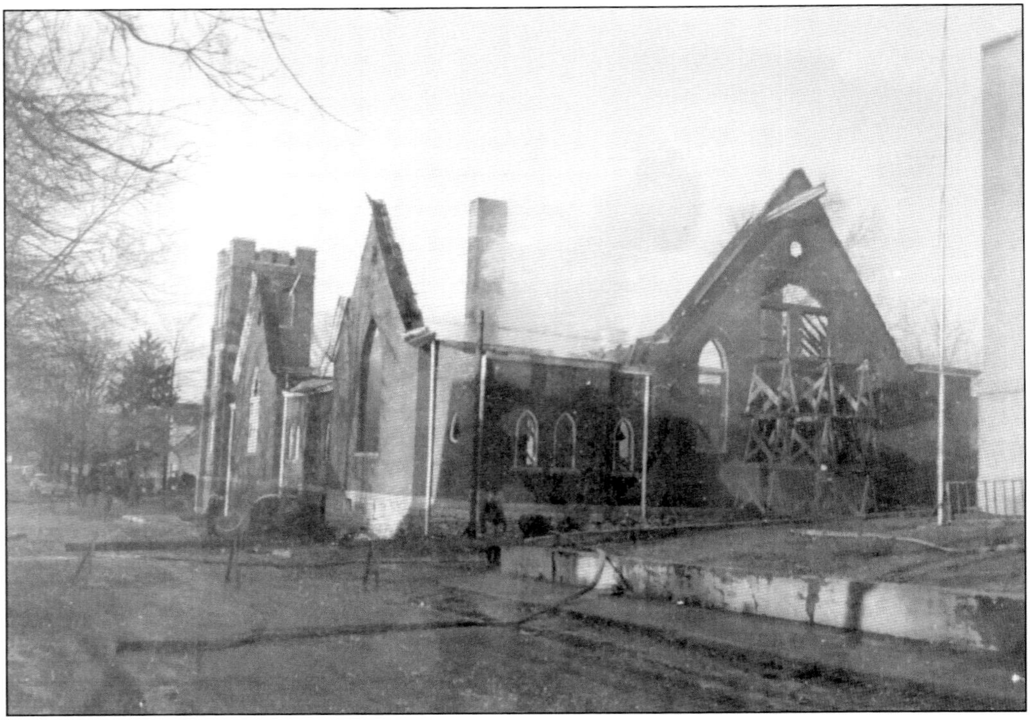

On Christmas Eve 1950, smoke was seen curling from the south end of the Yorktown Methodist Church and firefighters quickly rushed to the scene. It is now believed to have been an electrical fire related to the ongoing project to modernize the heat and lighting systems. While the interior of the church was burned out, the outer brick shell remained standing but had to be demolished. Below, firemen are seen entering the building through a small side door. Despite this and other efforts, they were unable to stop the fire. Due to the quick response of the fire department and community members, many items were removed, including pianos, the organ, and pews. Until a new building was erected, the church used the gym and classrooms of the nearby Yorktown School for Sunday services. (Both, Marylou Schmidt.)

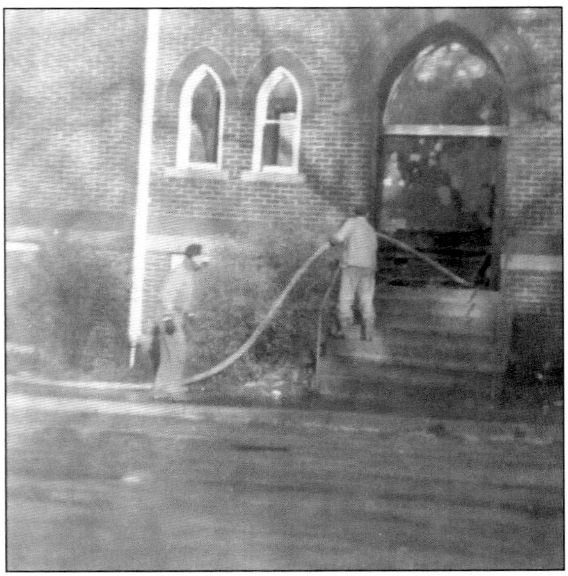

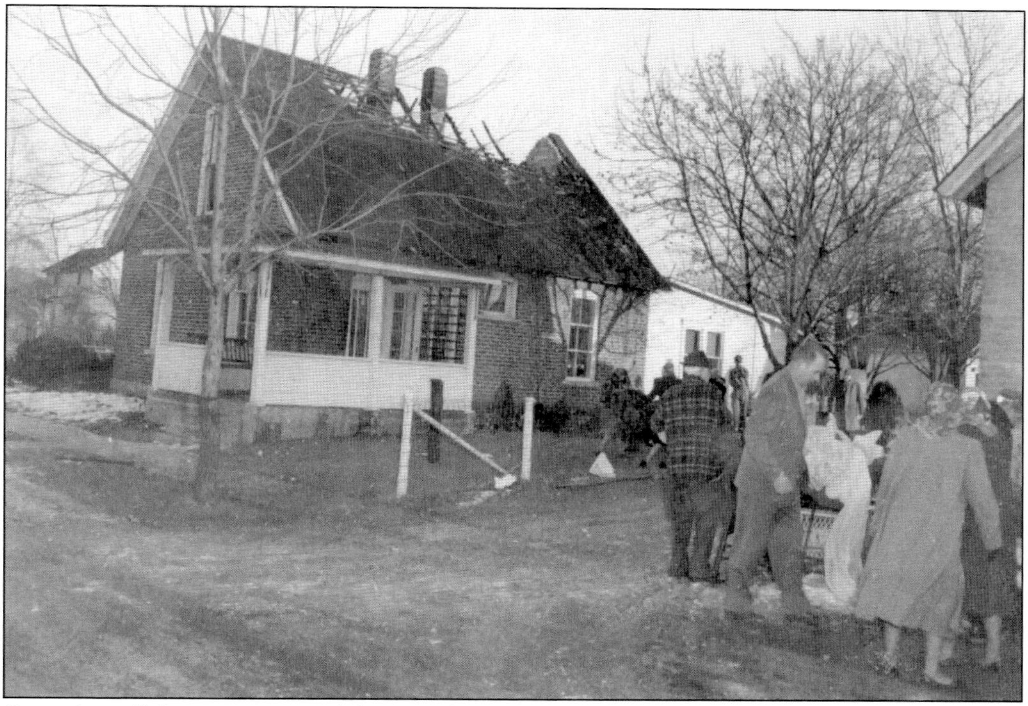

Several small fires were started due to a large amount of ash from the Methodist church fire. This house located on Mill Street (more than three blocks away) suffered a good deal of damage. Pictured here are neighbors who helped salvage items from the house. (Marylou Schmidt.)

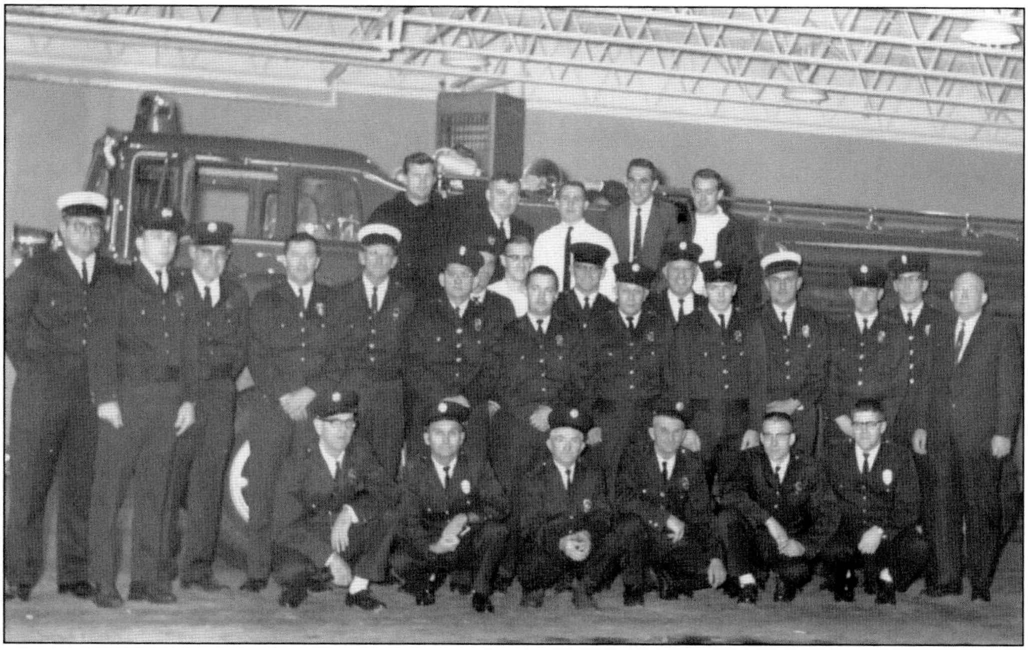

Inside a station built in 1963 at the northwest corner of Arch and Broadway Streets is a much enlarged department. Not only did this building allow for a larger crew, but it also provided room for additional equipment. Among those pictured on the second row are Capt. Ed Luzader (far left), Asst. Chief H.C. McVicker (fifth from left), and Chief Gib Fuller (fourth from right). (YMPTHA.)

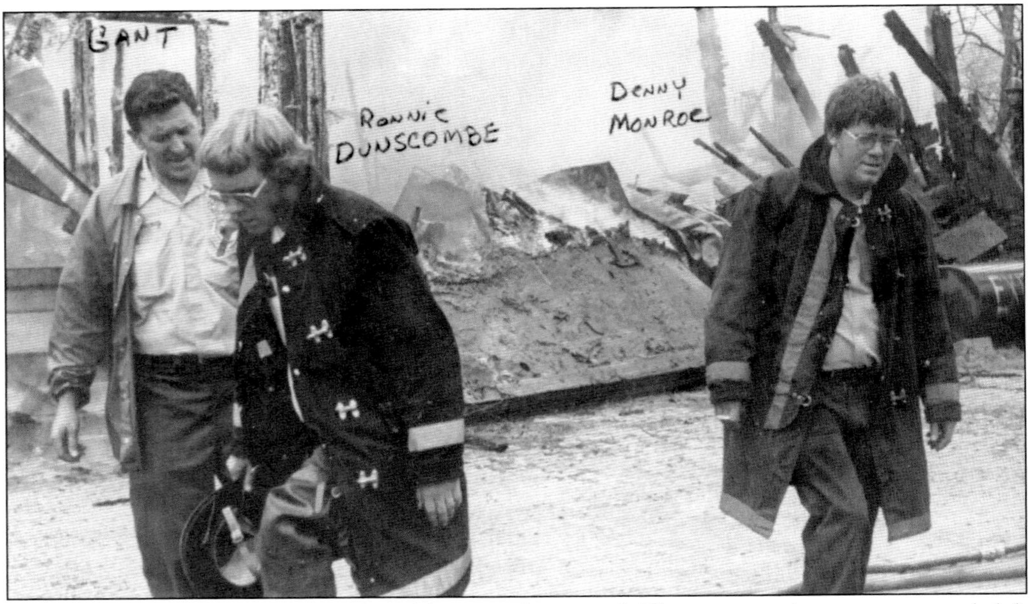

May 1974 saw a longtime area landmark burn to the ground. The ever-popular restaurant and club was located on Highway 32, southwest of Yorktown. The Top Hat served as a place for dances, banquets, or just a good Sunday meal. Here, former fireman Raymond "Sonny" Gant (left) comforts Ron Dunscombe. Dennis Monroe is at far right. (Jim Proudfoot.)

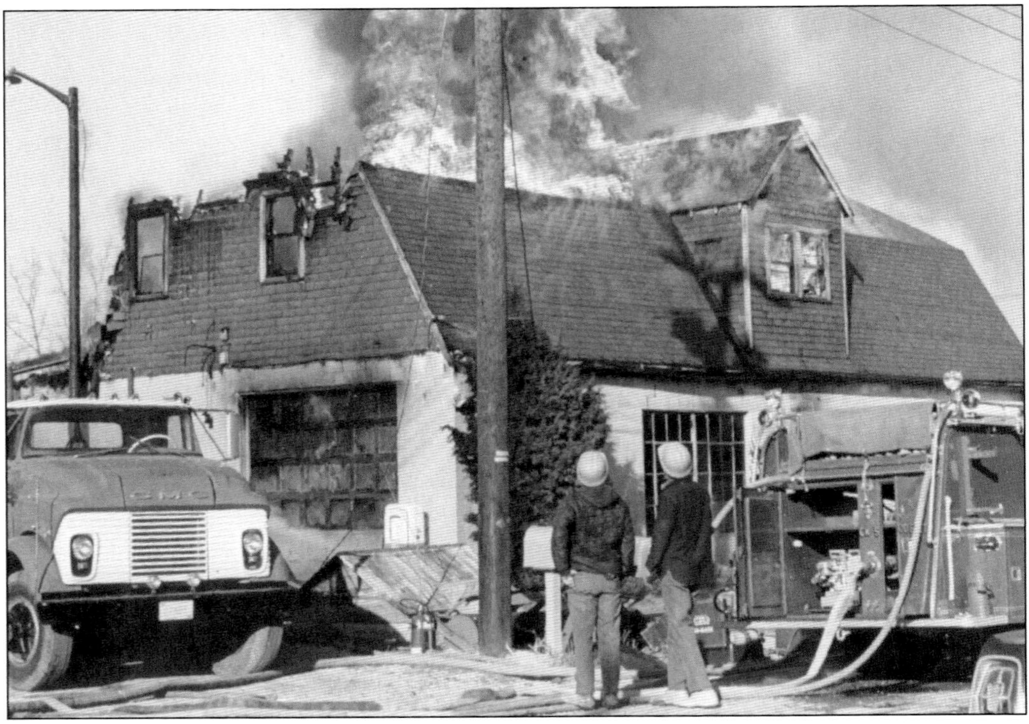

When the All State Landscaping Company called in a tractor fire, the Yorktown Fire Department sent out a single truck, only to scramble for reinforcements when it turned out the tractor was parked inside the company's warehouse. The warehouse suffered extensive damage, but the firefighters managed to prevent the blaze from spreading through the town. (Jim Proudfoot.)

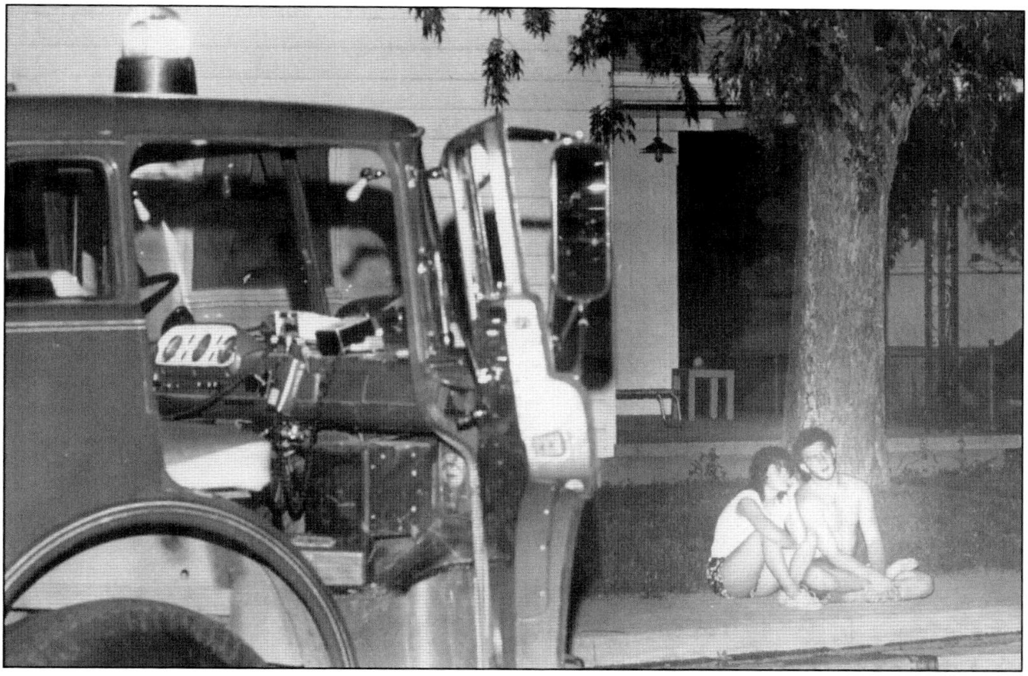

Neighborhood children Jenny Wagner and Joe Holman watch as volunteer firemen extinguish a fire in a house on South Broadway. Below, fireman Bruce Monroe awaits instructions, while the chief and assistant chief assess the situation. Heavy smoke appeared to hinder the operation. (Both, Bruce Monroe.)

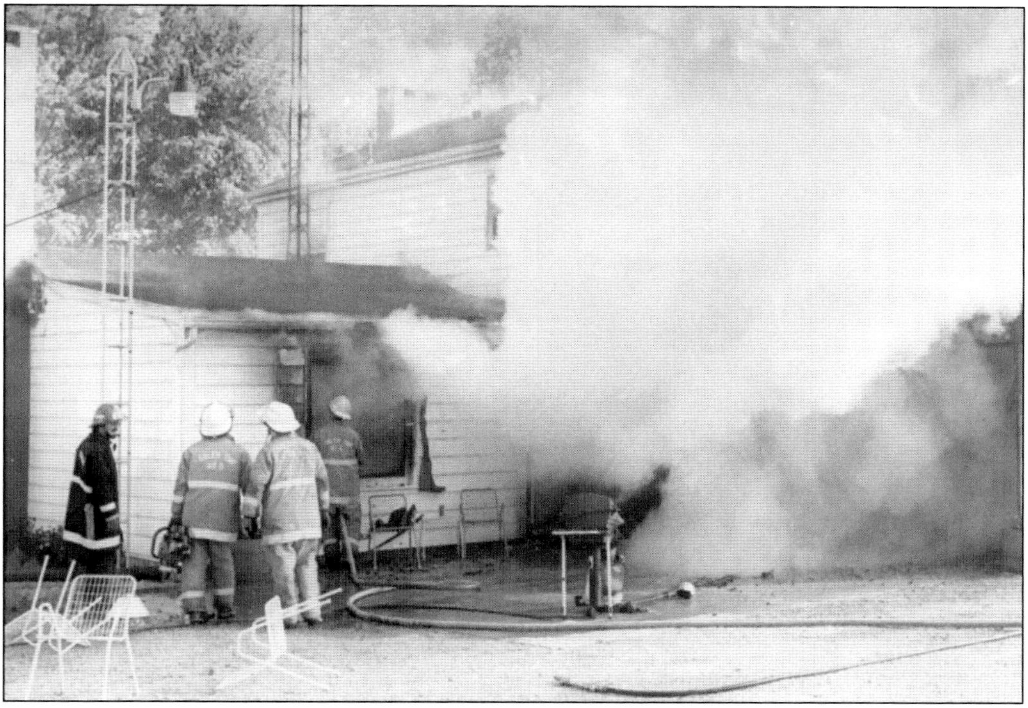

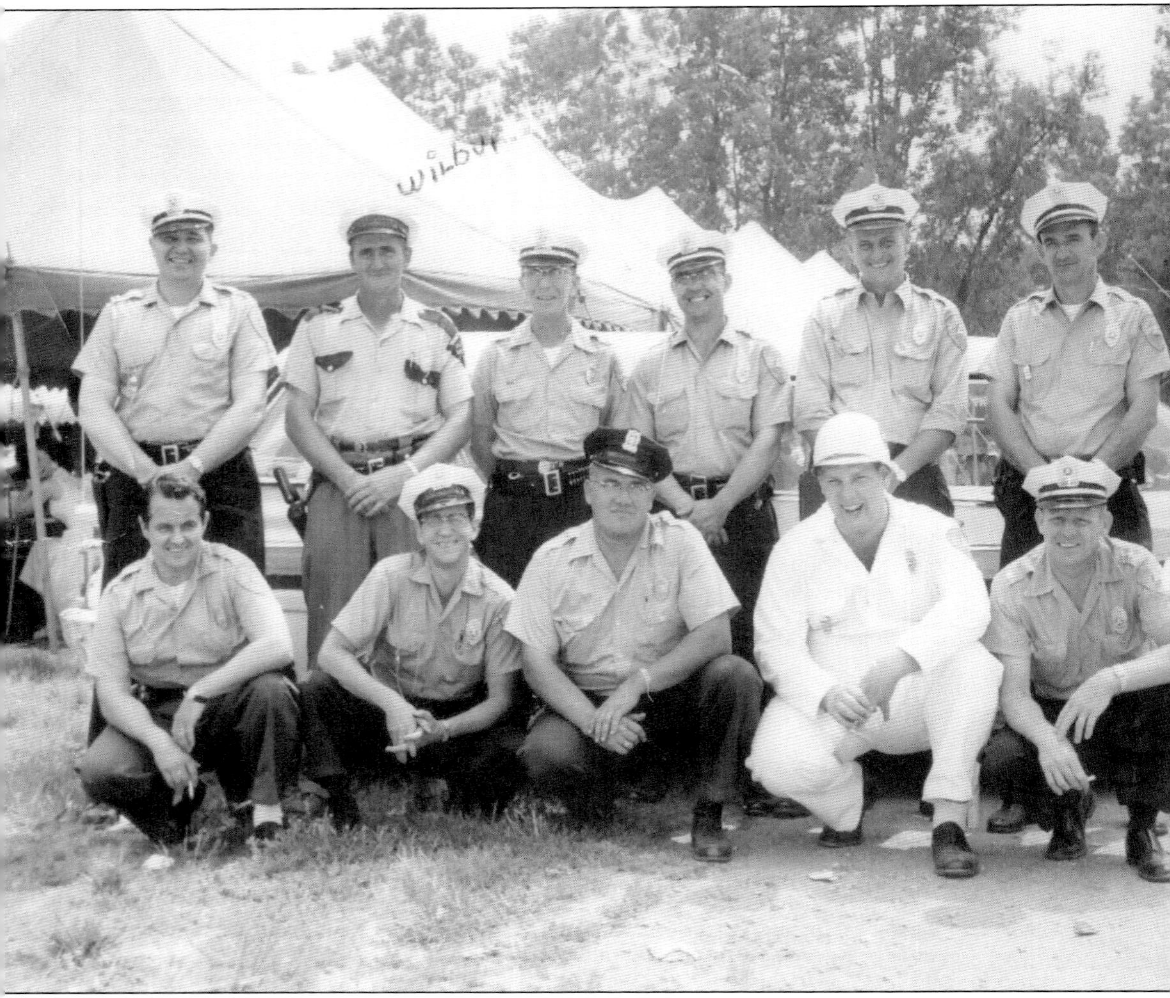

This civil defense team appears to have been at a training session; unfortunately, only four members have been identified: in the front row, Lunda Johnson (left), Dal Ellis (second from right), and Jerry Pennybacker (at right); in the back row, Wilbur Beeman (second from left). Pennybacker was a Yorktown native, serving the department for several years during the 1950s. After attending school at Yorktown, he joined the Air Force, was shot down over Germany, and was a prisoner of war for one and a half years. After he left the police department, Pennybacker drove a truck for Marsh. Beeman was born just over the county line in a little village called Moonsville. Along with his brothers and sisters, he attended school in Moonsville. Beeman and his wife, Wilma, moved to Yorktown, where they raised their children. Beeman spent several years as Yorktown town marshal during the 1950s and 1960s. Pennybacker also held the position of town marshal. (Yorktown Police Department.)

Dick Donovan was a native of Yorktown and the son of John and Ruth Palmer Donovan. After leaving school, he joined the Navy and served for 12 years, part of it during the Korean War. He was a member of the US Navy Reserves and retired from E & B Paving. Dick and his wife, Marian, continued to live in Yorktown and raised their family here. (Marian Donovan.)

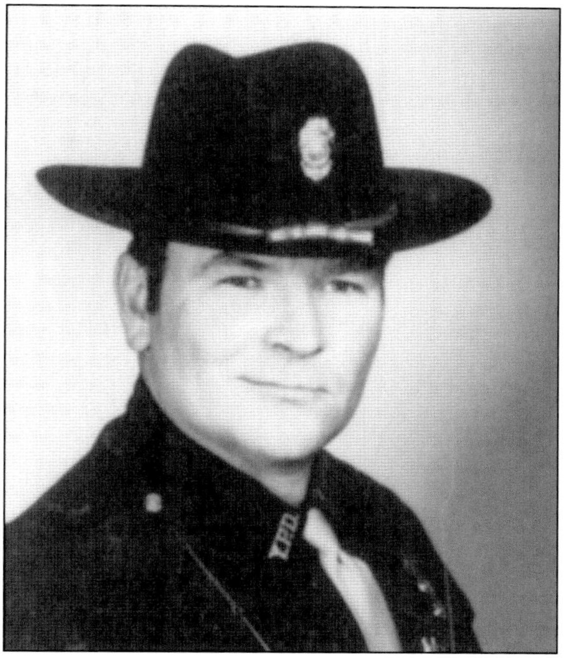

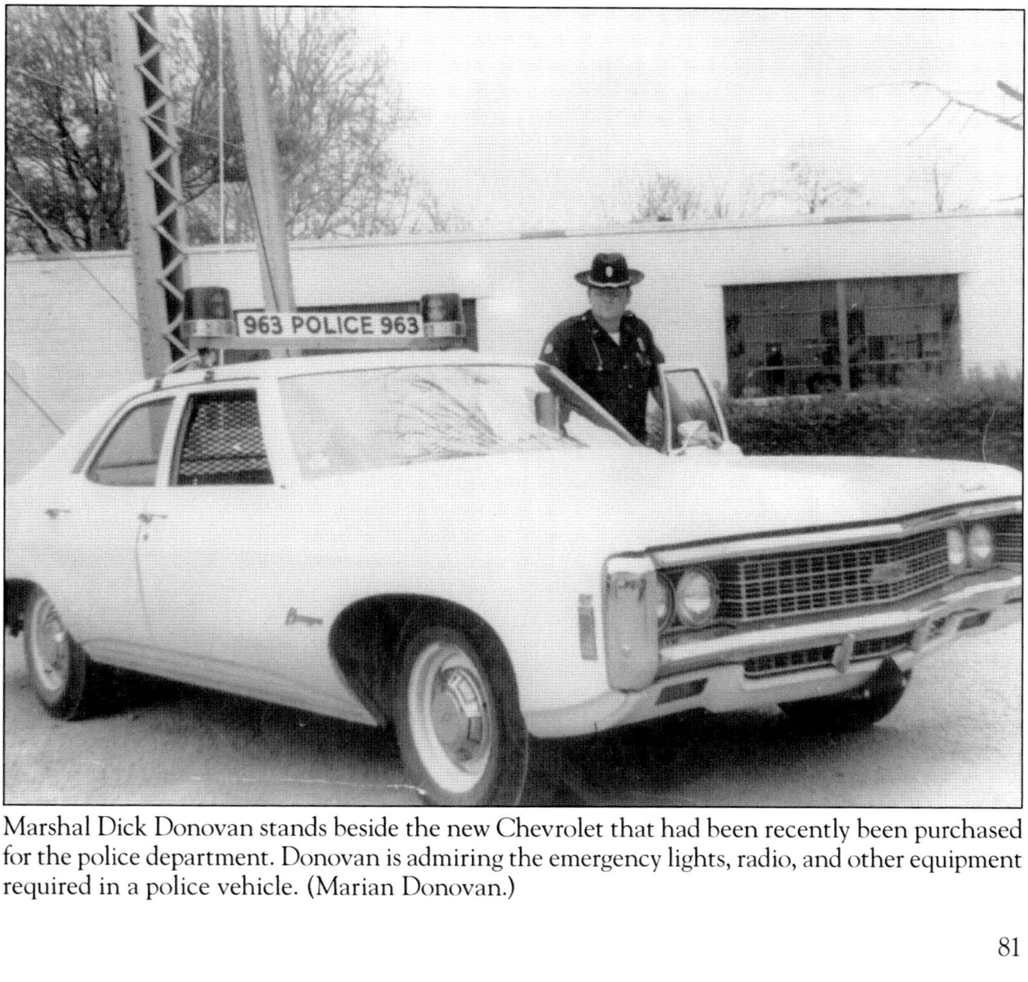

Marshal Dick Donovan stands beside the new Chevrolet that had been recently been purchased for the police department. Donovan is admiring the emergency lights, radio, and other equipment required in a police vehicle. (Marian Donovan.)

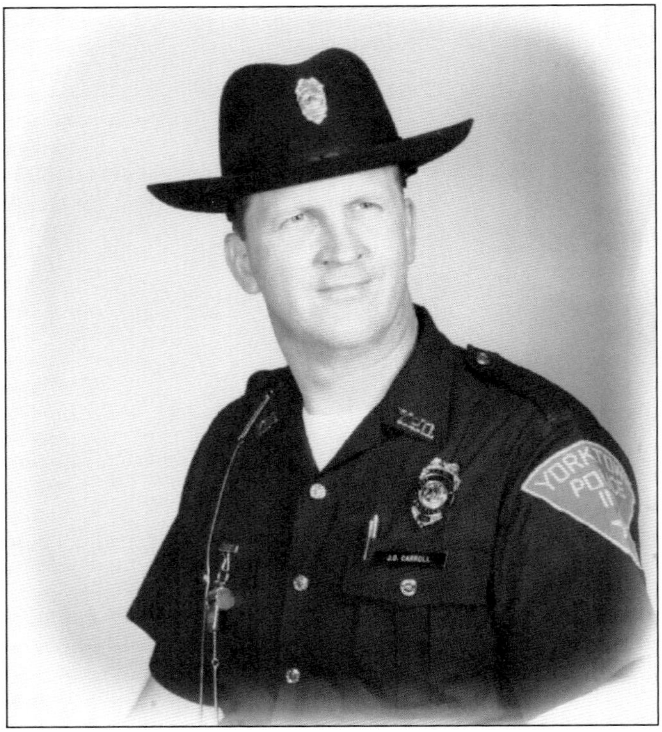

Jerry Carroll, a longtime Yorktown resident, was born in Hammond, Louisiana, and graduated from Wendell L. Willkie High School in Elwood. He served for five years as a Yorktown deputy town marshal and 15 years as a Delaware County reserve officer. Jerry and his wife, Estelle, raised their children in Yorktown. Jerry retired from Marsh as a forklift operator. (Sherry Lake.)

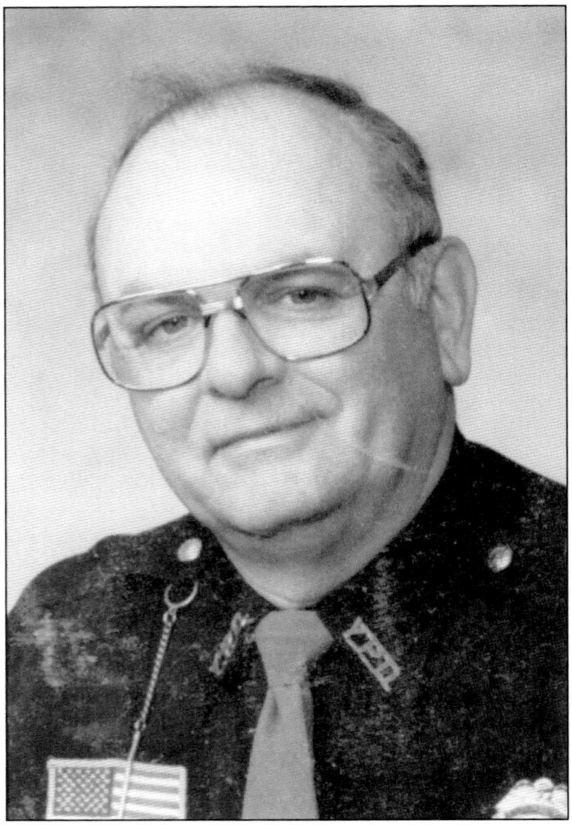

Gordon Grubbs grew up in the Portland and Cowan areas. After a brief tour in the Army, he came to Yorktown and served as the town marshal. He attended the police academy in 1978, there riding out the blizzard that hit central Indiana. After 21 years of service, he retired and went into the auction business. He also had a meat market in Yorktown. (Billie Grubbs.)

Six

Clubs and Activities

Many have questioned the origins of the unusual name of the Independent Order of Odd Fellows (IOOF). Early records indicate that a group of men banded together to form an association for mutual fellowship and help. Generally, society in those days did not function this way, so they were referred to as odd. The members accepted this tag and called themselves the Odd Fellows. As far as records show, this organization began in England in the 1700s, has continued since, and has also become a benevolent society that help the widows and orphans of members. There have been other explanations for the name, such as that these were men who had odd trades. Women of the Odd Fellows are call Rebekahs.

The Knights of Pythias was the first fraternal organization to receive a charter in 1864 under an act of Congress. Members stress loyalty, honor, and friendship. They aid disaster victims nationwide, provide camps for underprivileged youth and homes for their aged members. They are involved in blood drives, sponsor scholarship funds, and are noted for their funding of cystic fibrosis research.

In 1917, business leaders in Chicago formed a fellowship of businessmen who wanted to also reach out to improve their communities. Similar groups across the country came together to form the Association of Lions Clubs. Later, women formed the Lady Lions. There were, in addition, a number of women's clubs in Yorktown. Many were home economics clubs to teach homemaking skills. Others organized community events and helped the needy.

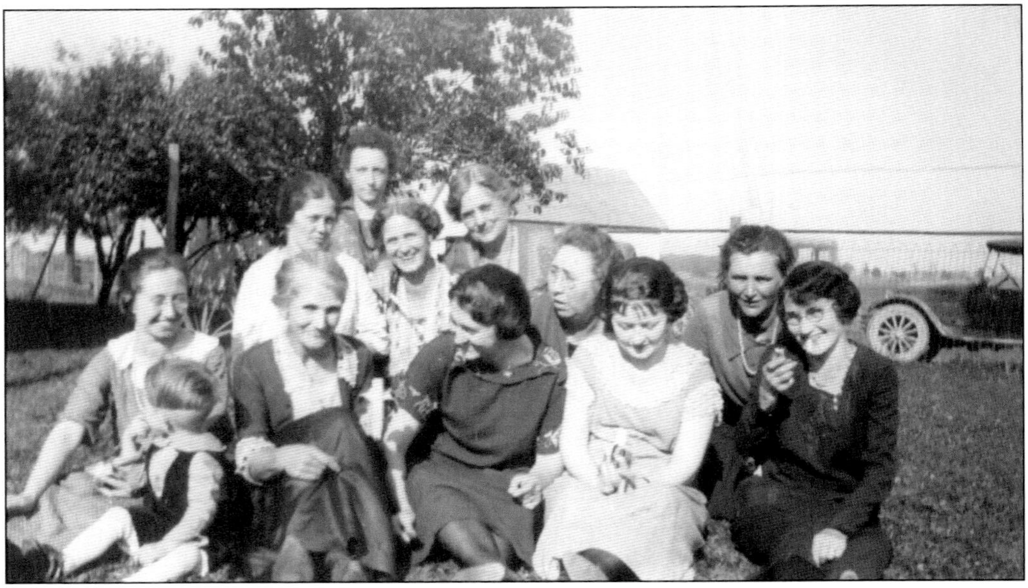

The Jolly Workers club was formally organized in 1914. These women are pictured around 1937. Weekly gatherings would find the members quilting, mending, canning, rolling bandages, or knitting socks, hats, scarves, and the like for the soldiers or needy. Much of the latter was done during wartimes. (YMPTHA.)

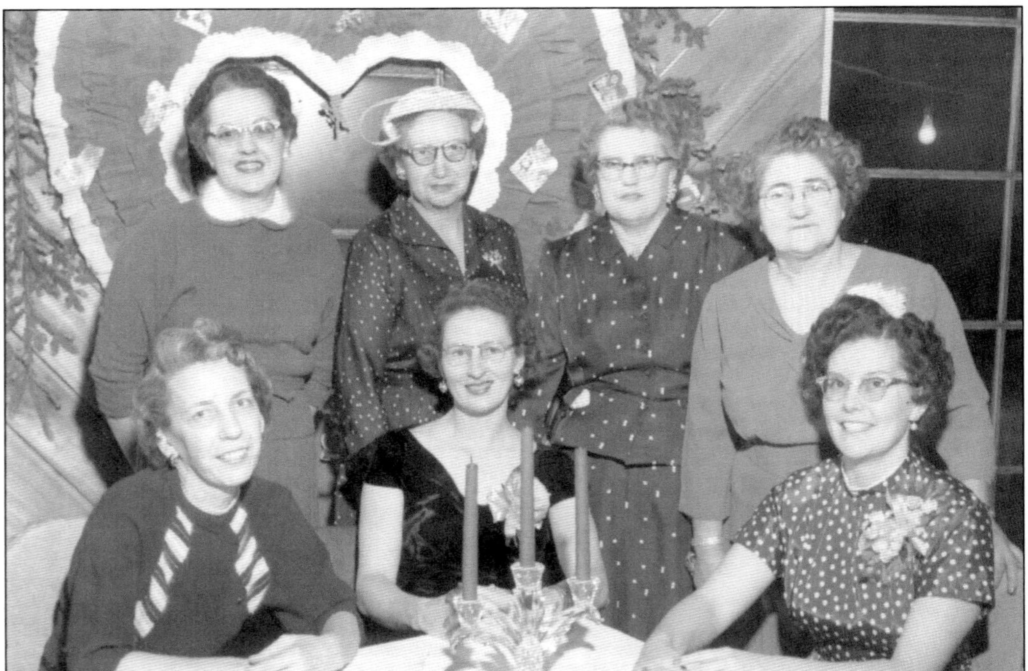

In 1955, the Yorktown Women's Club celebrated Valentine's Day at the Top Hat. Pictured are, from left to right, (first row) Dorothy Hamilton, Margaret Waymire Fuller, and Miriam Parkinson; (second row) Lois Bowers, Mary Hofherr, Eva Bilby, and Ocie Jordan. The Yorktown Women's Club remained active in the Yorktown community for many years. (YMPTHA.)

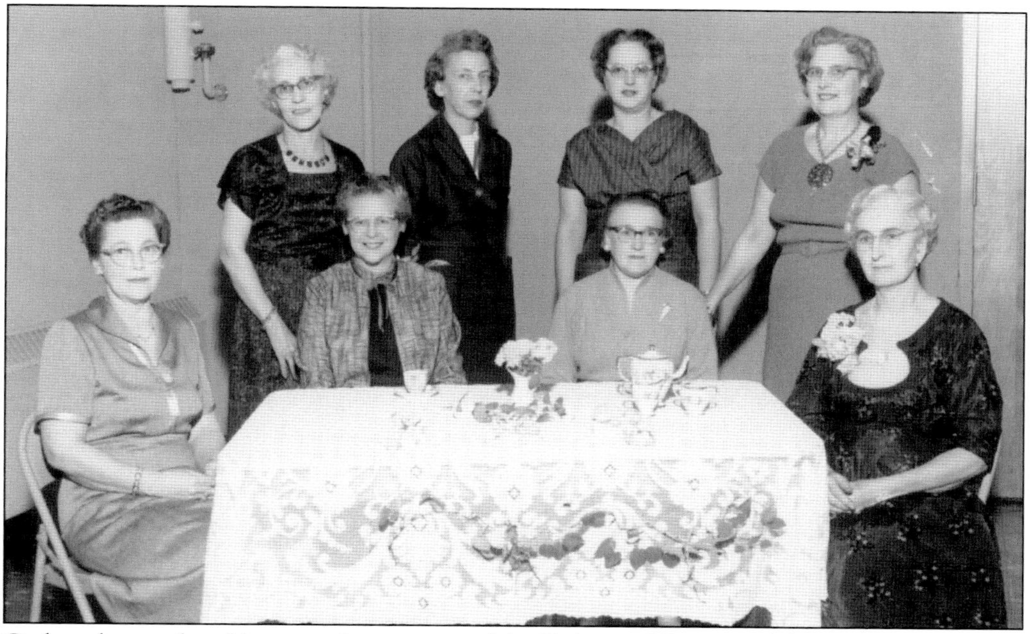

Gathered around a table at another meeting of the Yorktown Women's Club in the late 1950s are, from left to right, (first row) Edie Marsch, Audrie Williamson, unidentified, and Lucille Luke; (second row) Elizabeth Staggs, Dorothy Hamilton, Lois Bowers, and Geneva Grimes. This group of women often supported events sponsored by other organizations. (YMPTHA.)

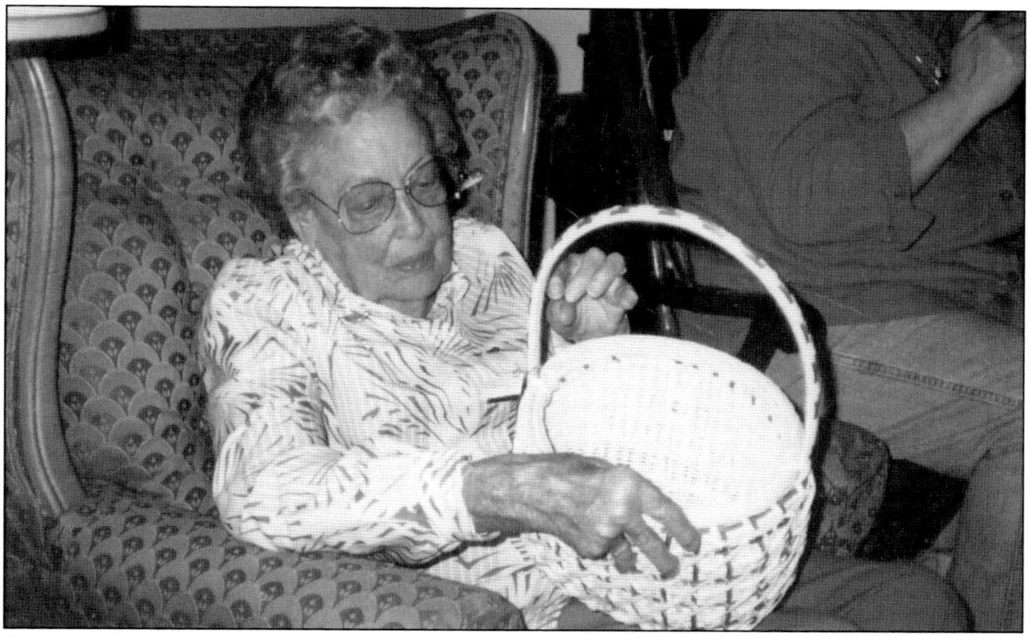

On June 23, 1948, a new home economics club was organized under the sponsorship of the Jolly Juniors Club. Meeting at the home of Lillian Young, the group called itself the Thrifty Thirty, limiting its membership to 30 women. The first officers were Eileen Crouse (president), Pauline Johnson (vice president), Valeta Mann (secretary-treasurer), and Etta Lois Miller (assistant) They met monthly to learn modern techniques related to the home. Etta Lois is shown here celebrating the club's 50th anniversary. (YMPTHA.)

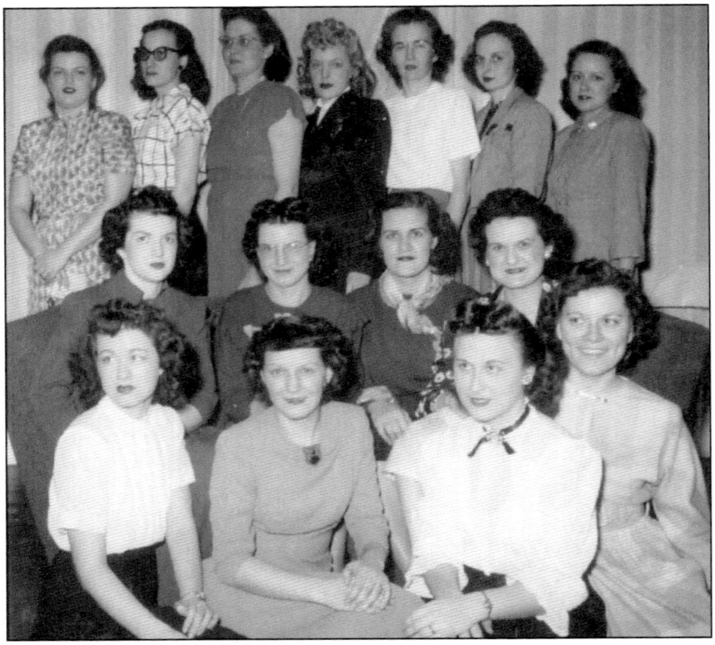

Pictured in the early 1950s, this group of women, believed to have been members of the Thrifty Thirty, includes, from left to right, (first row) Patty Miller, Evelyn Hofherr, Marcy Elliott, and Bertsie Parkinson; (second row) Helen Klophenstine, Ada Sears, unidentified, and Gerry Rodebaugh; (third row) Betty Greely, Patricia Ray, unidentified, Marge Shivley, Evelyn Hole, Ruth Hood, and unidentified. (Becky Monroe.)

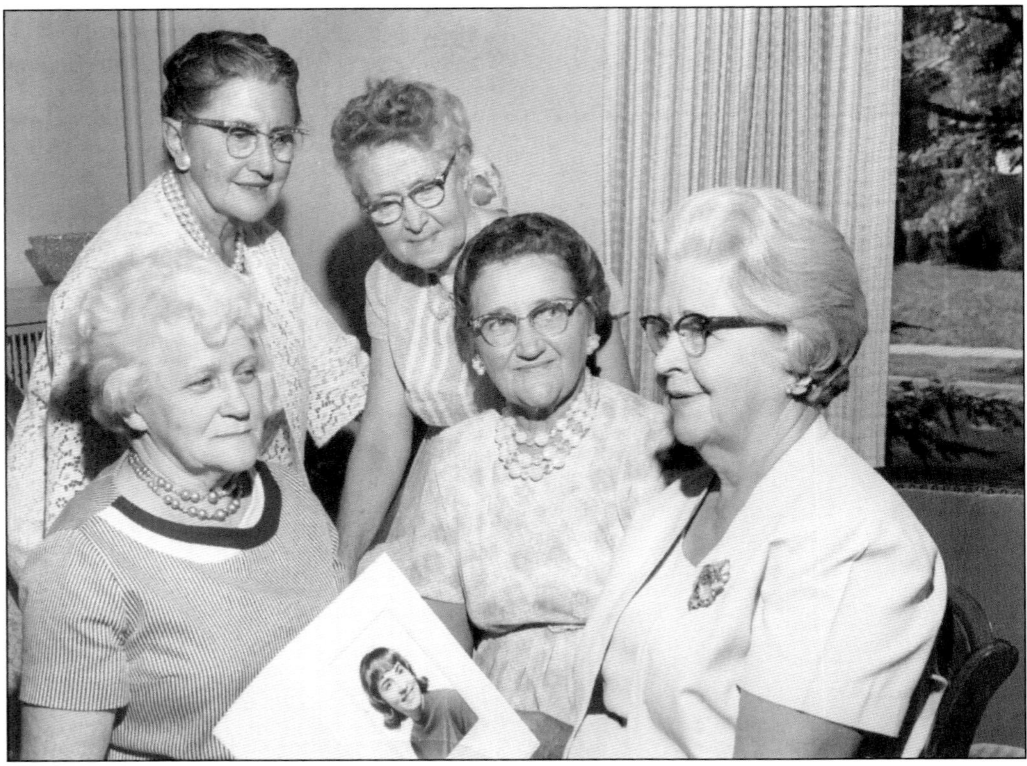

Organized in 1969, the Yesteryears Group, composed of friends and former classmates at Yorktown High School, continues to meet each fall for lunch and to visit with former schoolmates. The ladies pictured as they plan the event for 1966 are, from left to right, (first row) Opal Priest Jacobs, Martha Jones Lillie, and Janet M. Benton VanMatre; (second row) Belle Keys Jackson and Gladys Clevenger McFarland. (Bob Ellis.)

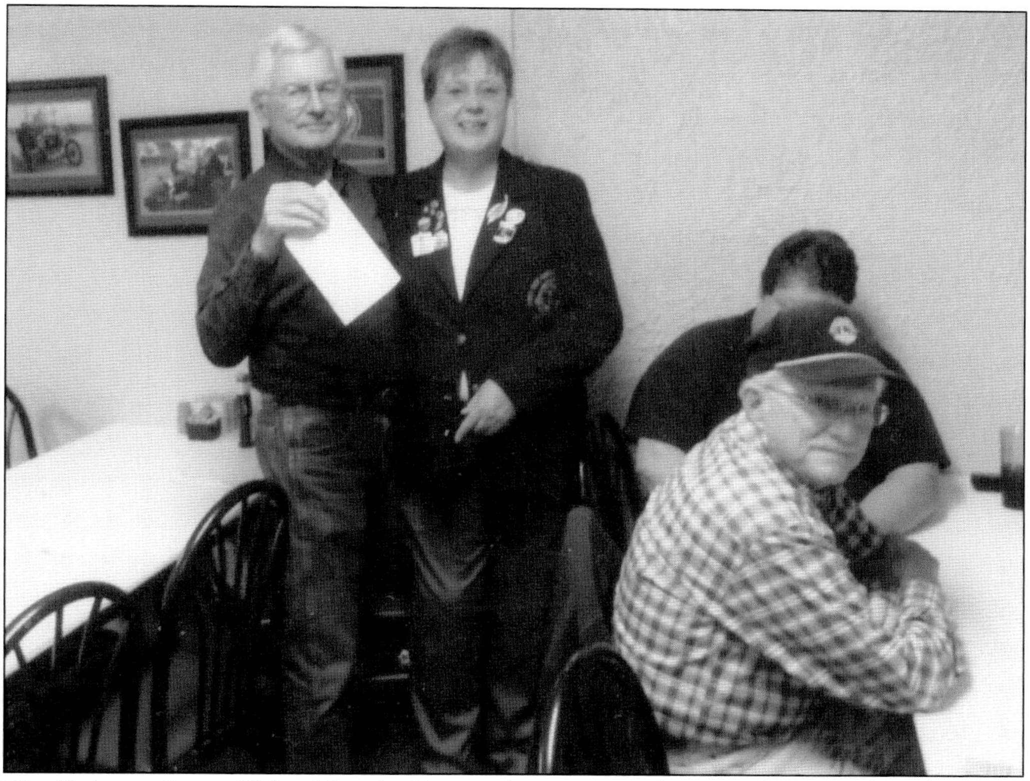

The Yorktown Lions Club sold its building and property to the town, but its still holds regular meetings and often contributes financial assistance to other organizations or community events. Shown here is Harold "Junior" Gale receiving his 50-year certificate of membership. Ron King is pictured at the right. (Yorktown Lions Club.)

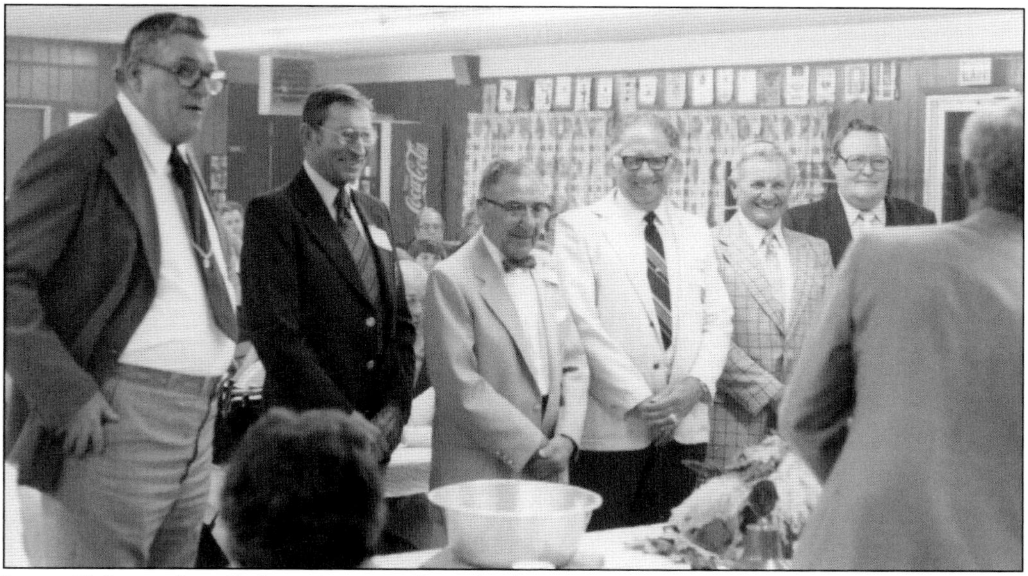

Lions Club members Robert "Moe" Fadley, Floyd Sollars, Fritz Marsch, Howard Gregory, Eugene Finley, and Vernon Williams line up in 1983 to watch the burning of the mortgage on the club's property. (Becky Monroe.)

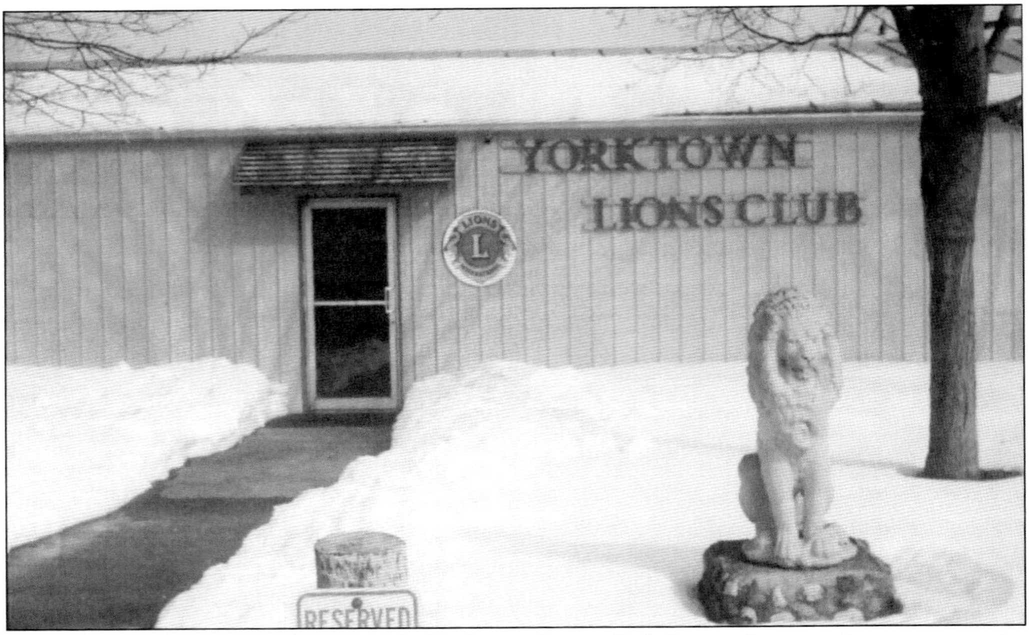

Not only was this building home to the Yorktown Lions Club, but it also served as a community center for local residents. It was not uncommon to see weekends booked full. It was used for everything from class reunions to wedding receptions, family reunions, and many more community functions. Of course, it was in high demand during Lions Club events. (Becky Monroe.)

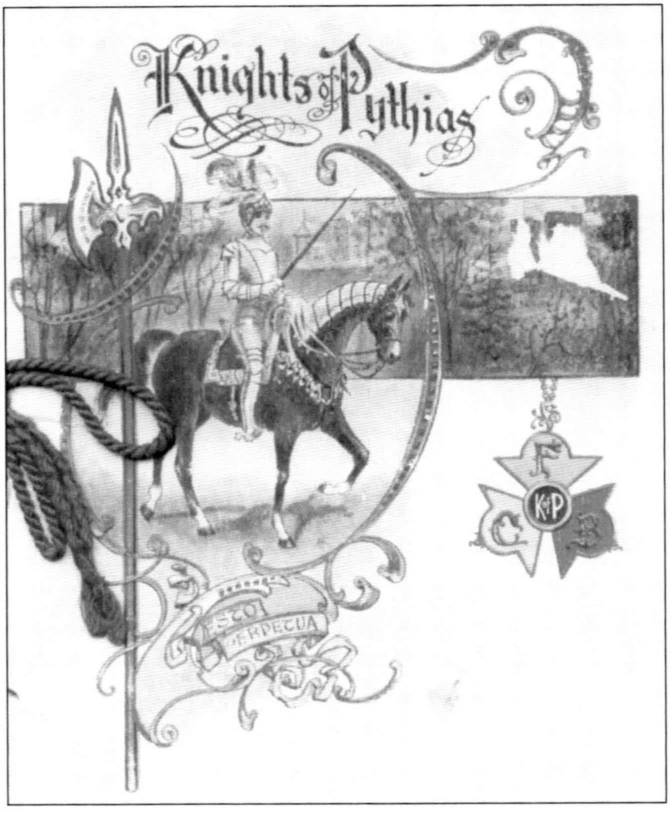

The Knights of Pythias are no longer active in Yorktown but used to meet above Byerley's Drug Store at the northeast corner of Smith and Walnut Streets. Espy Luce was a member at one time. Shown is a program for one event held in Anderson. (YMPTHA.)

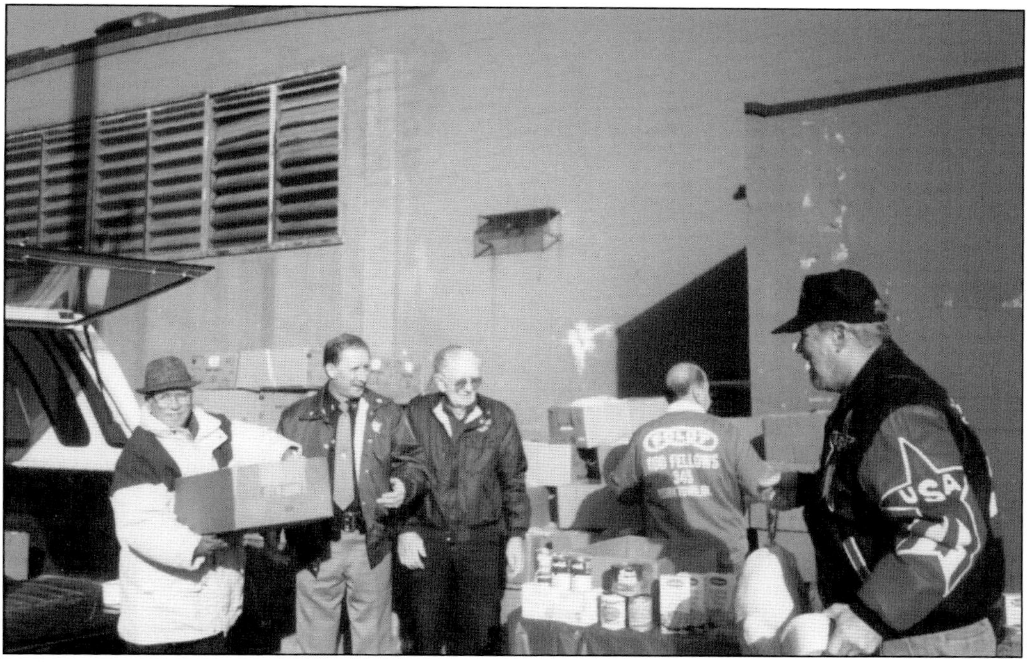

Each Thanksgiving and Christmas, the local Odd Fellows lodge collects money from area residents. These funds enable the lodge to purchase food and gifts for distribution to needy families in the Yorktown community. Above, lodge members are shown picking up cases of food for their baskets. Below, lodge members and guests are pictured enjoying a meal celebrating 255 years of Odd Fellowship. (Both, IOOF.)

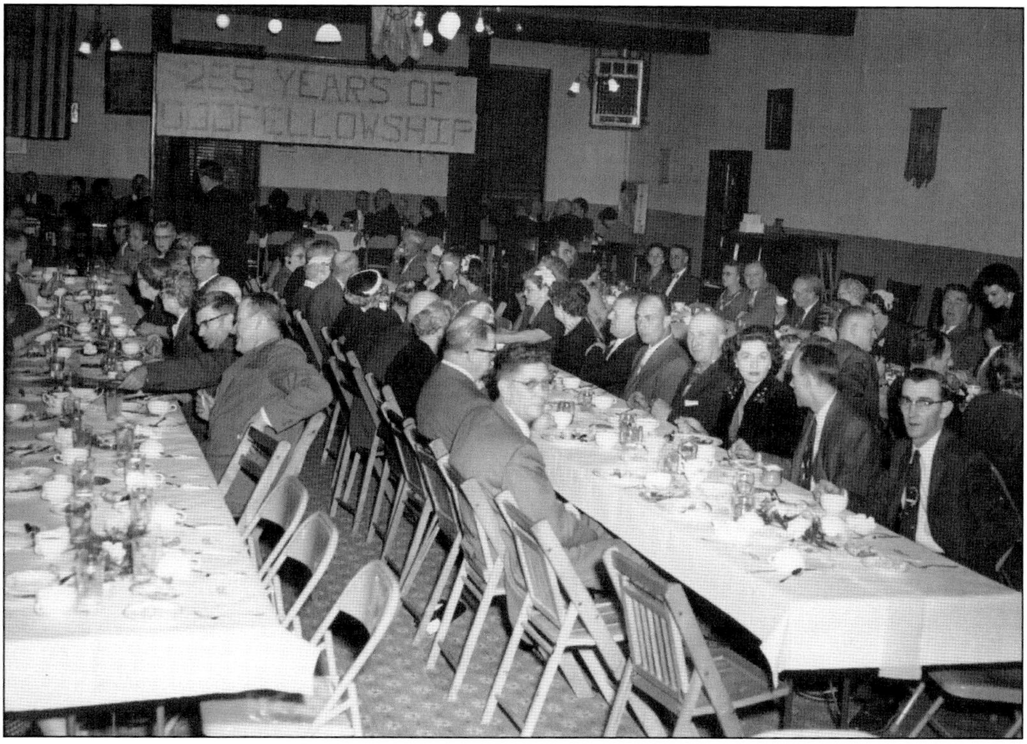

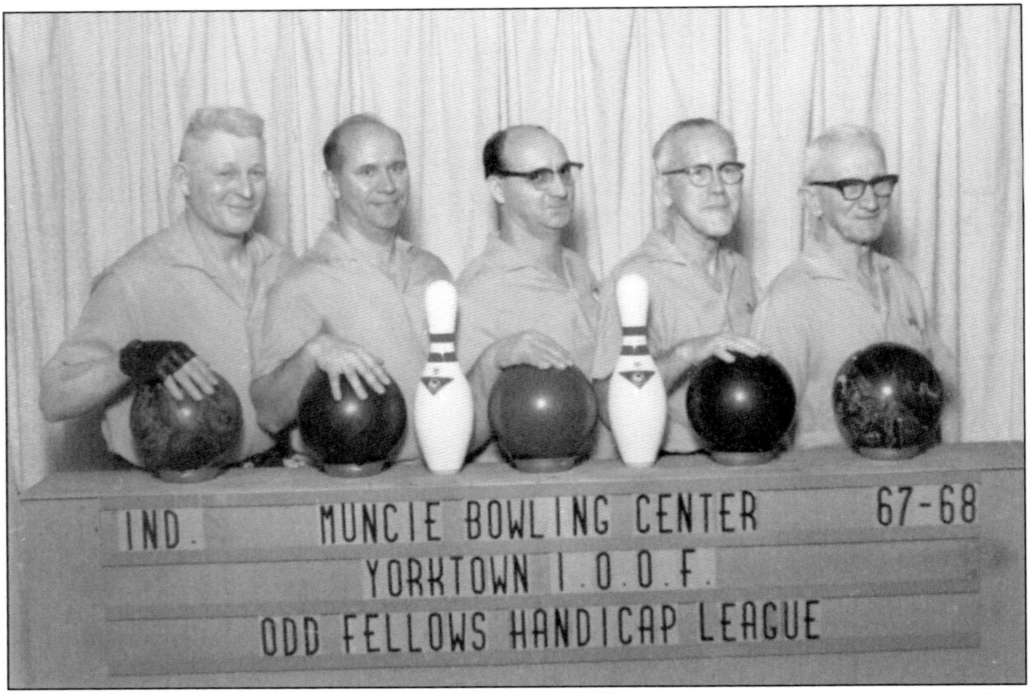

Just for fun, members of the IOOF lodge bowling team pose for their annual photograph. Identified are Bob Reed (far left), Paul Metzcar (second from right), and Merel Swanger (far right). (IOOF.)

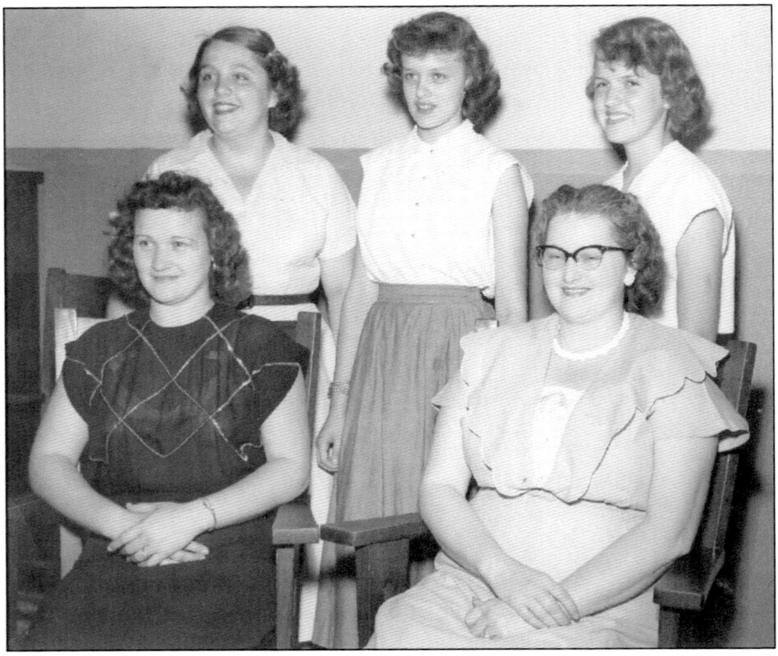

Theta Rho was an organization for young girls affiliated with the IOOF. Pictured around 1953 are, from left to right, (first row) Maxine McVicker and unidentified; (second row) Pat Dolin, Jerry Lennington, and Darlene Miller. (Bob Ellis.)

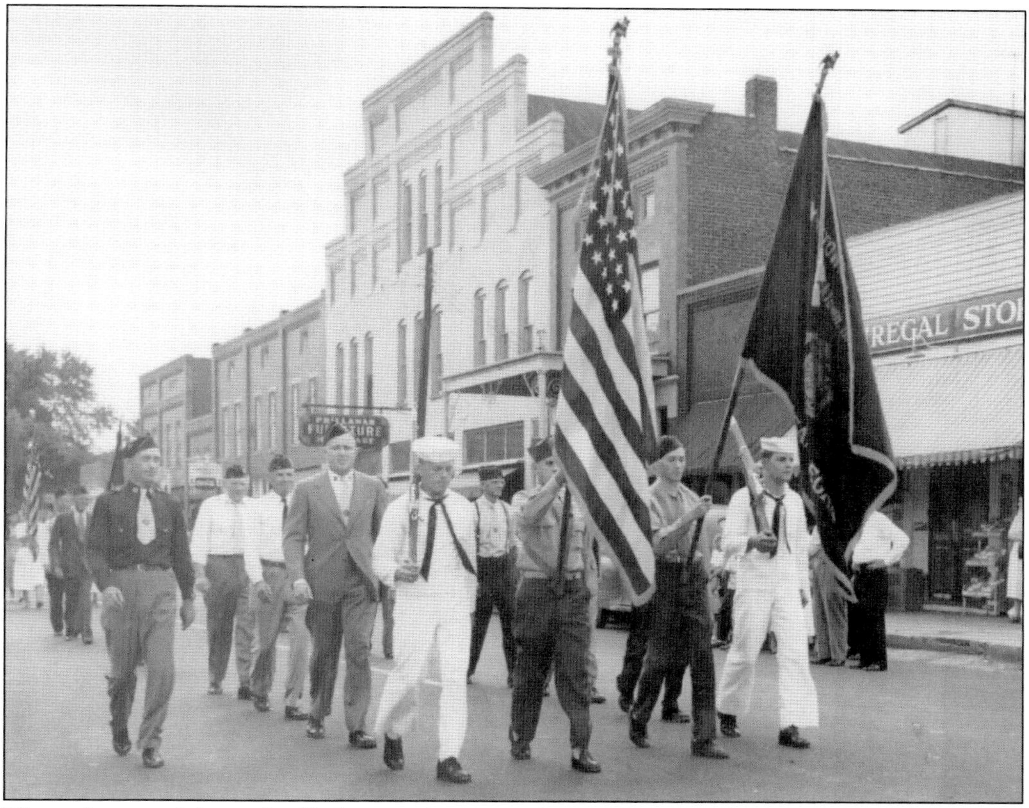

The color guard from the Yorktown American Legion Post 123 leads a parade in the early 1950s. In the second row, former high school teacher Kent Trempala is dressed in a business suit. Boyle Brothers' Regal Grocery is on the corner. The sign for Prillaman's furniture and hardware store is visible. Note the ladies' color guard directly behind the American Legion group. (Don Williams.)

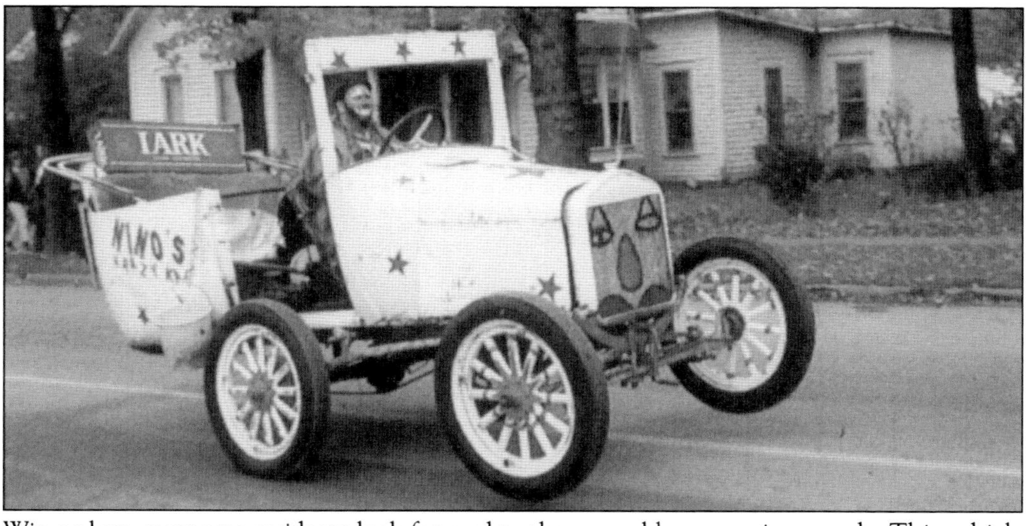

Win or lose, most area residents look forward to the annual homecoming parade. This vehicle was built and driven by Joe Sherman, better known in parade circles as Nino the Clown. This car would occasionally stop along the parade route and spray water into the crowd. (YMPTHA.)

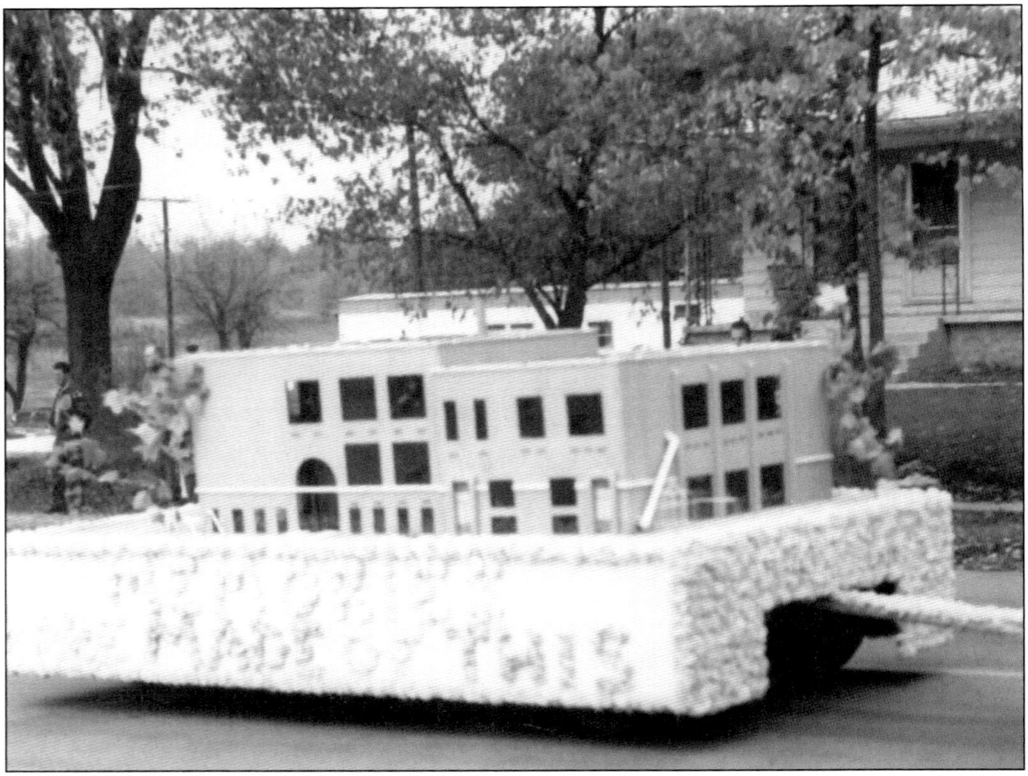

Bill Wilhoite and other members of the class of 1951 created this replica of the Yorktown School that was torn down in 1957—complete with playground and the tube-style fire escape. The actual building was used from 1898 until 1956. (Paul Vise.)

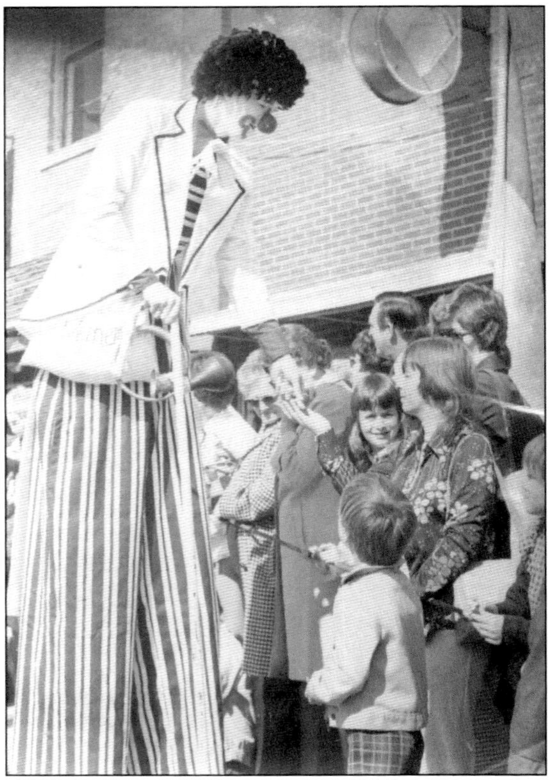

A very tall Jeff Gant, dressed in his clown outfit, passes out candy along the route of the 1975 homecoming parade. Gant, a mortician by trade, found an outlet by acting the part of a clown; he is also an artist and has a large assortment of drawings and paintings featuring his clowns. (Judy St. John.)

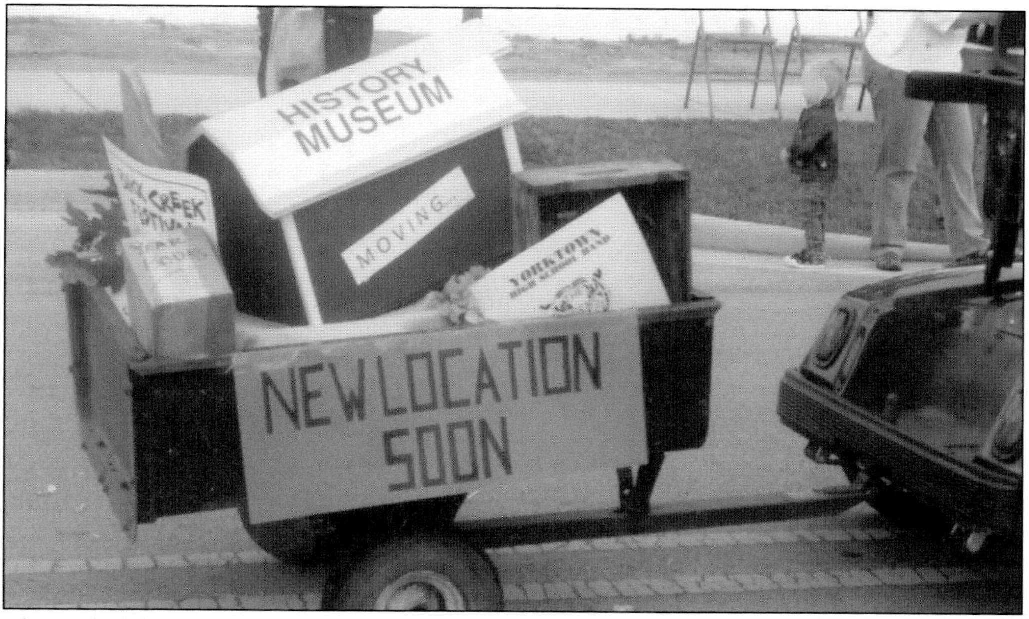

The goal of this tiny float was to let people know that the Yorktown–Mount Pleasant Township Historical Alliance was moving to a new location. Originally housed in the office area of the former fire station, it relocated to 9132 West Smith Street by the fall of 2011; this larger property is owned by the Odd Fellows organization. (YMPTHA.)

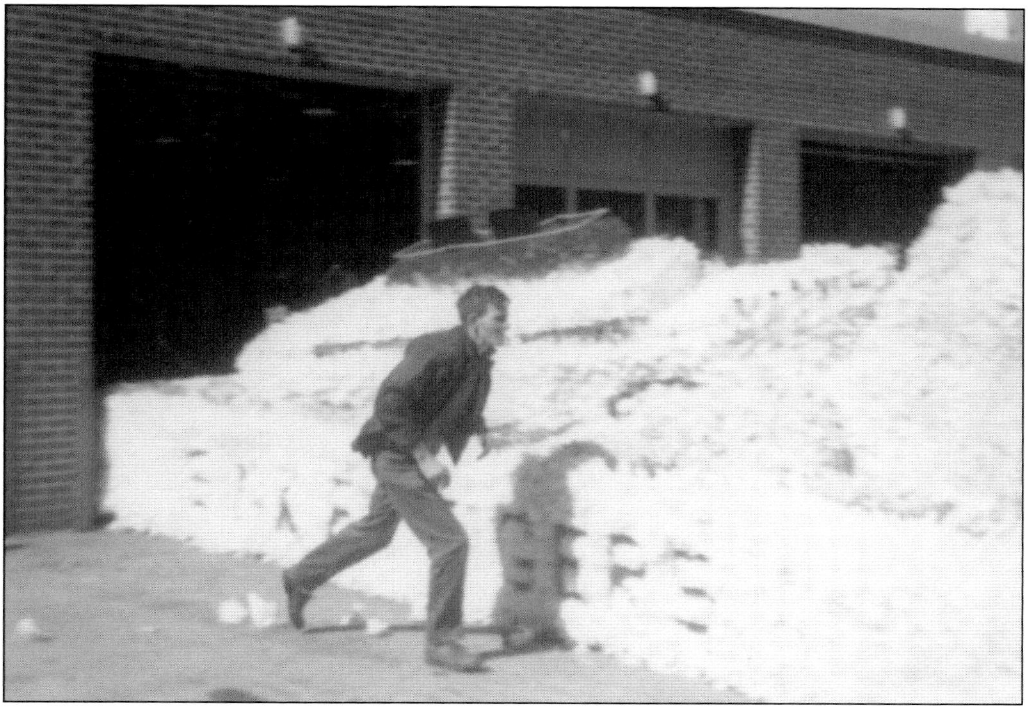

Volunteer fireman Dana Hannah conducts a final check of the fire department float for the homecoming parade. A rowboat was used as the base for this float. It was covered entirely with chicken wire with tissues stuffed into the holes. Text along the side of the float reads, "Sink Em Tigers." (Bruce Monroe.)

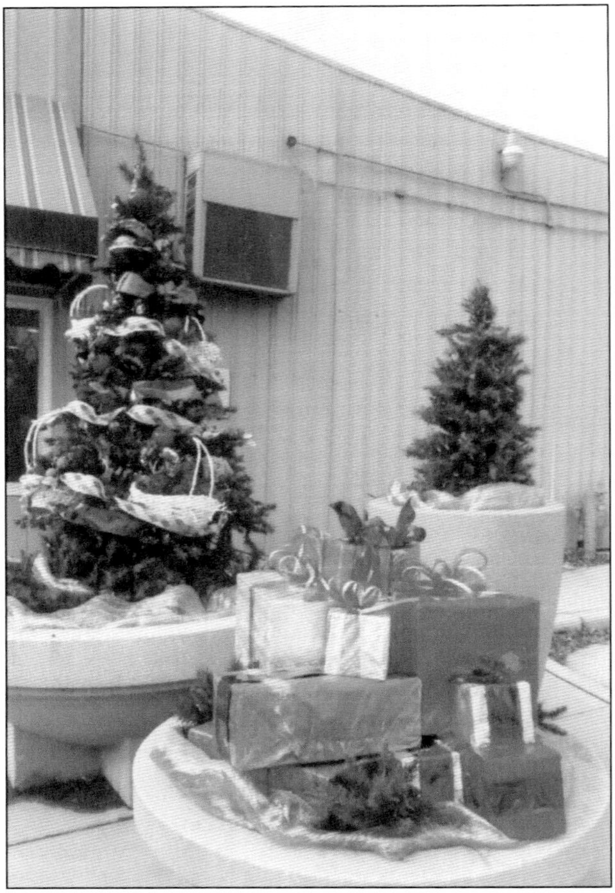

For several years, the Yorktown Luminary Festival, an annual Christmas event, has taken place under the umbrella of the Yorktown Chamber of Commerce. The main focus of the event is, of course, luminaries that run the entire length of Smith Street. Other events take place prior to nightfall, when the luminaries come alive. There are a large number of vendors in the gym of the middle school and a parade in the afternoon. During recent festivals, the organization has sponsored a planter-decorating contest, utilizing flower planters the town has placed along Smith Street. Examples of the 2013 decorations are featured here. The tree and gifts were done by the Cardinal Capital Management; the snowman planter, by Flour, a local bakery specializing in cupcakes. (Both, YMPTHA.)

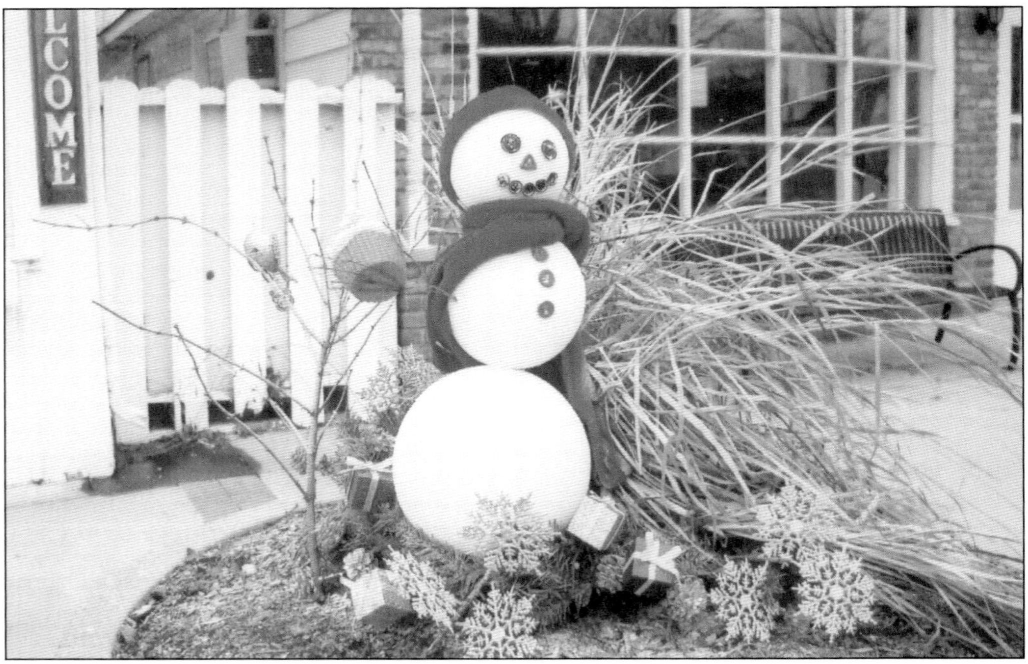

Seven

TAKING A TOUR

From the beginning, Yorktown has seen many modes of transportation. Early settlers arrived by foot, horseback, and soon enough by wagons filled with trade goods. Following were families with the few household goods they could fit into the wagons. Families and businesses need supplies, so more wagons followed. Eventually, the town saw progress that brought conveniences such as the attractive surreys—some with the proverbial fringe on the top. Later, Yorktown was fortunate to have a train system, the Indianapolis and Bellefontaine Railroad, which ran through the south side of the original platted area of Yorktown. Frequent changes in railroad ownership would soon see it called the Bee Line. The interurban system arrived shortly after, also providing passenger and freight service, and ran conveniently down the main street of town. This interurban entered Yorktown from the west, crossed Buck Creek, then turned south to West Muncie. The automobile and commercial bus service followed the interurban. All of these forms of transportation required bridges of various types, and the automobile and bus service demanded a need for service stations.

Oliver H. Smith, Yorktown founder, and judge David Kilgore were both active in political affairs of the day. Their positions afforded them early knowledge of any railroad expansion through Delaware County and headed to the early settlements out West. Consequently, rail systems stretching through the Yorktown area crossed property owned by both men. It was later found that Oliver Smith owned property in many areas where the railroads expanded.

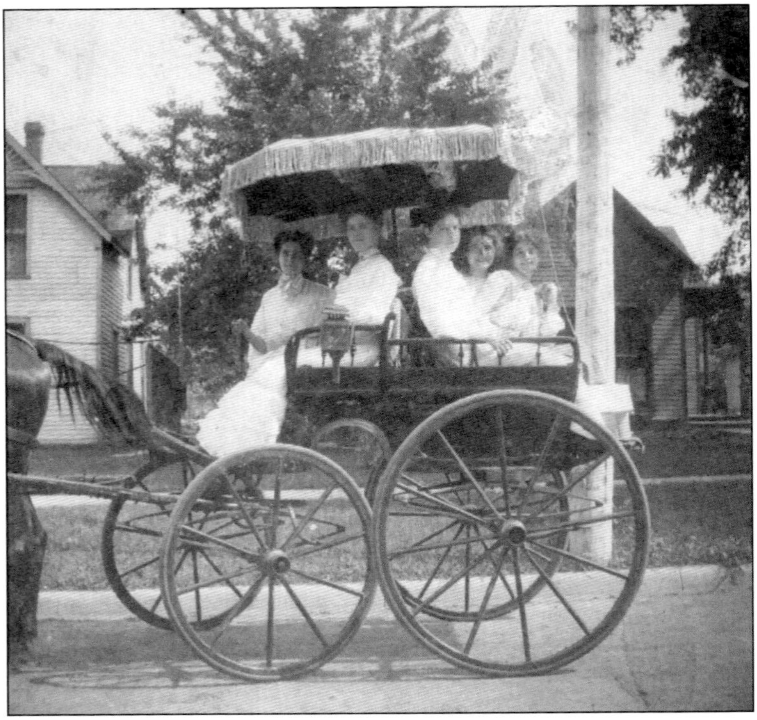

The ladies in this fringed surrey appear to be enjoying a Sunday afternoon ride around town. The photograph was taken at the intersection of Depot and Broadway Streets. The names on the back of the original photograph have unfortunately faded; however, the last name Mahoney can be seen. (YMPTHA.)

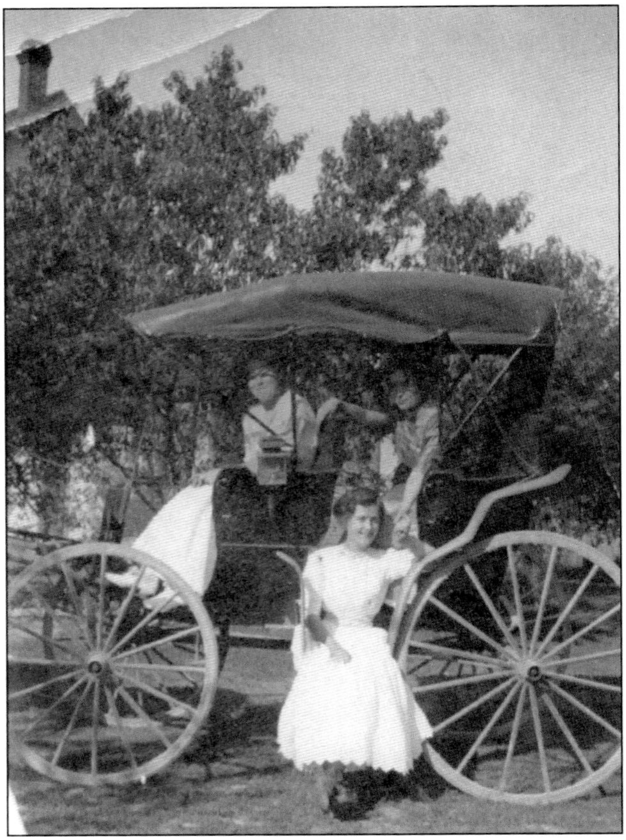

Harriett Hughes, Midge Hollis, and Lena Luce appear to be waiting for a young man to drive them to the scene of the next big adventure of the day around 1910. (YMPTHA.)

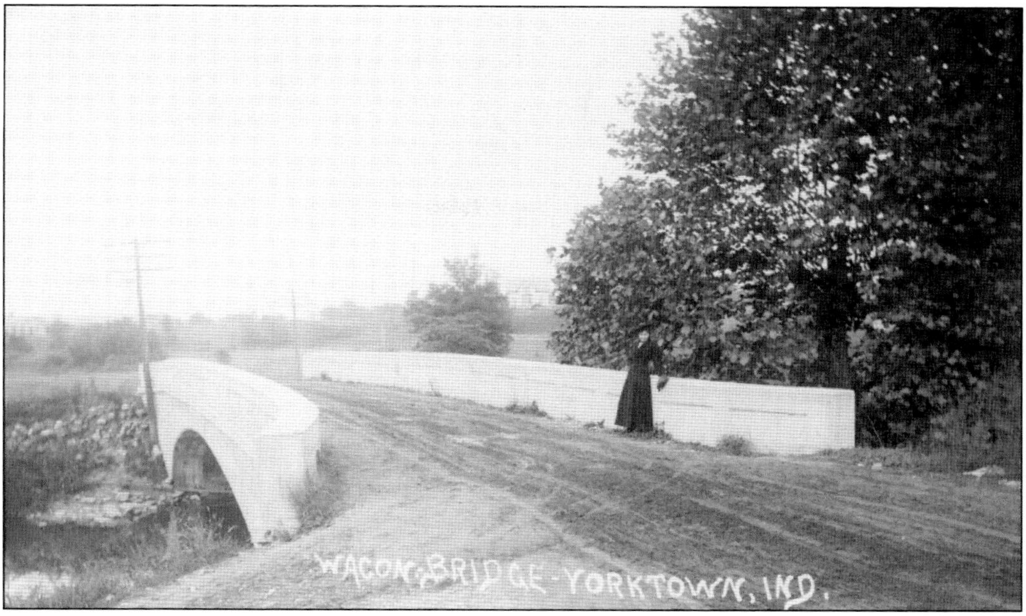

The Wagon Bridge, constructed over Buck Creek, connected Yorktown with what was then known as the Yorktown-Gaston Road. This bridge served the farmers and community members well until the automobile grew in popularity. Since this bridge was little over one lane wide, the increased number of vehicles created the need for a larger bridge that would allow an easier flow of traffic. (YMPTHA.)

The decision was made to add a bridge on the highway and keep the wagon bridge, since each provided direct access to different roads. The upper bridge, served only traffic on State Road 32 (Smith Street), while the lower continued to connect the Yorktown-Gaston Road with State Road 32. Both bridges were torn down and replaced with one four-lane bridge. (YMPTHA.)

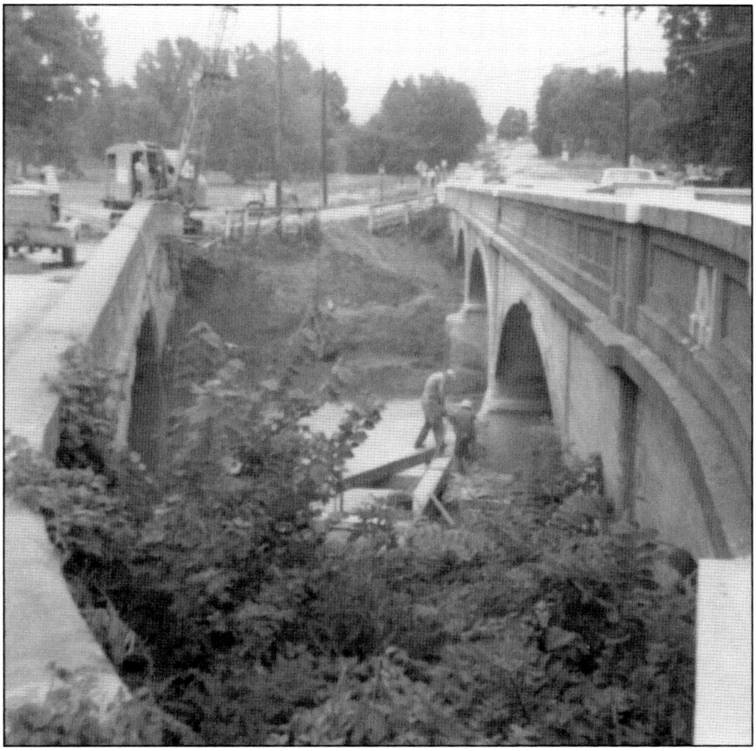

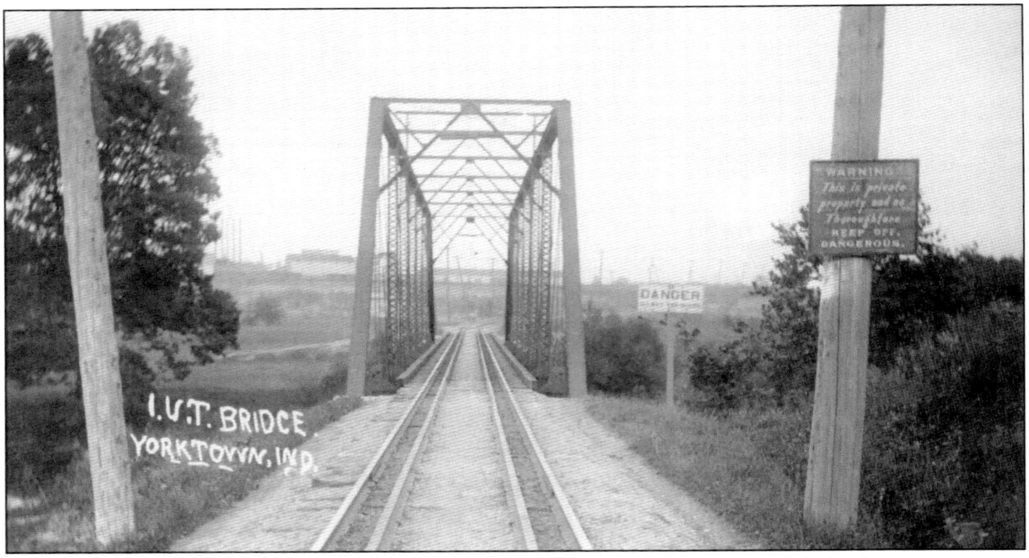

The interurban bridge spanned Buck Creek, connecting the Muncie and Anderson stations. The sign on the right reads "Warning: This is private property" and "No Thoroughfare. Keep off. Dangerous." A second sign restates the hazards. Despite this, the Historical Alliance has photographs of people sitting on the bridge. (Jeff Koenker.)

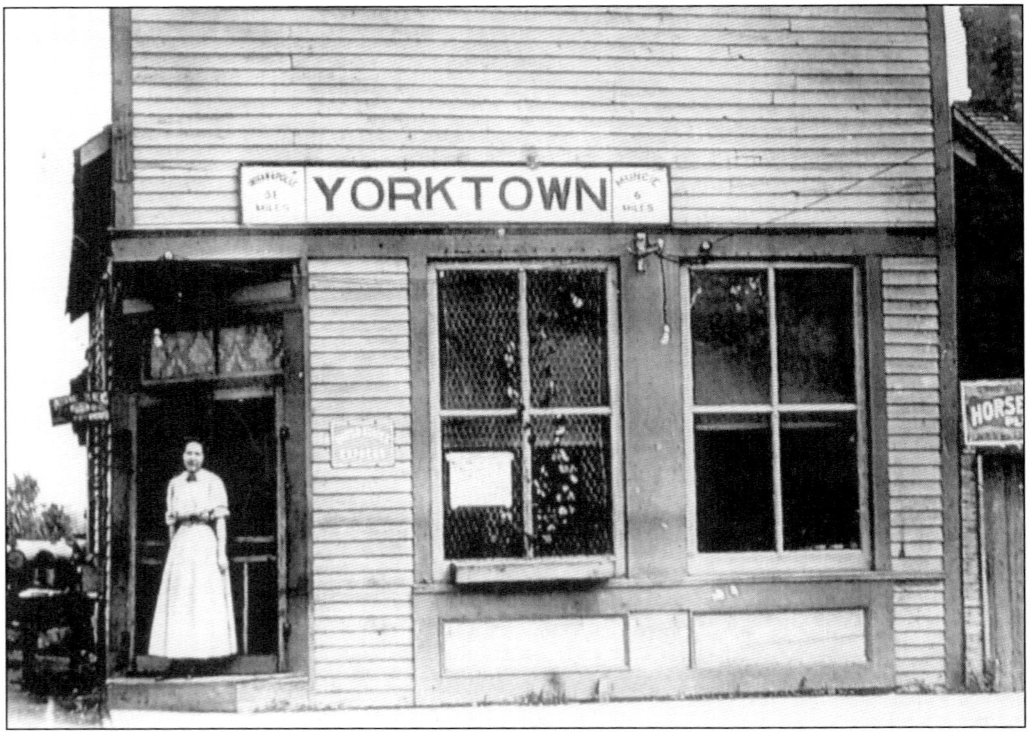

Located at the corner of Broadway and Smith Streets, the interurban office was a place to purchase tickets to one of the many stops on the line. This office also served as a telephone switchboard and telegraph office. There was also a turnaround on Broadway where the cars could unload cargo. Pictured here is Ruth Dickerson, who served as a clerk as well as a telephone operator. (Shirley Pearson.)

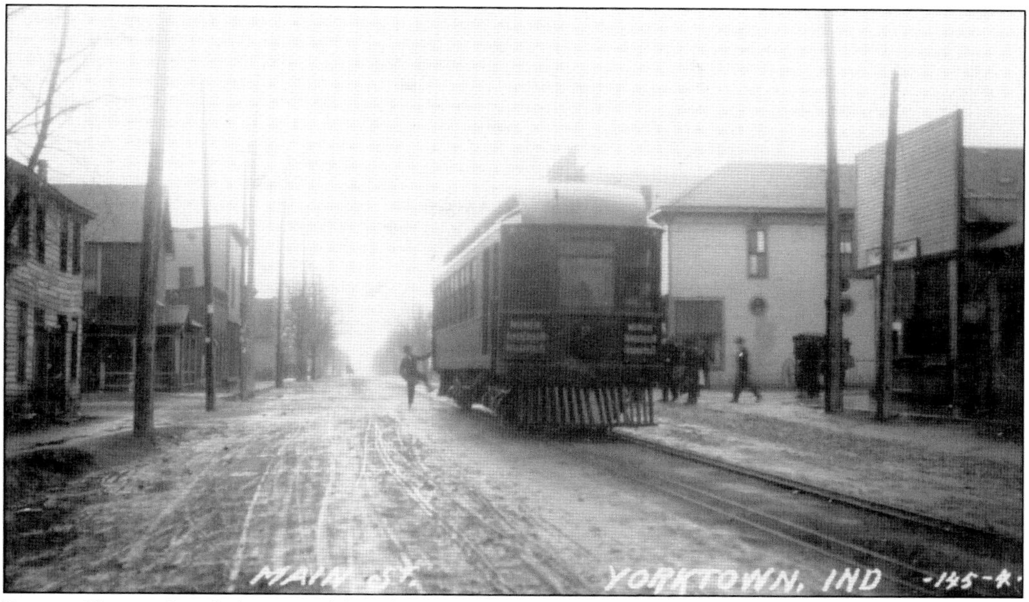

Powered by overhead electric cables, the interurban railway connected the majority of Indiana with regular trolley service. The tracks ran down the center of Smith Street; at the intersection with Broadway, a spur went to the north, allowing the trolley to unload shipments or turn around. The interurban ran until the 1940s, when the highway system and the popularity of the automobile forced the interurban out of business. (YMPTHA.)

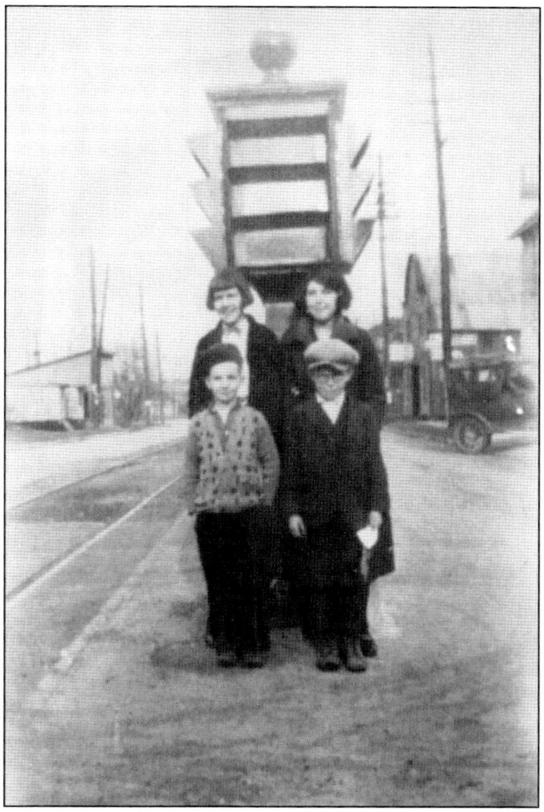

Evelyn Miller (back left) is pictured here with friends in front of this odd contraption, which served as a stop signal for the interurban. It signaled both trolleys and cars as to right-of-way usage of Smith Street. This is a rare view facing east. The building on the right, with the curved roofline, was the town livery stable. The building on the far right was a hotel. (Susan Clevenger.)

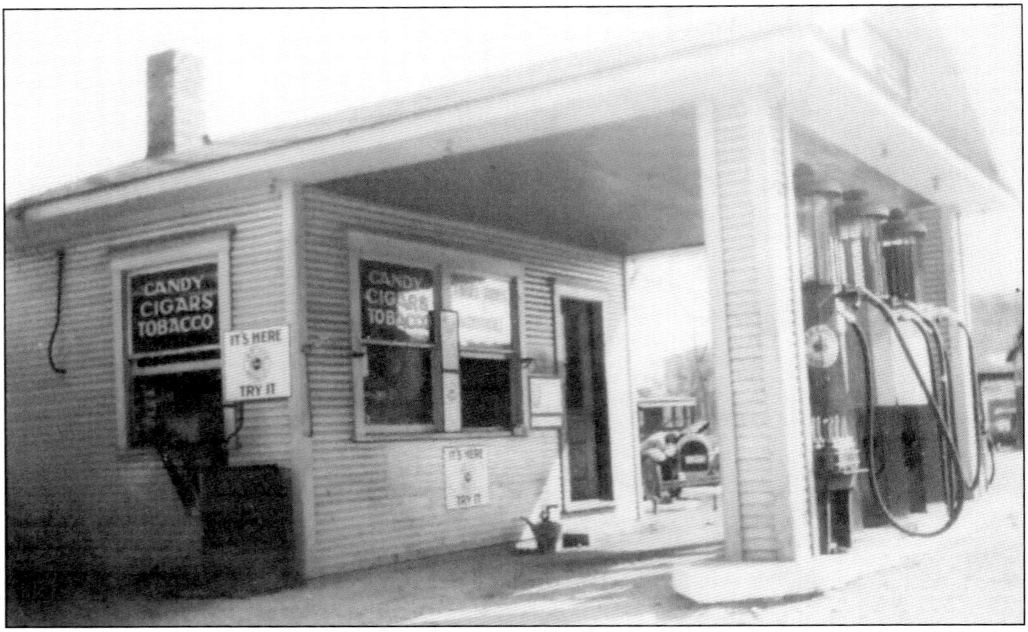

Jordan Reliable Store and Service Station was one of the first service stations in Yorktown. At the southeast corner of Broadway and Smith Streets through the 1920s, it sat at an angle and featured candy, cigars, and tobacco along with oil and gasoline. After Ocie and Joe Jordan retired, Joe dressed as Santa Claus and passed out candy canes to children downtown. (Tim Spangler.)

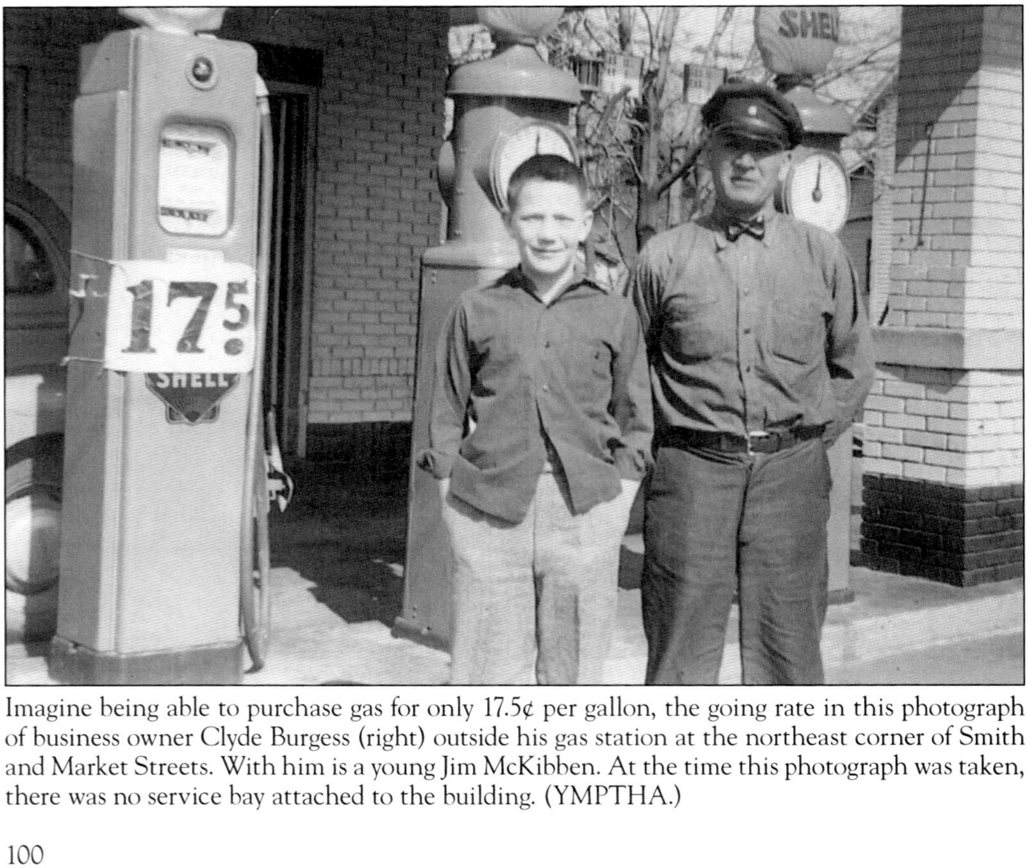

Imagine being able to purchase gas for only 17.5¢ per gallon, the going rate in this photograph of business owner Clyde Burgess (right) outside his gas station at the northeast corner of Smith and Market Streets. With him is a young Jim McKibben. At the time this photograph was taken, there was no service bay attached to the building. (YMPTHA.)

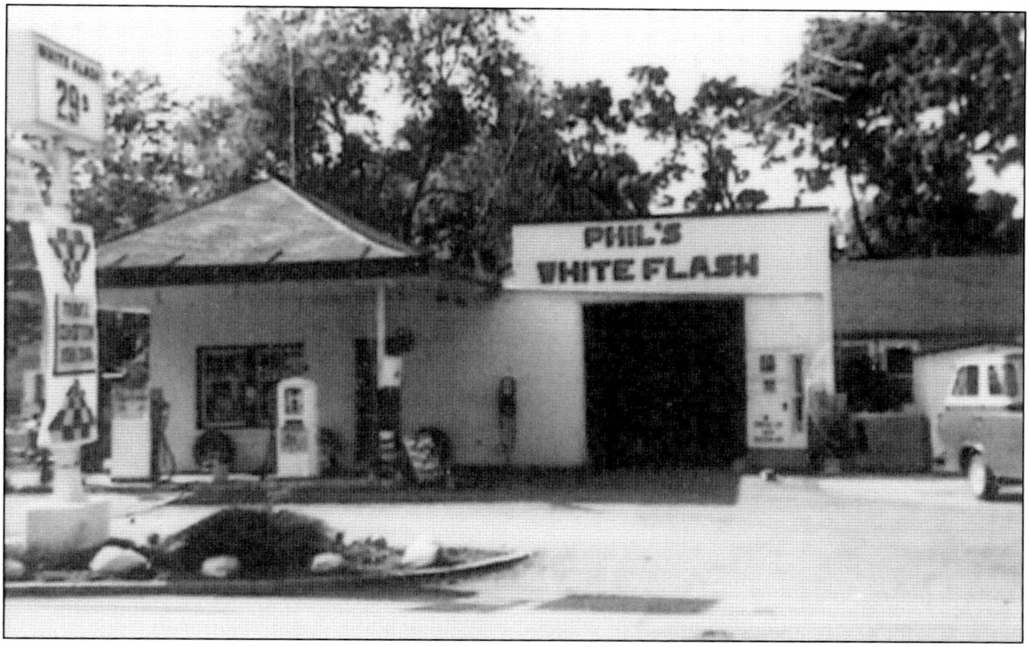

Pictured in 1959 is one of the first White Flash gas stations, which later became Gas America. Phil White moved from Shirley, Indiana, to run this station. His family had operated White Petroleum Company in the early stages of moving into the service station market. (Phil White.)

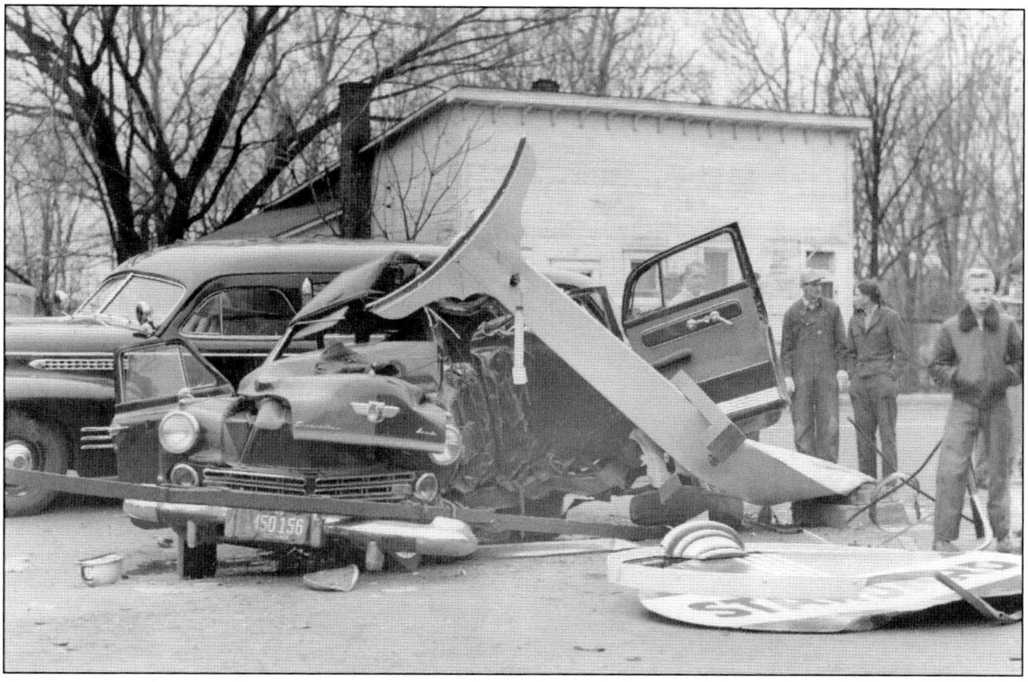

Sometime in the 1940s or 1950s, a car crashed into the Standard Oil sign on Smith Street. The car was destroyed along with the huge sign. Fortunately, the vehicle missed the gas pumps. Volunteer firemen H.C. McVicker (left) and Bill Martin are on the scene to assist. Sonny Martin is pictured at far right. The white building in the background served as both home and dental office for Dr. Langston. (Lois Henderson.)

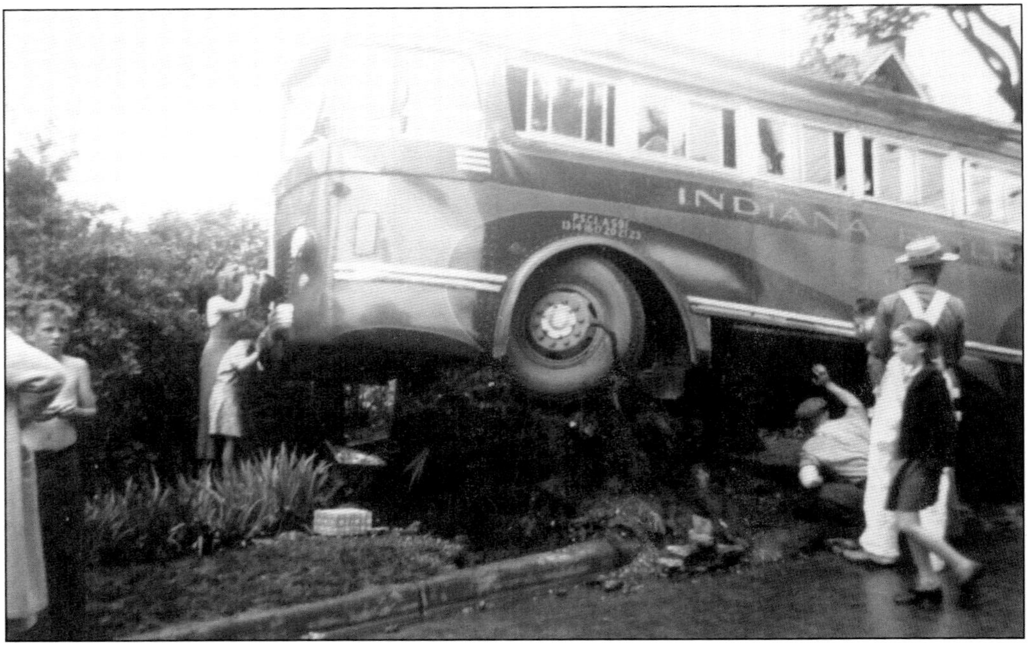

According to an article in the *Muncie Star* in the mid-1940s, a "huge inter-city bus" owned by Indiana Railroad skidded 100 feet down Smith Street and over a maple tree, resulting in the death of one man and the injury of several others. The accident was attributed to an intense rainstorm, which made the roads extremely slick and unsafe. (YMPTHA.)

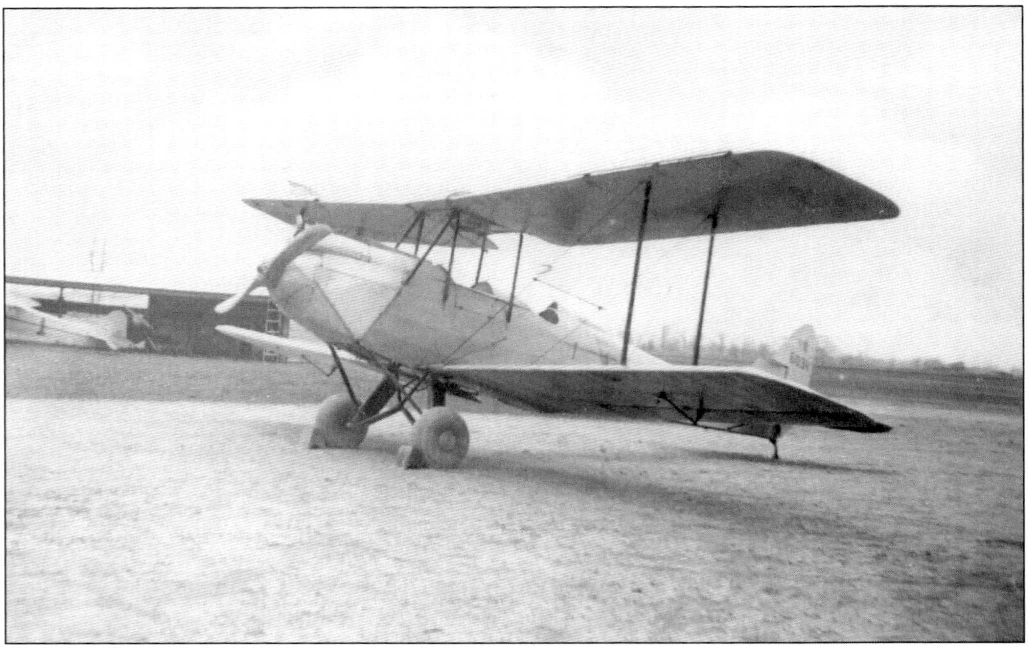

The Magic City Airport, owned by G. Warren "Wimpy" and Neal M. "Rody" Parkinson, was located in a field south of the railroad and west of Broadway. The Parkinsons offered flying lessons and a small commercial service. During World War II, most of their planes were used for military purposes. Wimpy served as a flight instructor and went on to become an air traffic controller. (YMPTHA.)

Eight

Learning the ABCs

From the early years, the education of Yorktown's young people has been a priority. Due to a lack of transportation, small school buildings were constructed throughout Mount Pleasant Township Students could walk to school or ride via horse or wagon.

In 1838, the first school was held in an abandoned log cabin on the Jonathon Bentley farm. By 1842, there were nine school buildings within the township. The nine area schools were McKinley; Antiock, destroyed by a storm and replaced with Cammack; Shepherd-Lincoln; Sycamore; Walker; Reed-Liberty; Center; Yorktown; and Kilgore School. The Cammack, Lincoln, Walker, and Kilgore Schools are still standing. Cammack is now the site of Aul Brothers Tool, and the others have been converted to homes.

By 1935, Cammack was the only rural school that remained open. All of the others had been closed, and students were sent to the largest school in Yorktown. Cammack School joined the others and closed in 1937, making the Yorktown School the only one in the township.

Since 1925, there has been a continued growth in the Yorktown School System, and in 1956 the students moved from a very crowded and outdated building to a larger modern structure located at the northeast corner of State Road 32 and Yorktown-Gaston Road (now Tiger Drive). By 1958, a small addition was made onto this structure. For many years, additions were built in an attempt to keep up with the growth.

By the mid-1960s, more than 1,000 students were enrolled in the elementary school. Again, it was time for an expansion. Instead of adding on to the current building, the decision was made to construct two additional buildings, one to be an elementary and the other a high school. Pleasant View Elementary was built at the southeast corner of River Road and Tiger Drive, and the high school building sits south of Pleasant View. Buildings started in 1956 were remodeled and expanded to house the Yorktown Elementary and Middle Schools. Both Pleasant View and Yorktown High Schools were completed in 1969. The students at Yorktown have always excelled in both academics and sports.

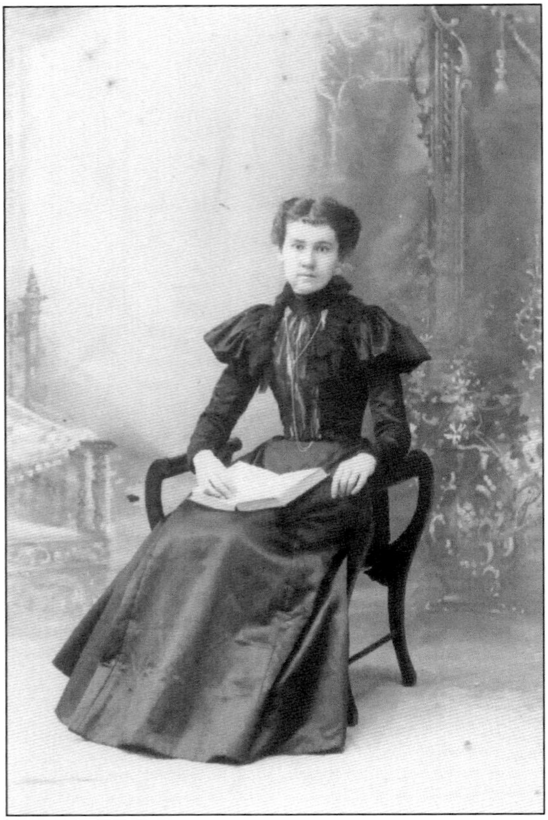

Ida Isanogel, daughter of John T. and Sara Isanogel, was one of the earliest teachers in the Mount Pleasant Township school system. Ida may not have been more than 16 years old when she began her teaching career. During this time period, most schools did not go beyond the eighth grade and teachers received very little training beyond their basic education. (Shirley Pearson.)

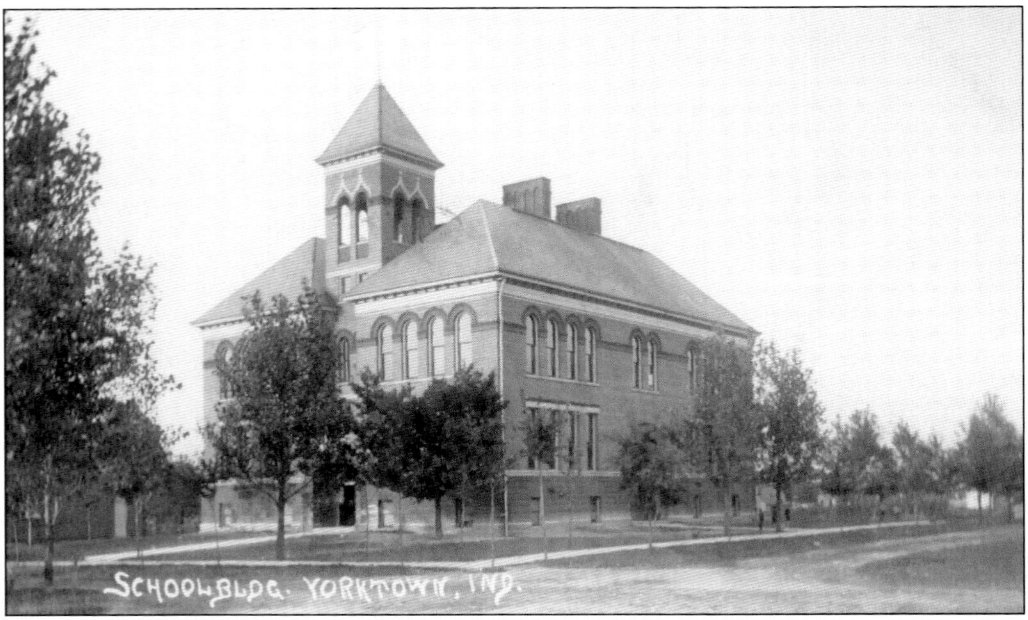

Erected in 1898, the second school building within the boundaries of Yorktown was known as School No. 8. It featured ramps instead of stairways connecting the three floors. In the days before electricity was available, classrooms were lit by a combination of gas lamps, oil lamps, and windows. In 1898, there were 185 students enrolled in both grade school and high school. (YMPTHA.)

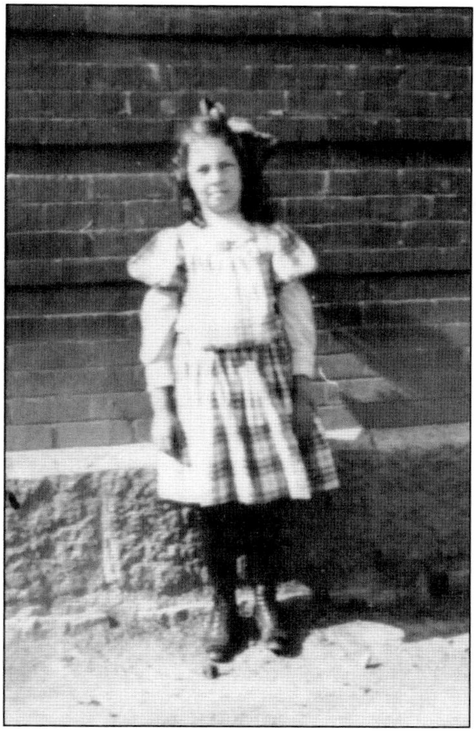

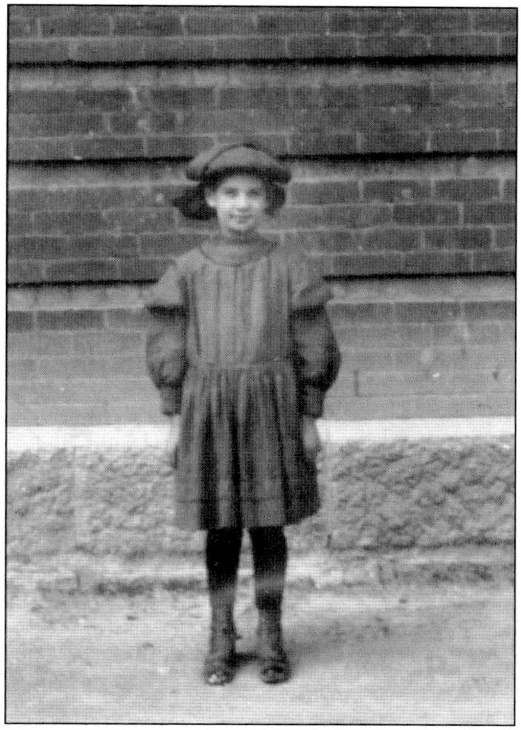

In 1908, Nanine Case (left) and Grace Sutton, dressed in their best, pose for their individual school photographs, which were typically taken outside. Below, J. Hofherr stands behind his class. The students pictured here are, in no particular order, Leo Taylor, Martha Cox, Norene DeBoise, Erma Ellis, Nanine Case, Gladys Phillips, Reba Wiggerly, Harry Case, Arthur Hensley, Daniel Goodin, George Warfel, Arthur Donovan, Elizabeth Sutton, Herbert Stewart, Joseph Koontz, George Carter, Ed Vance, Cleo Miller, George Carter, Ed Vance, Cleo McKinley, Elsie Everett, Pauline Babbett, Josephine Donovan, Walter Ellis, James Johnson, Laura Richie, Mary Sloan, and Mila Brown. Note the oil lamp hanging from the ceiling and the gaslight hanging along the wall. (All, Larry Stewart.)

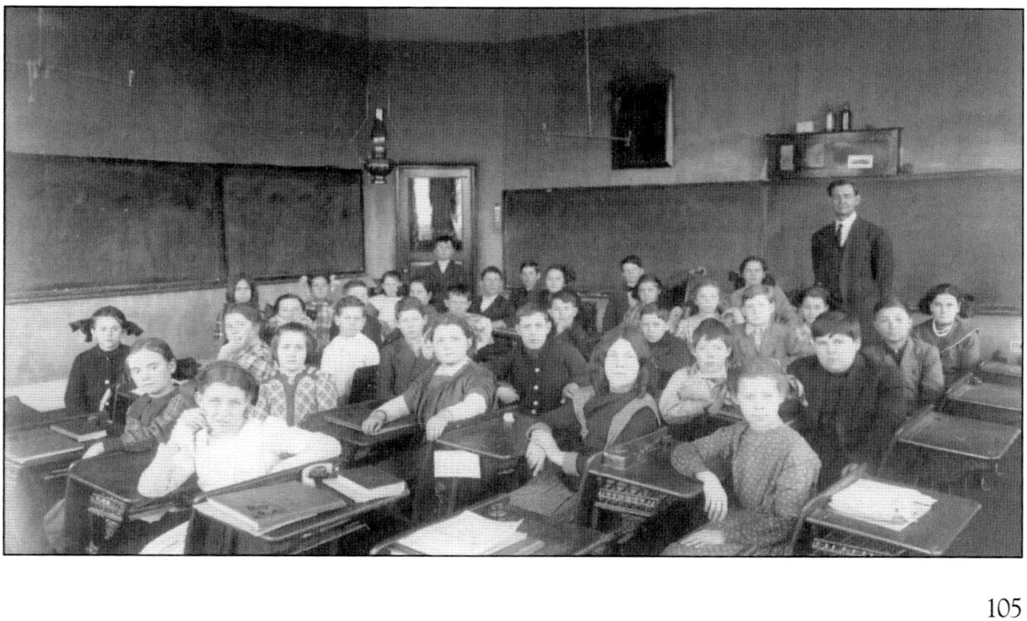

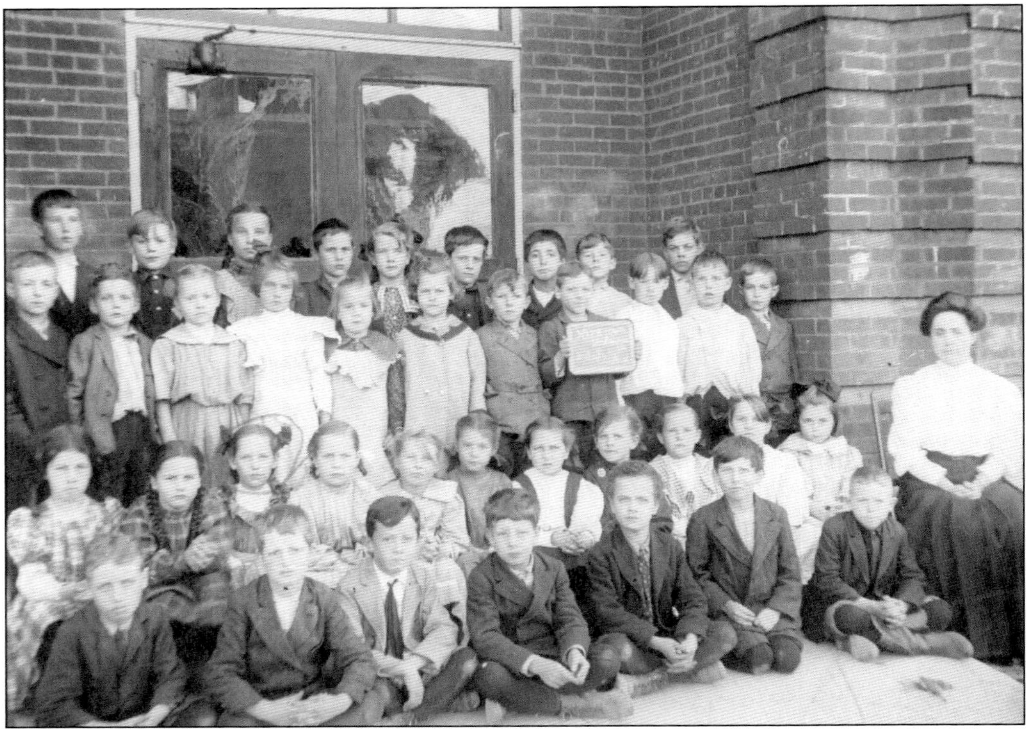

This unidentified teacher poses with her 38 second- and third-grade students. A class of this size was not at all uncommon for the time period. For the most part, each teacher handled the class without the assistance of an aide of any type. (Larry Stewart.)

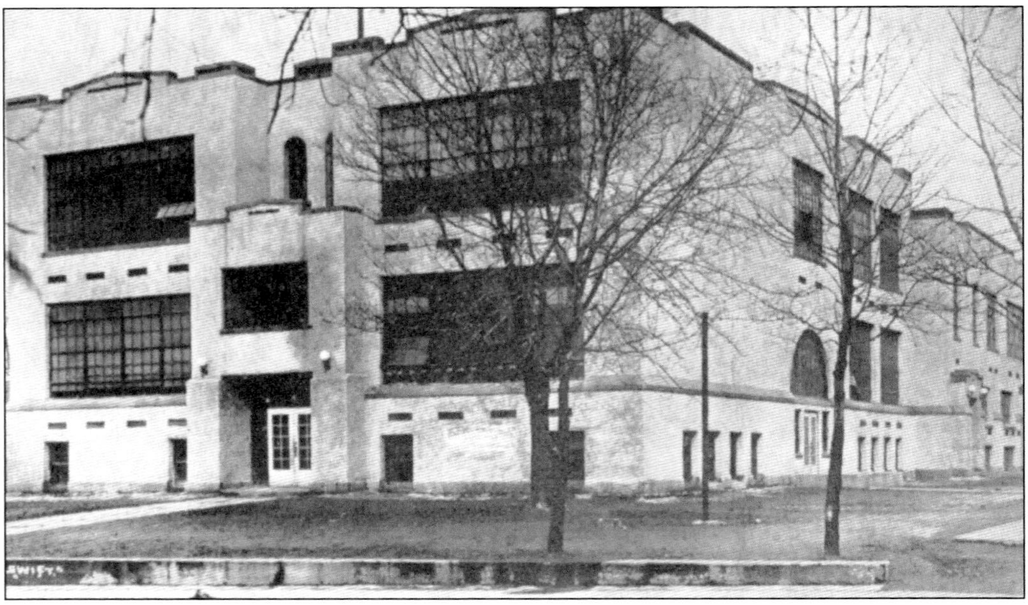

By 1925, enrollment at the Yorktown School had outgrown the building, calling for extensive renovation and expansion. A gymnasium and an assembly hall were added, along with new windows and a wing containing several new classrooms. With this project, the building almost doubled in size, giving the school district almost 30 years before needing to expand again. (YMPTHA.)

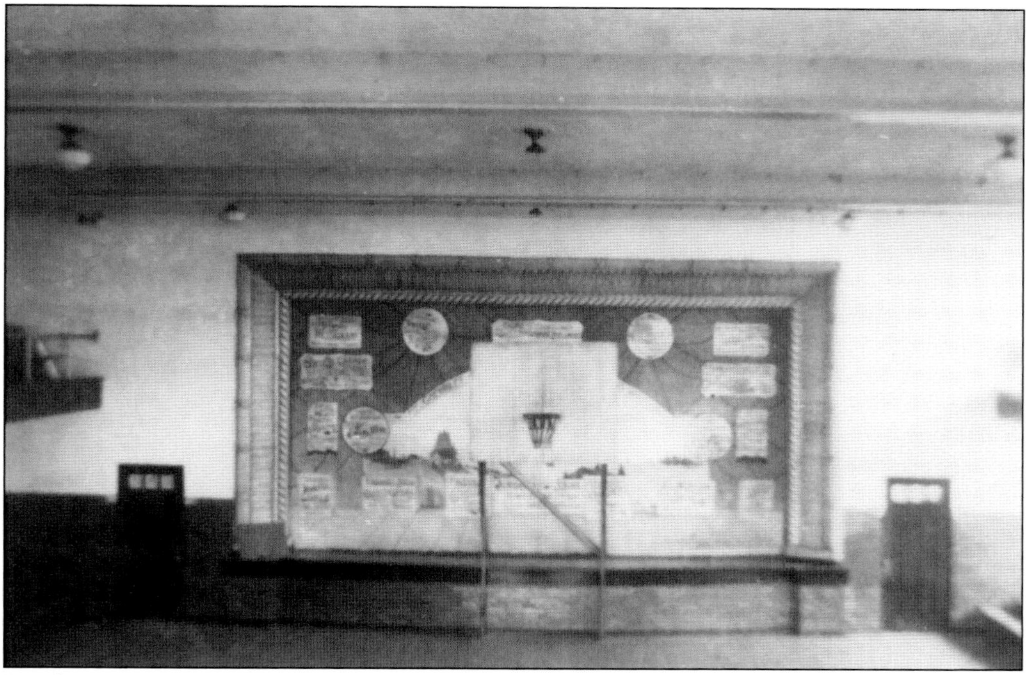

Besides sporting events, the gymnasium, pictured around 1938, was built with other programs in mind. Bleachers ran along the sides and one end of the main floor with a balcony above. A stage designed for plays or other programs was at the opposite end. The out-of-bounds line for basketball games was so narrow that spectators on the first row often had to move out of the way. (YMPTHA.)

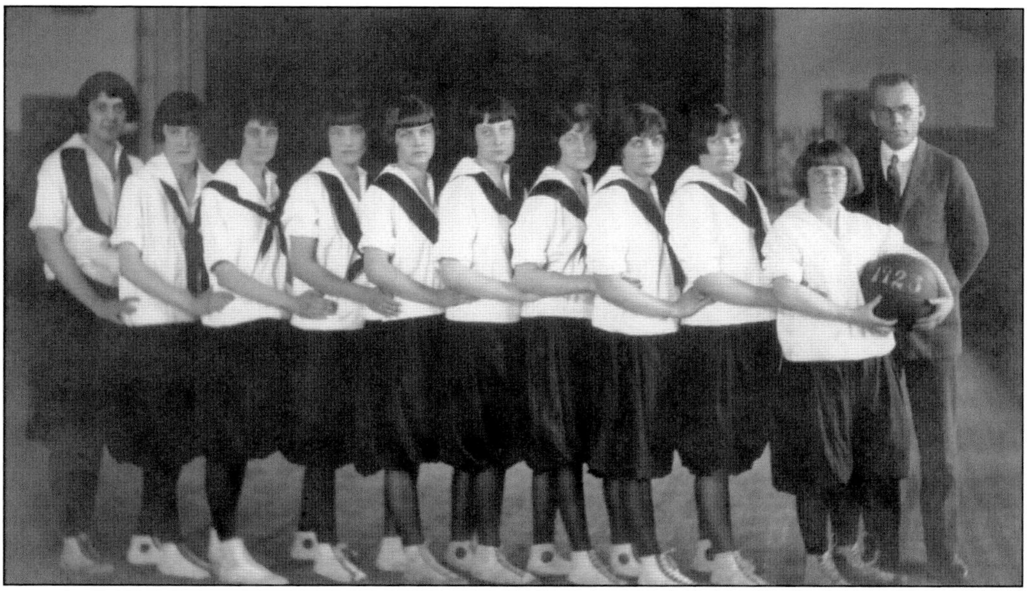

Coached by Frank T. Park (far right), the girls' basketball team of 1925 won six out of its eight games. Team members pictured are, from left to right, Mary Connelly, Evelyn Applegate, June Littlefield, Edna Kilgore, Evelyn Miller, Mary Donovan, Helen V. Donovan, Dora May Miller, Winifred Darter, and Mary Skinner. Prior to renovations done in 1925, ball games were played at the nearby Methodist church. (YMPTHA.)

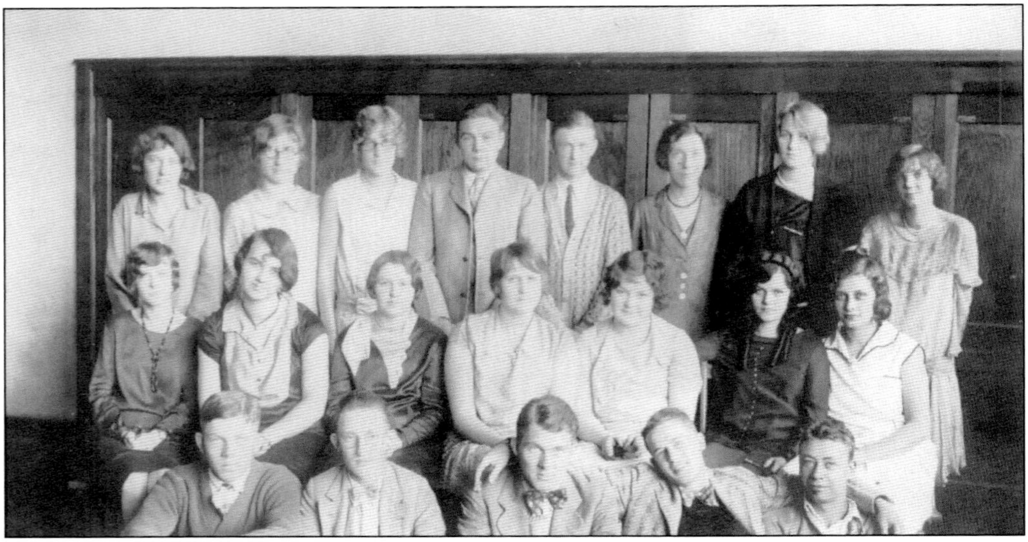

Members of the 1929 senior class pose for an informal photograph in their classroom. Pictured are, from left to right, (first row) Marshall McKinley, Merritt Jackson, Enoch Childs, Earland Sears, and Meredith Reed; (second row) Marie Estep, Cora Belle Yingling, Lennie Reed, Virginia Joliffe, Verah Thomas, Dainty Lennington, and Virginia Miller; (third row) Marie Duncan, Irene McKinsey, Mable Jackson, Ted Wright, Ralph McShurley, Ethel Klepfer, Irene Donovan, and Lorenna Cox. (Sheila Sheward.)

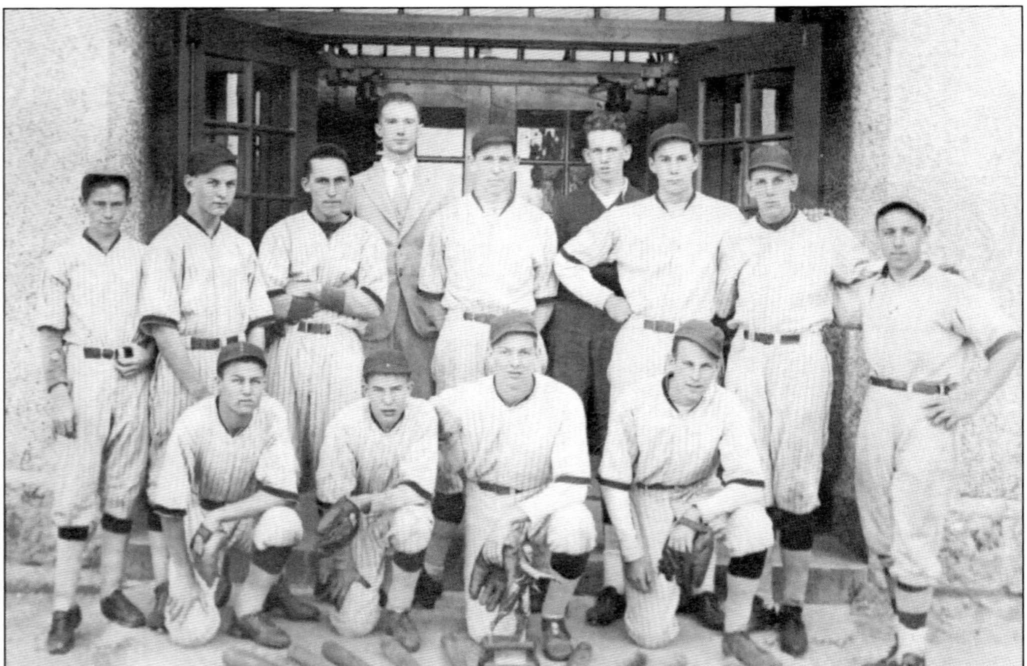

The baseball team from the 1930–1931 season was even more successful than the basketball team during the same time period. It batted an undefeated regular season, crowned by an unbelievable 35-1 victory over Cowan, and followed by a sweep of the county baseball championship to finish off a remarkable run. (YMPTHA.)

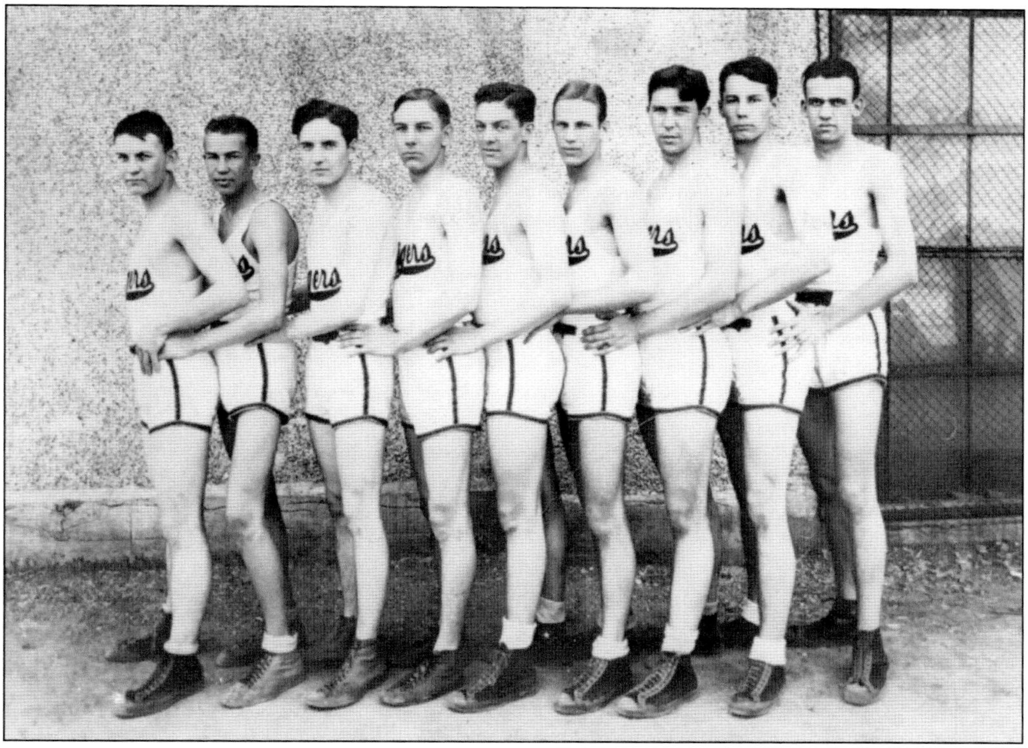

Pictured are the 1930–1931 Yorktown basketball team members. They are, from left to right, Robert McKinley, Kenneth Koontz, Gene Baldwin, Gleason Hodson, John Cox, Marcellus Wright, Dale Mann, Tom Sear, and John Mitchell. Under the direction of coach Leslie "Red" Reeves, the team had an overall winning season, taking second place in the county tournament. (YMPTHA.)

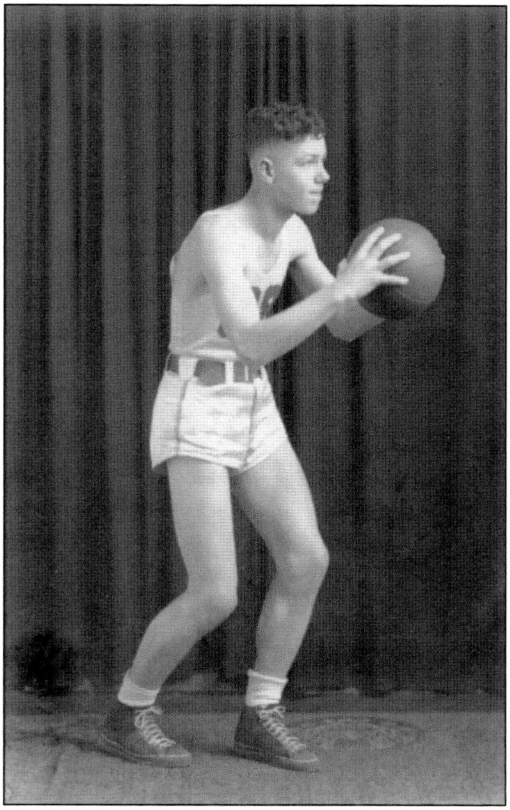

As a junior, Byron Ellis played center on 1937 basketball team under the leadership of coach Kenneth Sigler. Five other members of the junior class joined Byron on this squad. Although not as successful as teams in prior years, these boys worked hard to show their quality and were expected to make a contribution to the team the following year. (Bob Ellis.)

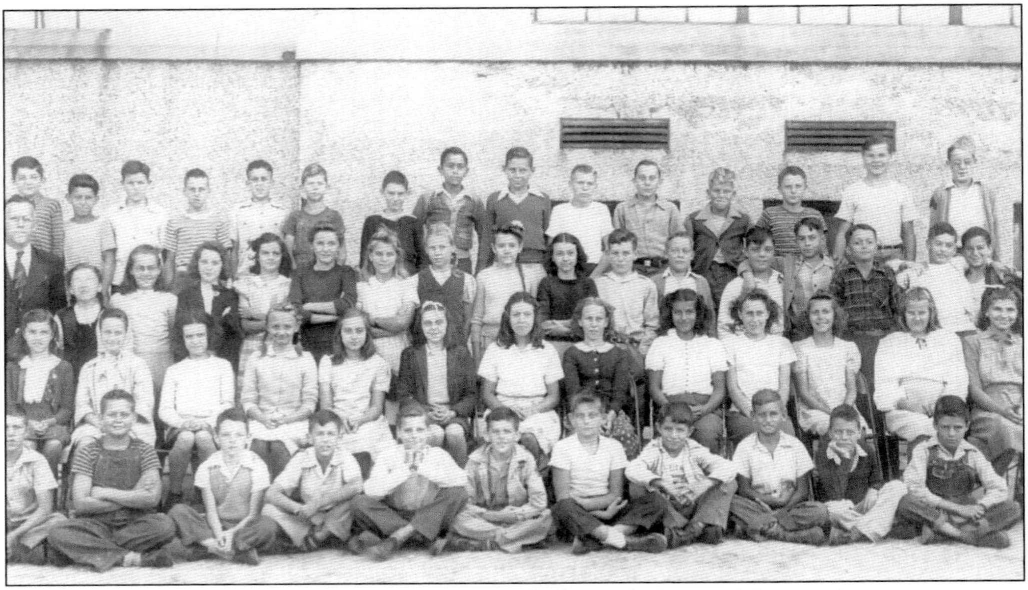

This large sixth-grade class of 41 students was taught by Paul Metzcar. Many in this group went on to graduate in 1944, with 10 of these students completing their grade-school educations entirely at Yorktown. (YMPTHA.)

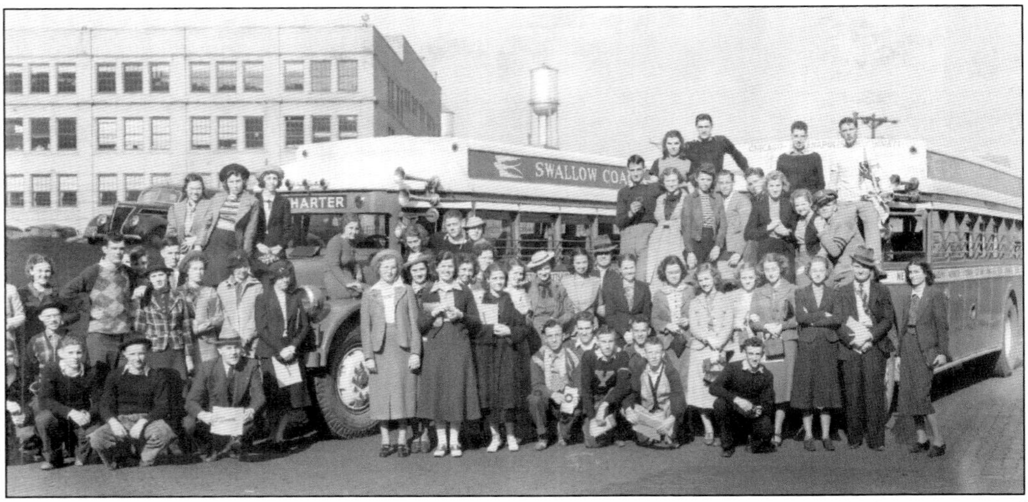

The junior-senior trip in 1938 to Akron, Ohio, was to see the tire industry. The large group of students was accompanied by principal Ray O. Burns and coach Claude Williams. Here, the group stands between and atop its charter buses at the Akron bus depot for a group shot. During this trip, the group toured at least one of the local tire companies. (YMPTHA.)

Kenneth Sigler began his coaching career at Yorktown in 1937, leading his baseball team to a county victory. The Yorktown Tigers won a good number of county championships during Coach Ziegler's career. In his last year at Yorktown, both the baseball and basketball teams secured county titles. (YMPTHA.)

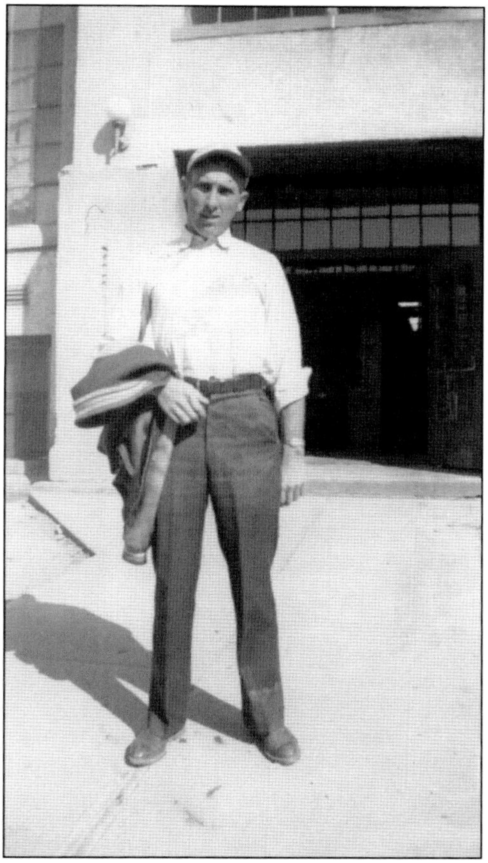

Ready for their next performance, the Yorktown Band members of 1941 are dressed in the uniform of the day. The uniform consisted of black-and-gold capes with envelope-style hats, dark pants for the boys, and dark skirts for the girls. The capes belonged to the Daleville School System before finding their way to Yorktown. The music instructor was Florence Anderson. (Wendell Conner.)

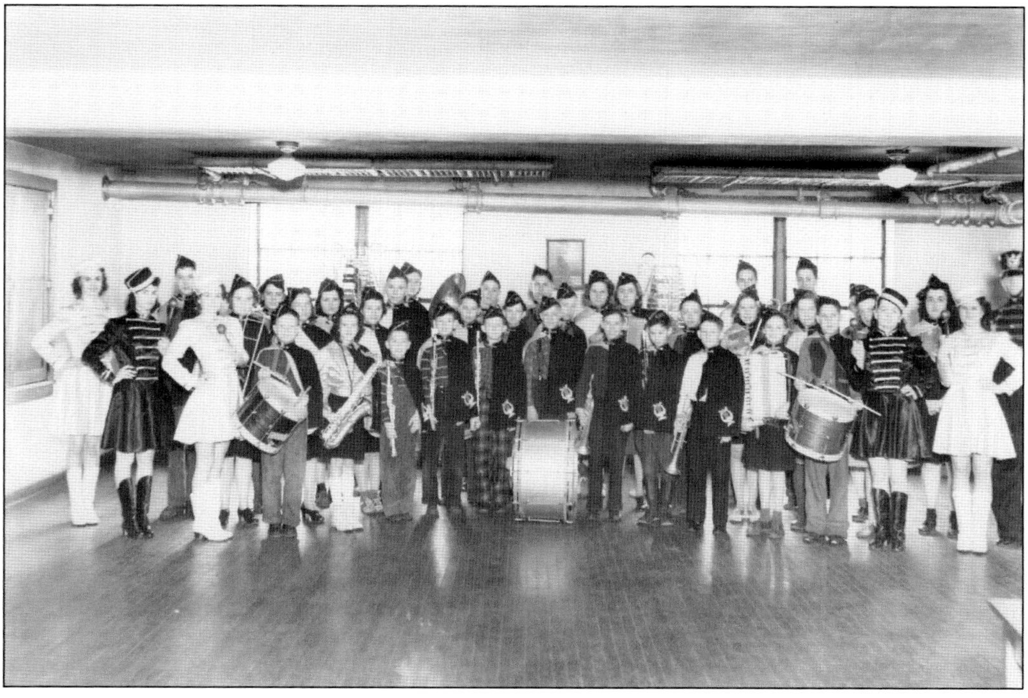

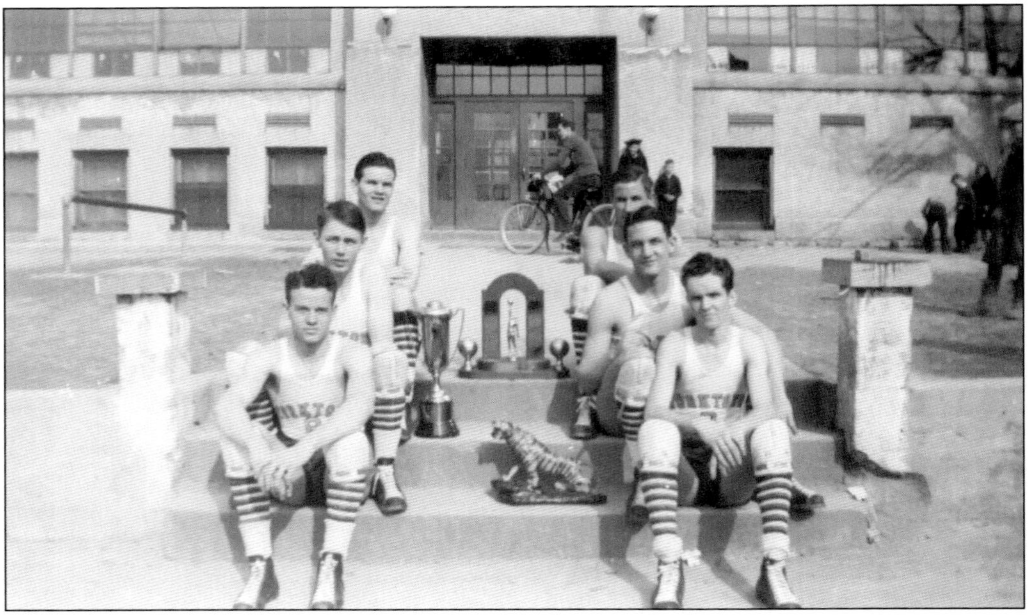

In the above photograph are, from left to right and bottom to top, Dort Richman, Monte McKibben, Clarence Cook, Bud Robertson, George McKibben, and Cliff Barker—the six seniors of the 1938–39 basketball team, as they sit on the front steps of the school showing off their trophies for a yearbook photograph. The team had won 20 out of its 25 games and topped off the season by capturing the county championship under the direction of coach Kenneth Sigler. This squad consisted of the six seniors pictured, plus three juniors and one freshman. The individuals in the photograph below are not identified. (Both, YMPTHA.)

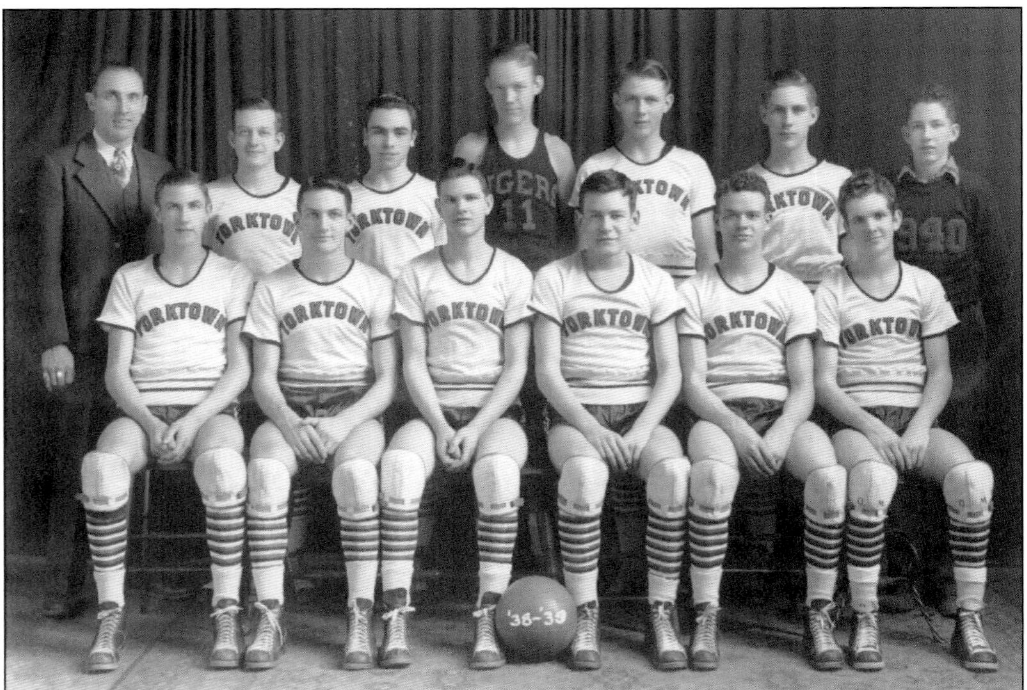

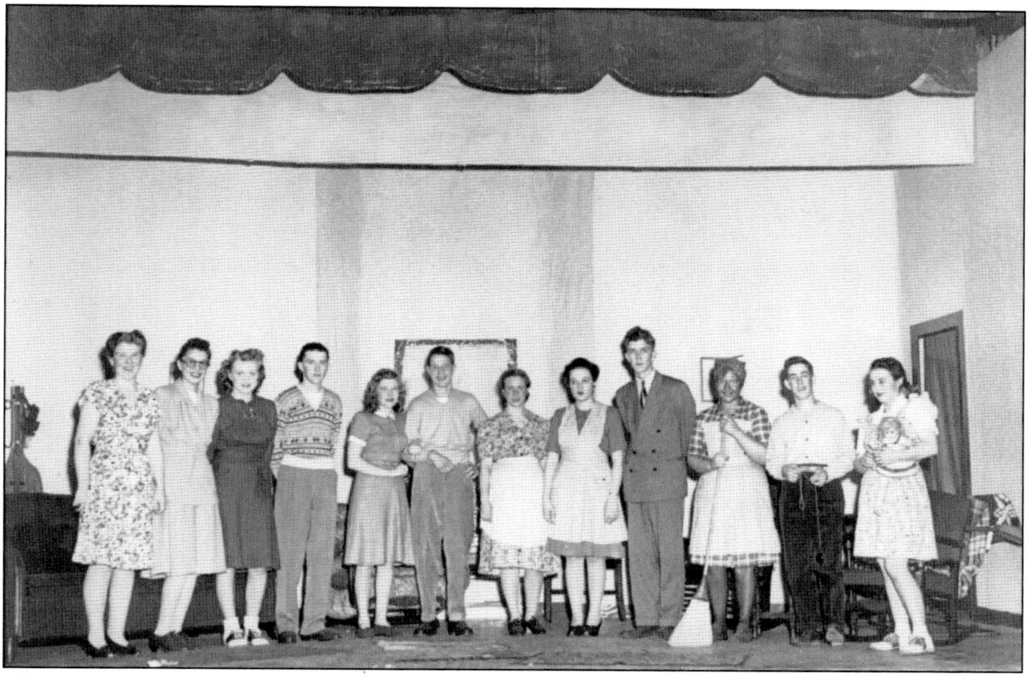

The cast of the 1946 class play, *The Daffy Dills*, poses for a curtain call. Featured here are, from left to right, Lois Ann Reed, Jean Hamilton, Lois Ann Payne, Dick King, Judy Broadwater, Keith Morrison, Beverly Burgess, Virginia Miller, James Watkins, Reva Mae Curtis, Norma Dragoo, and Vera Ingram. (Lois Ann Henderson.)

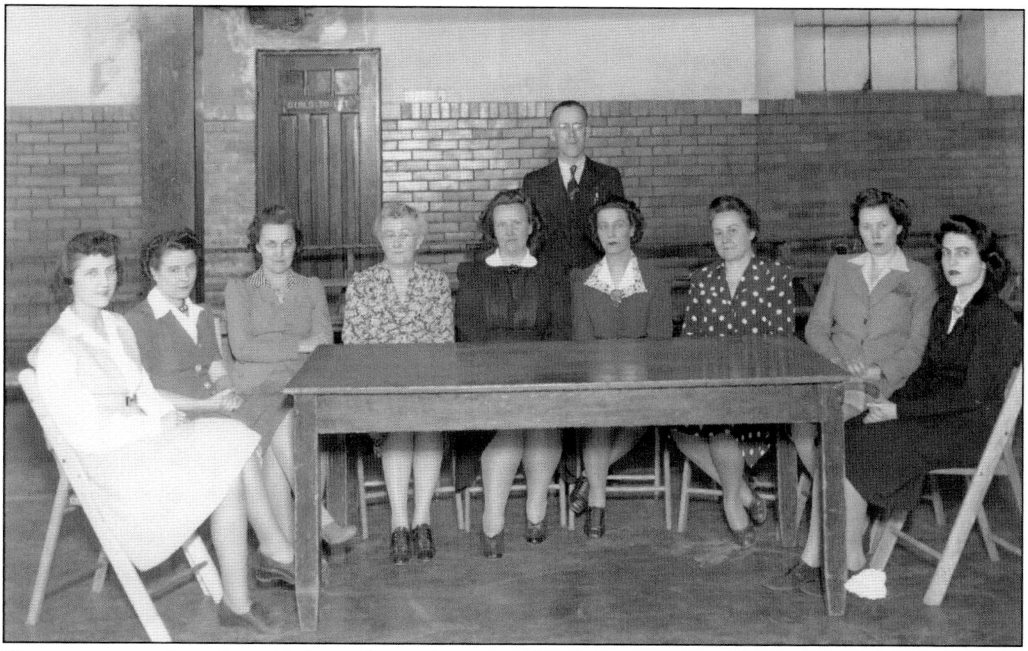

Elementary teachers from 1943 are shown between classes. Pictured are, from left to right, Kathaleen Reed, Irene Schirmer, Winnifred McKinley, Alma Robertson, Charline Spencer, Paul Metzcar, Louise Bush, Becky Miller, Margaret Shank, and Martha Sheets. Most of this group continued at Yorktown until retirement. (Rhonda Williams.)

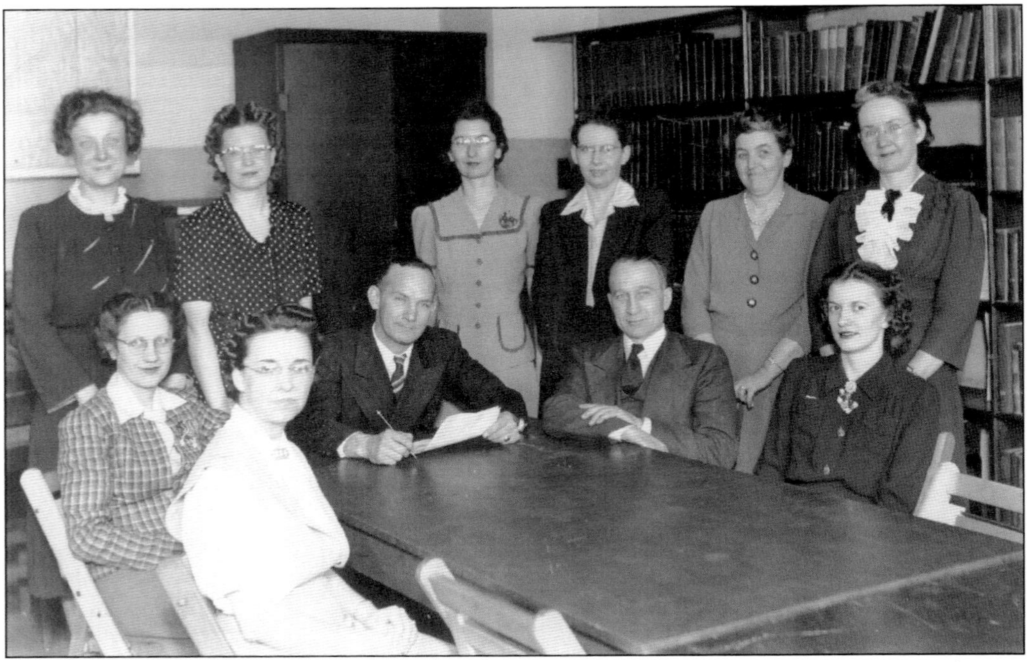

High school teachers for the year 1944 are, from left to right, (seated) Marie Dice, Catherine Rothhaar, Arthur Alexander, Claude Williams, and Genvieve Chambers; (standing) Mary Van Skyock, Marguerite Dunn, Crystal Rees, Bernice Sigler, Dorothy Henkle, and Bright Kimmel. Dunn, Henkle, and Kimmel remained on the staff until sometime in the 1960s. (Rhonda Williams.)

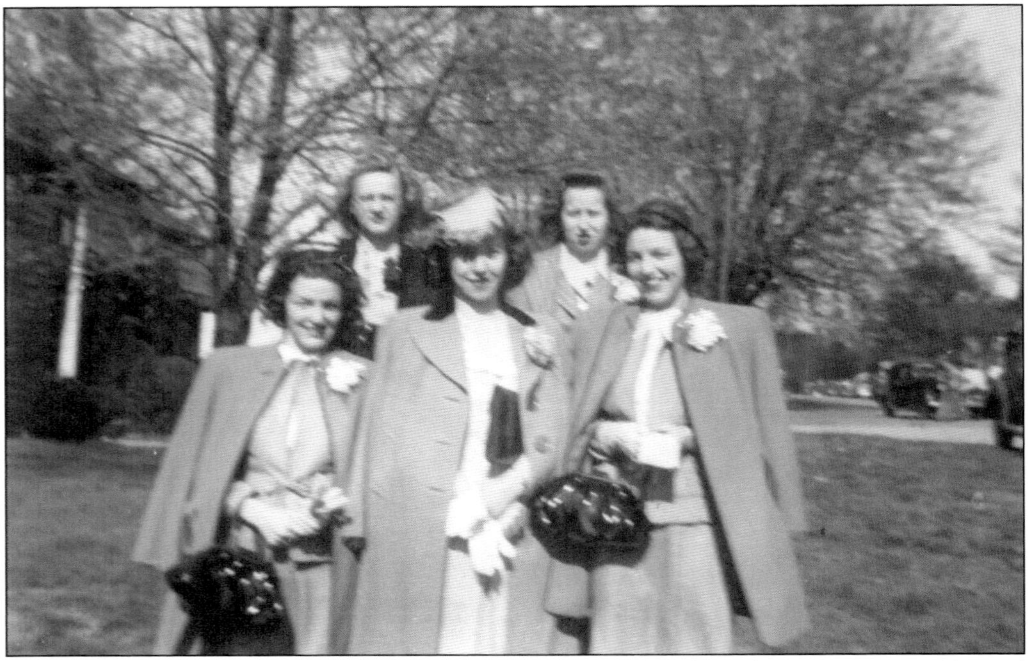

Friends from the class of 1945 pause for a photograph before their baccalaureate program. Dressed for the occasion are, from left to right, (front) Maxine Parkison, Evelyn Warfel, and Madge Parkison; (back) Mary Lou Hofherr and Betty Mae Fisher. The commencement ceremony itself was held in the Yorktown High School gymnasium in early May. (Betty Mae Fisher.)

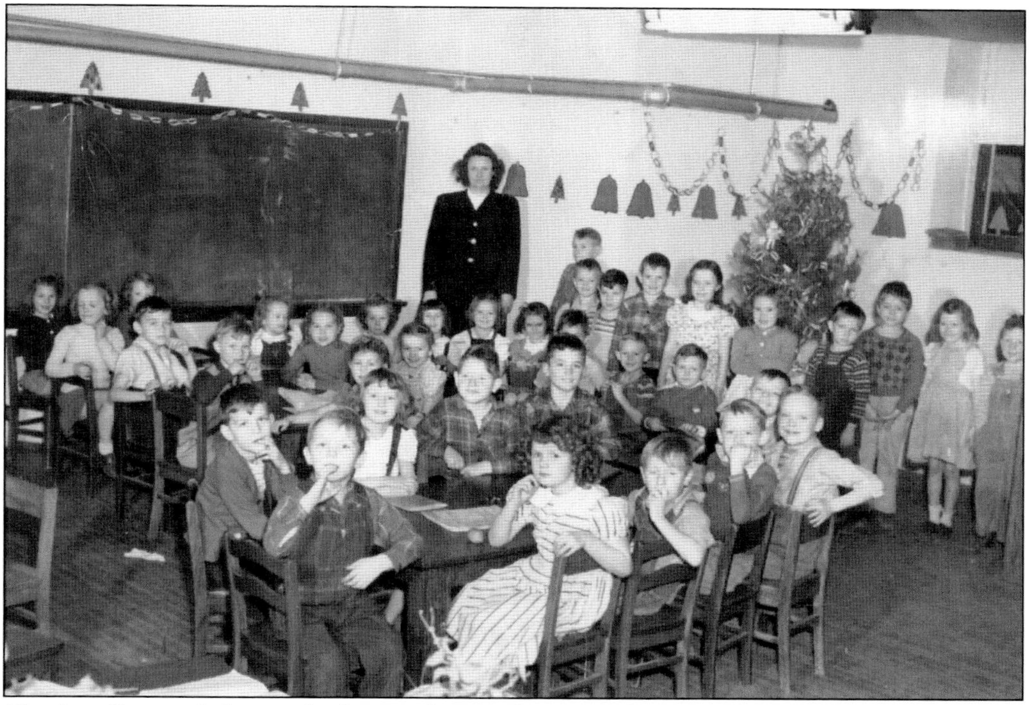

Charlene Spencer's first-grade class made time for some Christmas cheer near the end of 1946. The students all sit around large wooden tables, perhaps because of room size or large class size. This would become the class of 1958. Note there were still exposed pipes in some school buildings, but schools had advanced by then to fluorescent lighting. (YMPTHA.)

In 1948, Walter Stephenson started the Junior Athletic Association to train young boys in the sport of basketball by stressing sportsmanship and fair play. Members of the Pirates team in 1953 are, from left to right, (first row) Tom Monroe, unidentified, Dennis Monroe, and coach Jim Mitchell; (second row) Ron Plummer, unidentified, and Charles Music. Several years later, a baseball program was created. (Becky Monroe.)

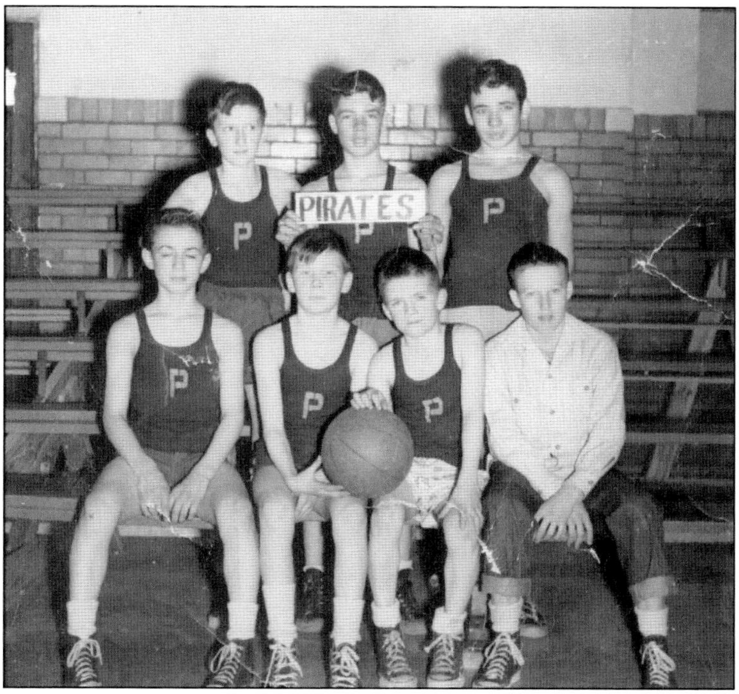

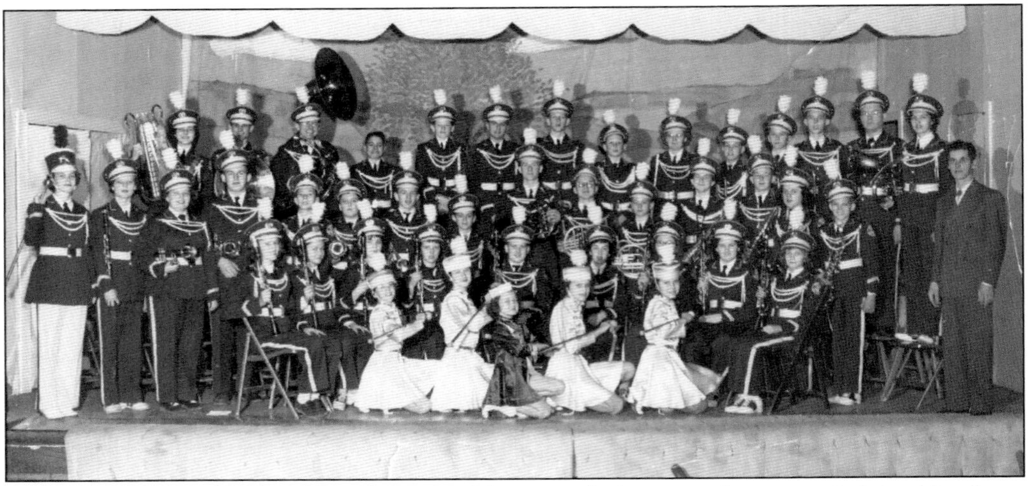

The Yorktown High School Band, pictured here just before a performance, is joined by drum major Joanne Thompson (far left) and majorettes (center, from left to right) Shirley Spencer, Nancy Burns, Carolyn Clevenger, Janice Phillips, and Joan McKinley. Standing at the right is director and music teacher Kenneth Wooley. (YMPTHA.)

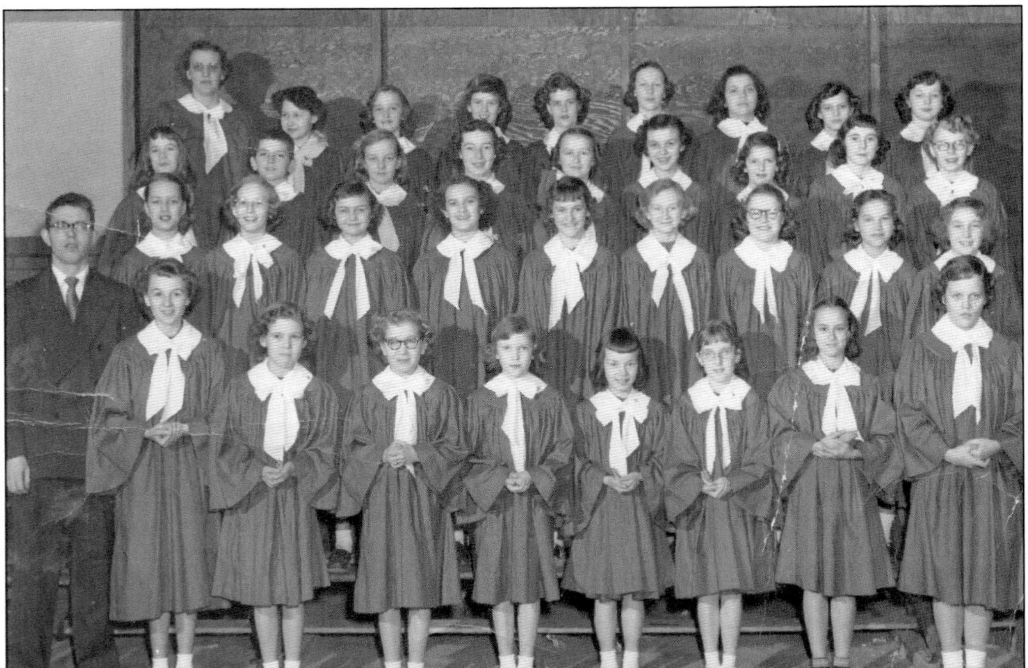

The 1952 Yorktown Junior Choir, with directors Thomas Ray (far left) and Mildred Armstrong (back row, left) standing proudly, prepares for a performance. The choir consisted of students from fourth to eighth grades and was one of the only extracurricular activities available for this age group. Members are wearing dark blue robes with white collars and bows. (Jerry Kay Davis.)

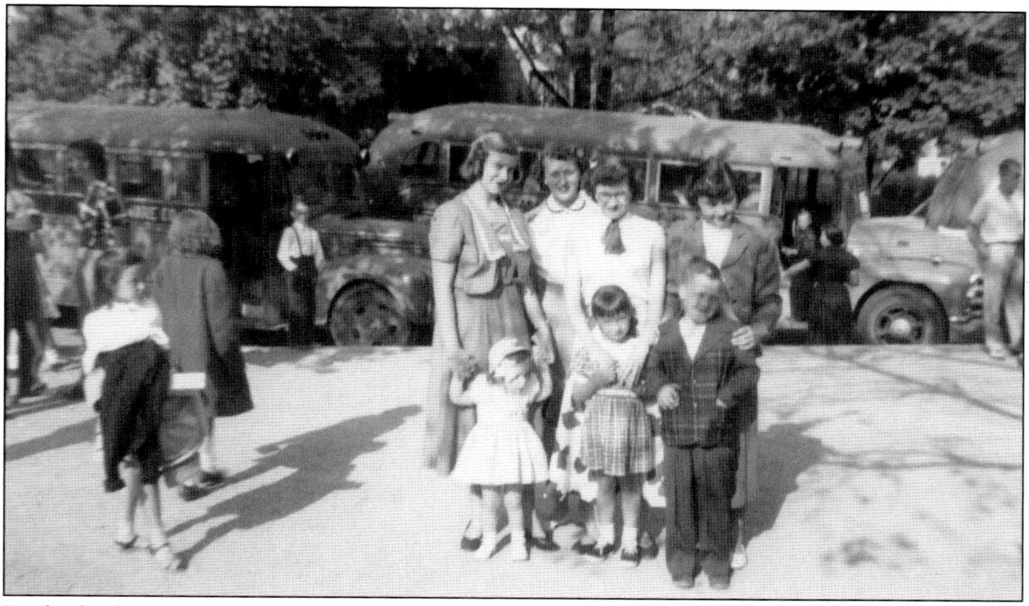

In the back row, from left to right, Deanna Thomas, Patty Davis, Sharon Johnson, and Joyce Moore, along with three young friends, take time to visit before boarding their bus on the last day of school. Note the size of the school buses compared to those of today. (Janice Ross.)

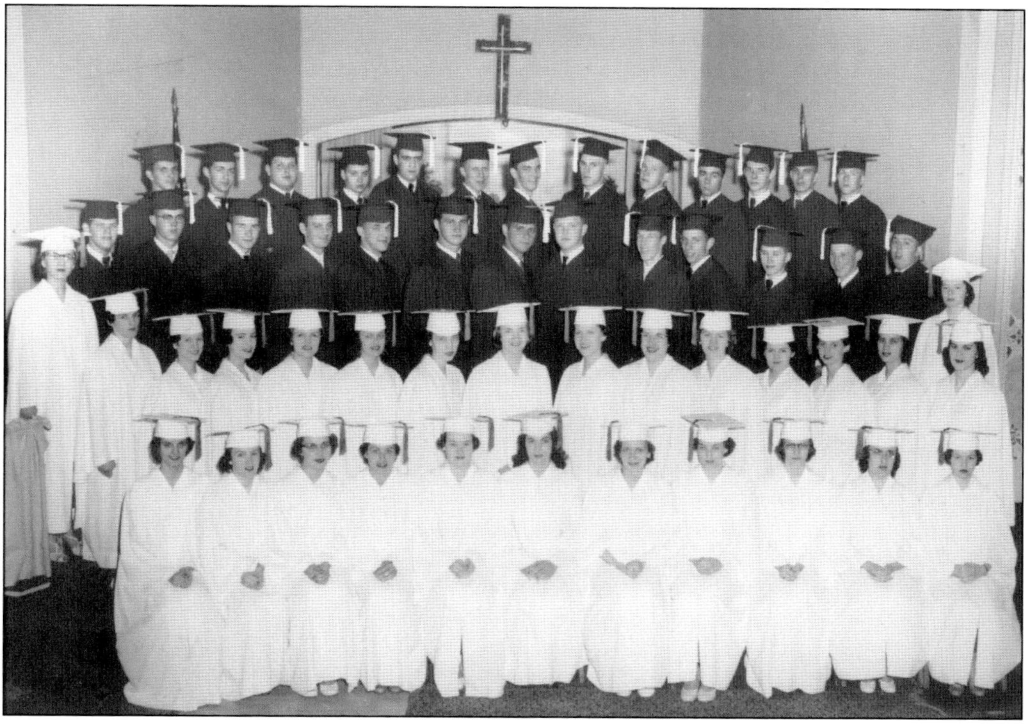

The class of 1955 poses for a photograph in Yorktown Christian Church before its baccalaureate service. It was common for the graduating classes to have a religious service at one of the local churches on the Sunday prior to the graduation service. Commencement was usually held in the gymnasium, with the county superintendent participating in every program throughout the county. (YMPTHA.)

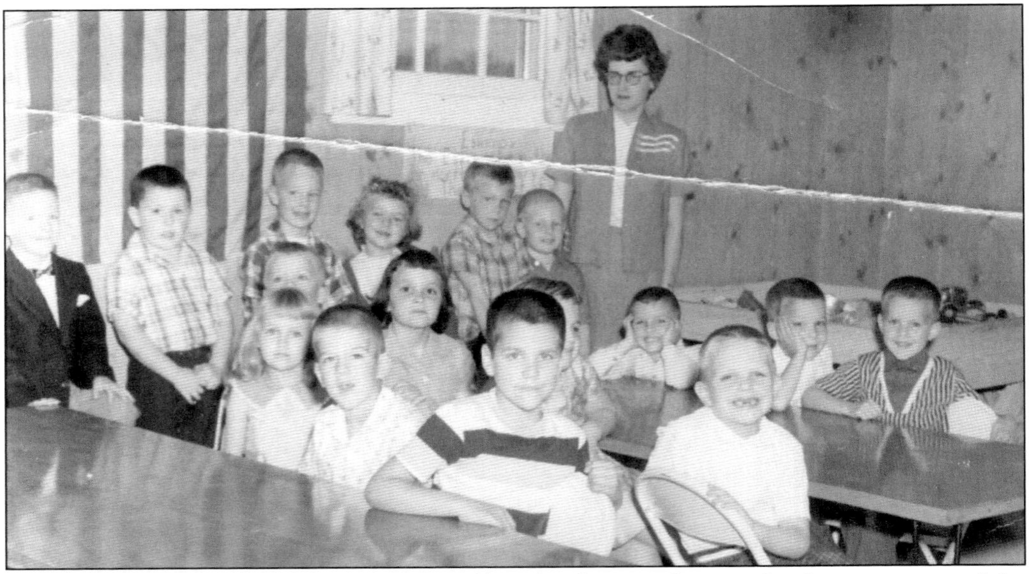

Prior to kindergarten being offered in the public schools, several private kindergartens served the community. Pictured here is teacher Peg Fight, supervising her class of 16 youngsters—Sherry Babb, Gary Reed, Marc Shores, Randy Schlegel, Kevin Darl, Melisa Marsh, Cindy Taylor, Jimmy Wallen, Mike Wilson, Bruce Reed, Barry Barnum, Michael Conningore, Steve Hood, Cathy Main, Dennis Nixon, and Steven Gentry. Several in this group went on to graduate from Yorktown in 1971. (Terry Reed.)

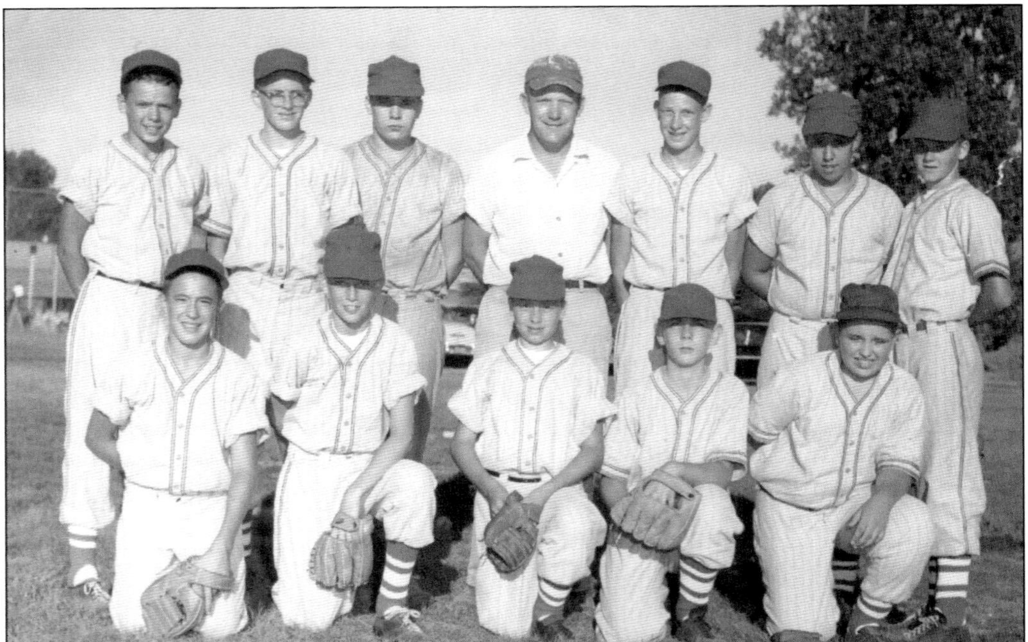

A junior high baseball team, with coach Jim McKibben, prepares for a game. Pictured are, from left to right, (first row) Preston Cross, Ronald Small, Jim Turner, Sidney Mitchell, and Richard Flick; (second row) Gary McKinley, Jerry Snider, Boyd Hopper, McKibben, Mike Niccum, Dale Stephenson, and Steve Noward. (YMPTHA.)

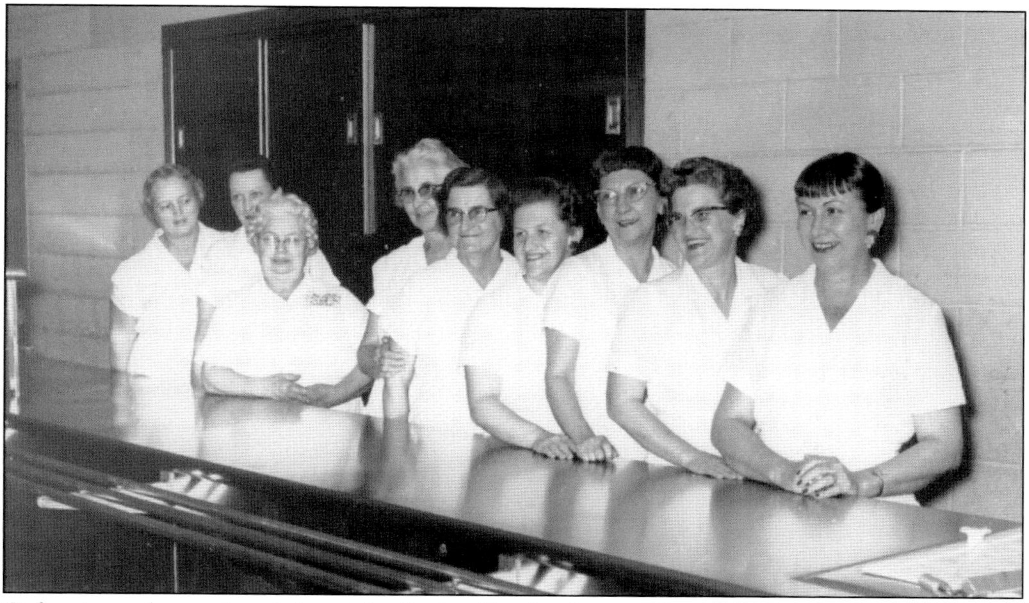

Cafeteria employees, from left to right, Evelyn Hensley, Lorine Clore, Edna Patty, Josephine Hamm, Jessie Reynolds, Sue Woods, Jeanette Stewart, Glenna Lennis, are Vivian Belcher are pictured here before the start of the lunch hour. These dedicated women prepared and served many wholesome and tasty meals, serving all 12 grades within a short period of time. (Kathy Mattingly.)

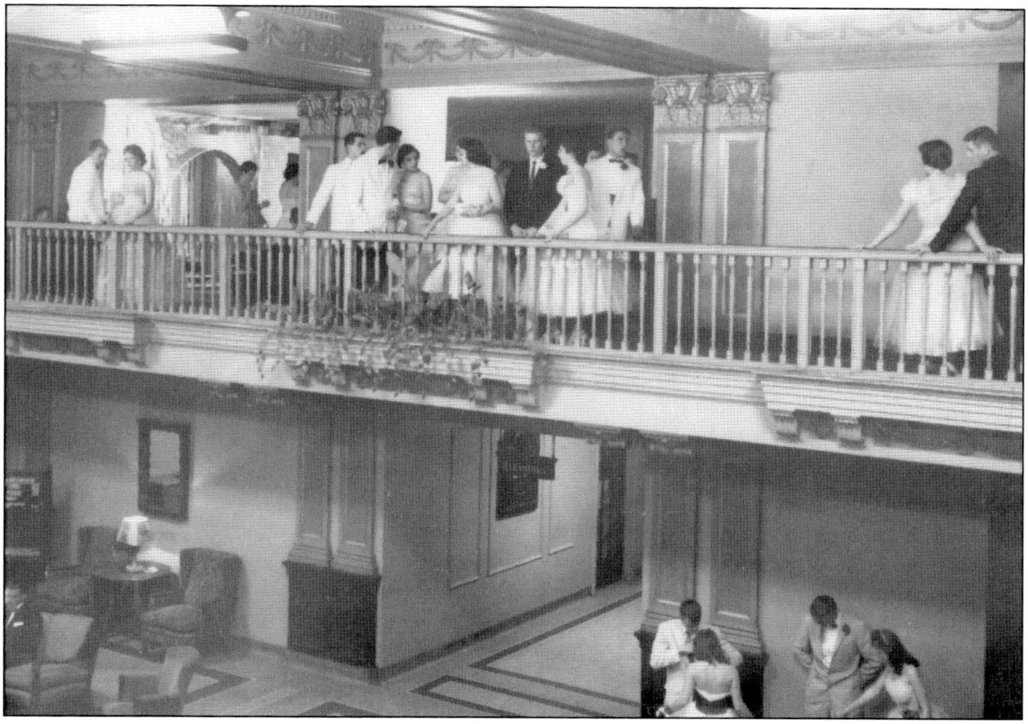

The Roberts Hotel was a popular place to hold high school proms and other formal dinners and dances. Guests are shown taking a break on the second-floor balcony. Through this elegant area, couples could enter the ballroom or lounge while watching friends and other guests in the large lobby below. (Jerry K. Davis.)

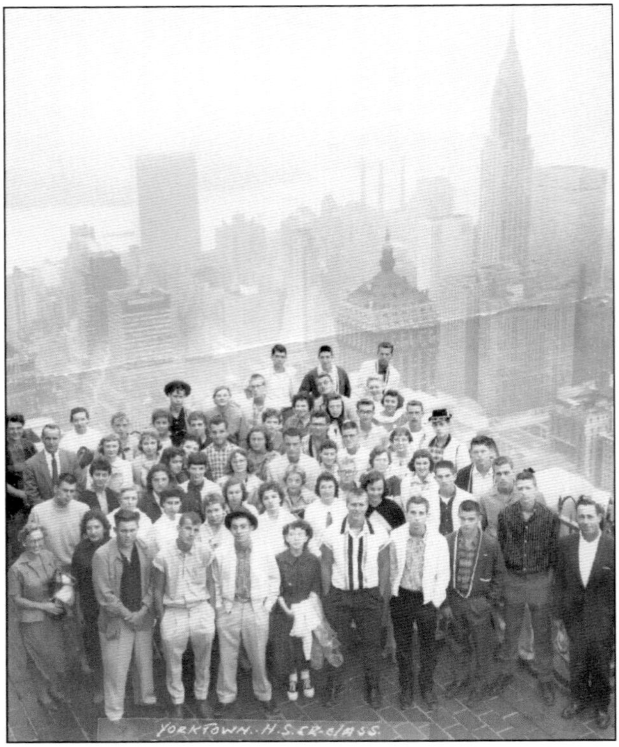

Pictured on top of the RCA Building in New York City, members of the class of 1959 are enjoying the last few days of their senior trip. The class left Richmond, Indiana, via train and traveled to Washington, DC, where students visited the usual historical attractions. From there, they went to New York, where they enjoyed the sights and some free time. (Becky Monroe.)

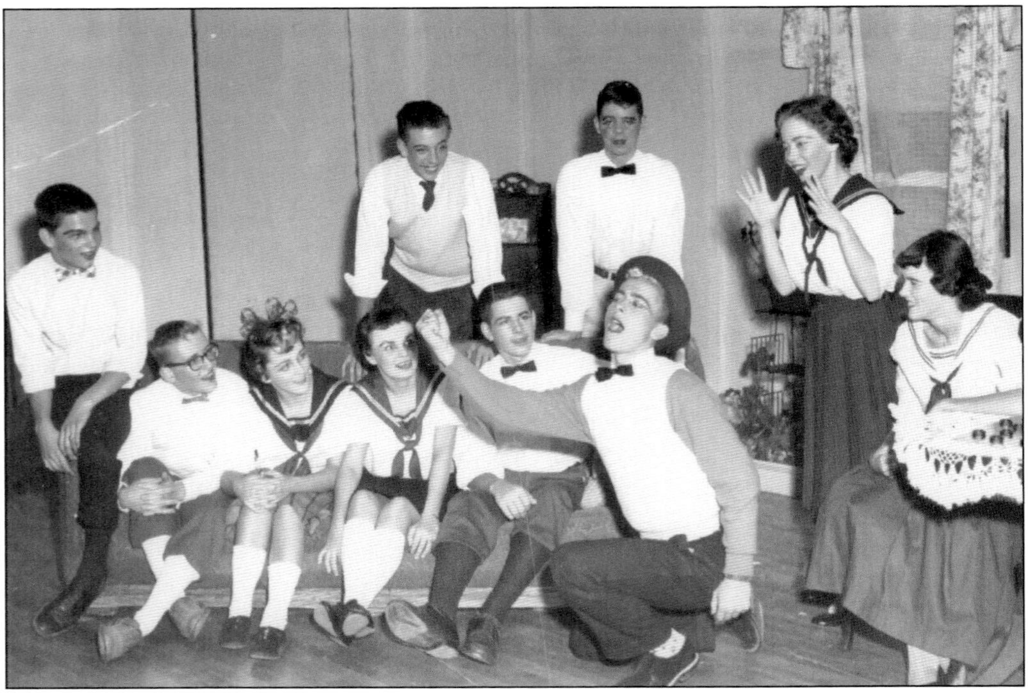

In 1959, *Cheaper by the Dozen* was selected by the senior class for their final play. During a dress rehearsal, cast members watch as Ned Rigsbe leads a cheer. Seated on the couch are, from left to right, Mikel Thornburg, Mike Spangler, Carmelita Kowalski, Pat Watkins, and Tyrone Judkins. Others are Bill Mudd, Jim Bailey, Judy Goodwin, and Becky Sears (far right). (Jerry K. Davis.)

The opposing team in this photograph from 1960 is unidentified, but Laury Cross, from the Tigers, appears ready to block a shot while teammate Jack Neal stands ready to rebound. Coach Bob Swander was successful in leading this Tiger team to a county tourney victory. (Kathy Mattingly.)

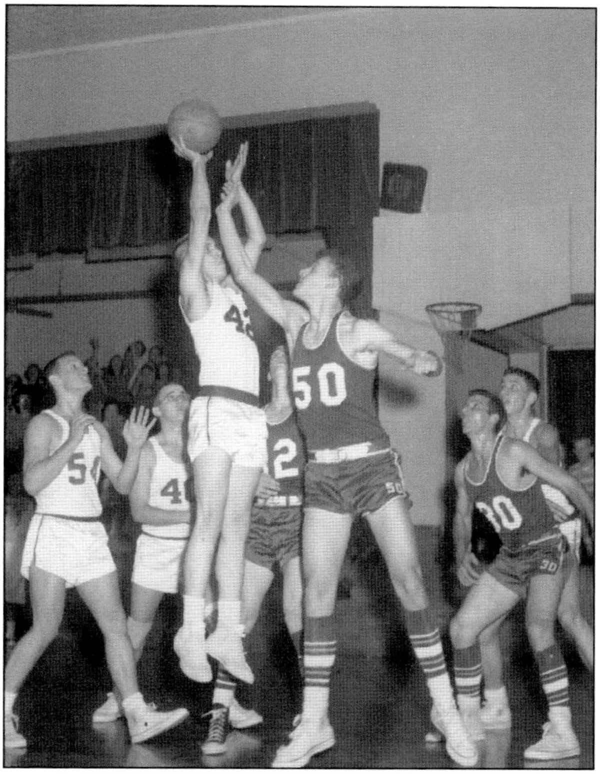

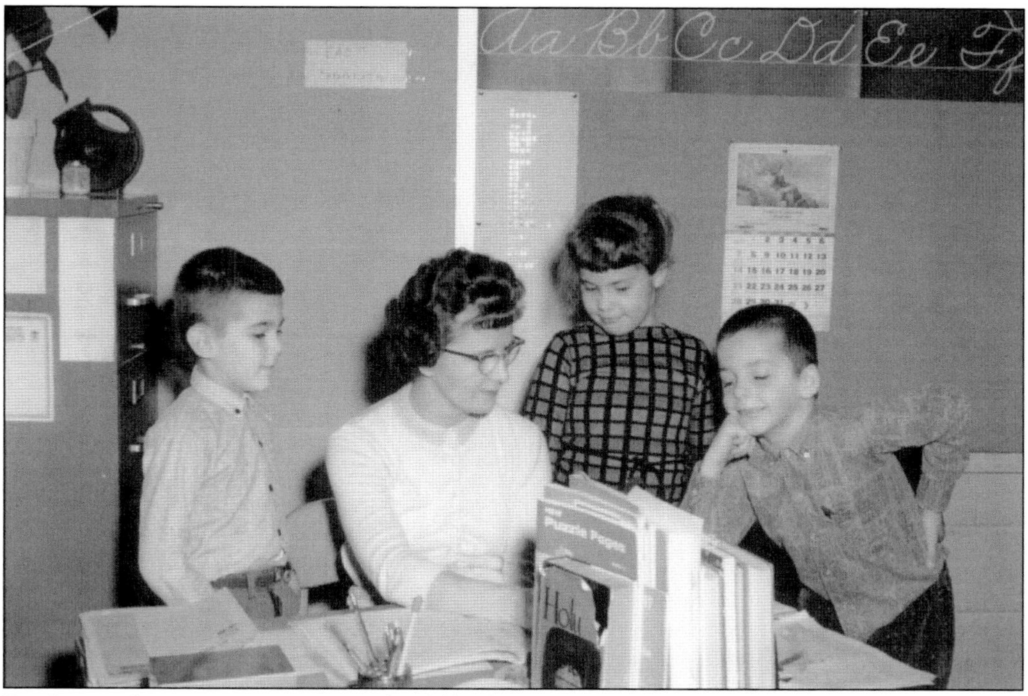

Reading and writing can sometimes be difficult. Second-grade teacher Theresa Luttrell takes the time to explain a problem to her students. Gathered around to get information on their assignment are David Burton (left), Debbie Crosley, and Bruce Parkinson. (Laurie Swartz.)

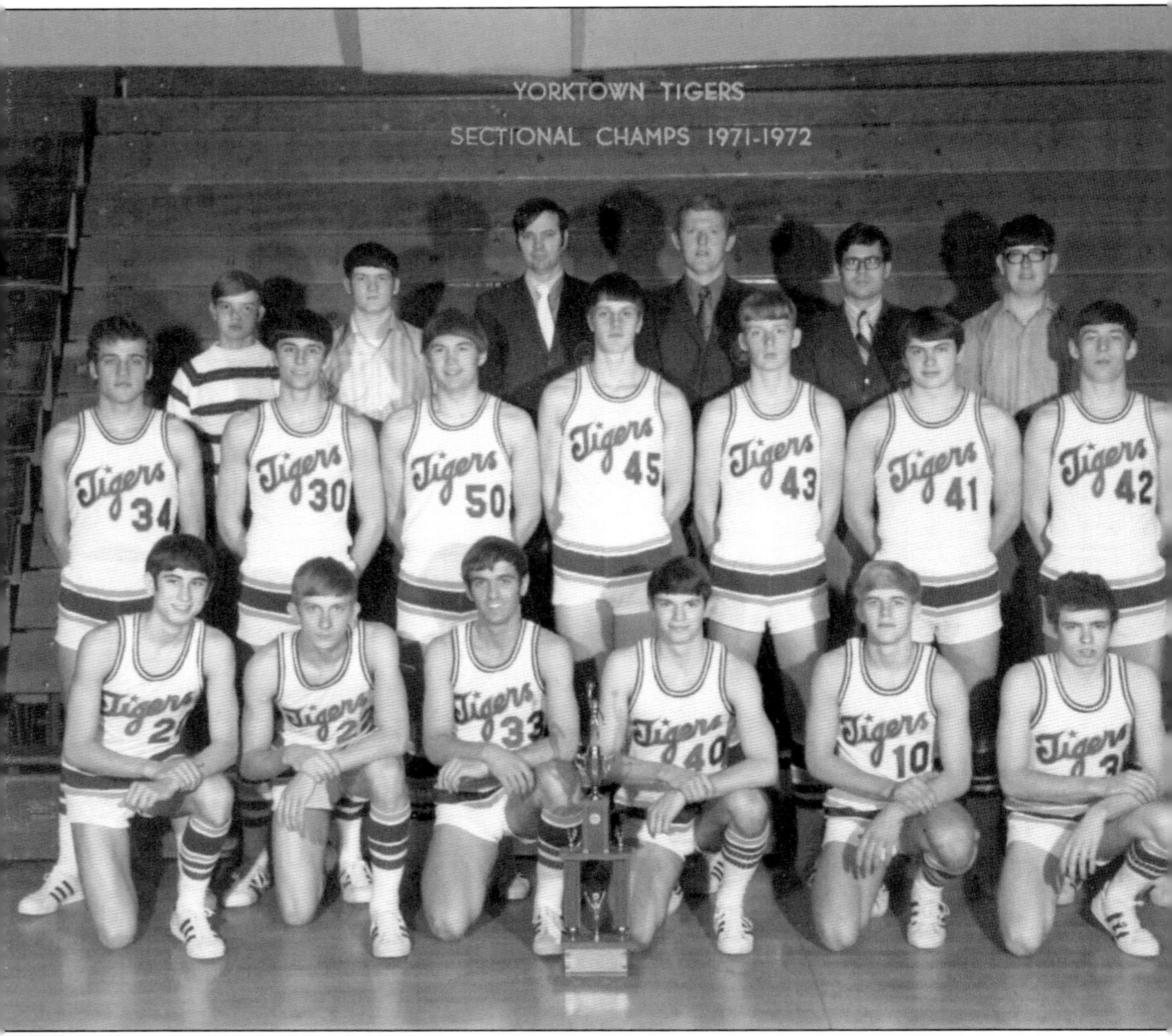

The 1971–1972 basketball team is probably the most celebrated team in the school's history. Not only did it win every game of the scheduled season, but it went on to accomplish what no Tiger team before had been able to do. The men capped off the season by defeating three Muncie schools to secure the 1972 Sectional Championship. From there, the Tigers went to the regional at New Castle, where they won the Friday game against the New Castle Trojans but were defeated on Saturday by the Richmond Red Devils. Pictured are, from left to right, (first row) Rick Day, Sam Crisswell, John Stephenson, Randy Sollars, Ed Winningham, and Brent Reed; (second row) Steve Hilton, Bruce Parkinson, Craig Charles, Cliff Bell, Rod Harman, Kurt Humes, and Jeff Guy; (third row) student managers John Mohler and Jeff Mahoney, coach Don Rogers, assistant coach Mike Kelly, assistant coach Dwight Michaels, and student manager Gary Wilson. Following the sectional win, fans of all ages filled the gym to overflow status. (YMPTHA.)

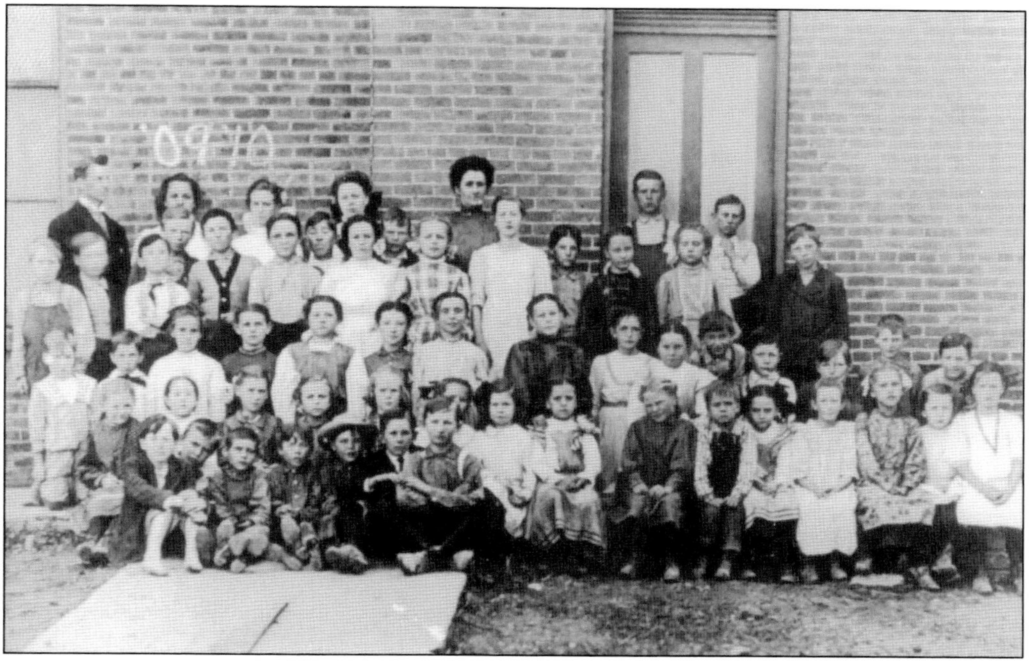

In 1910, students in the Cammack area attended the Antioch School, which sat on the west side of Yorktown-Gaston Road, where it joins Jackson Street. This unidentified group of students poses for what may be one of the last photographs showing any portion of this building. A storm in 1911 totally destroyed the Antioch School. A new and larger building was erected on the east side of the Yorktown-Gaston Road. The Cammack School, built in 1912, served the area students in grades one through eight until it was closed in 1937. The building is still standing and houses the office and operations of Aul Brothers Tool. (Both, YMPTHA.)

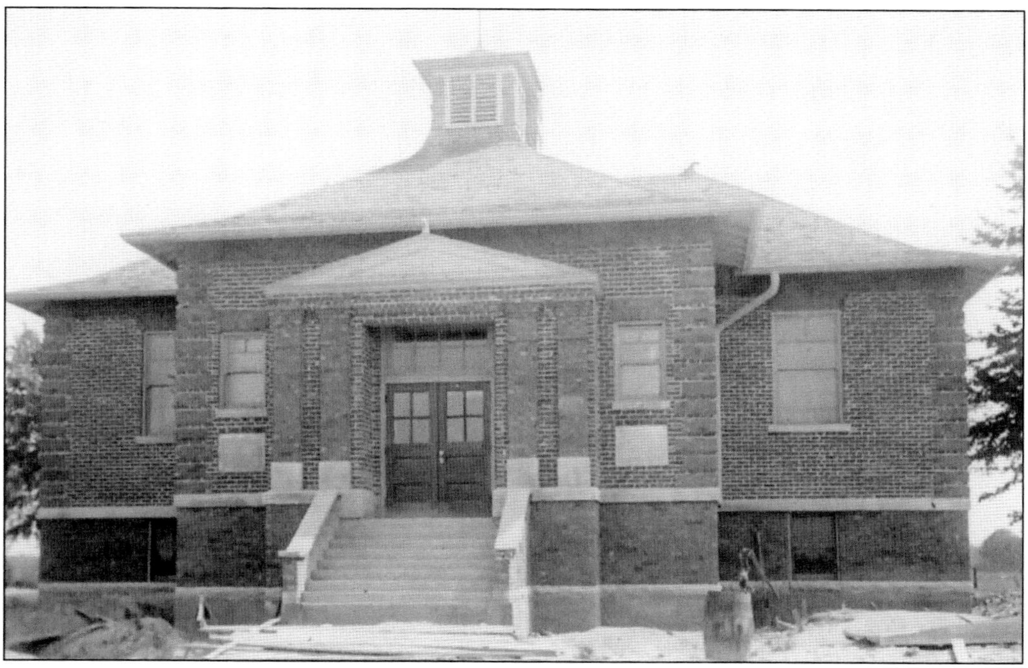

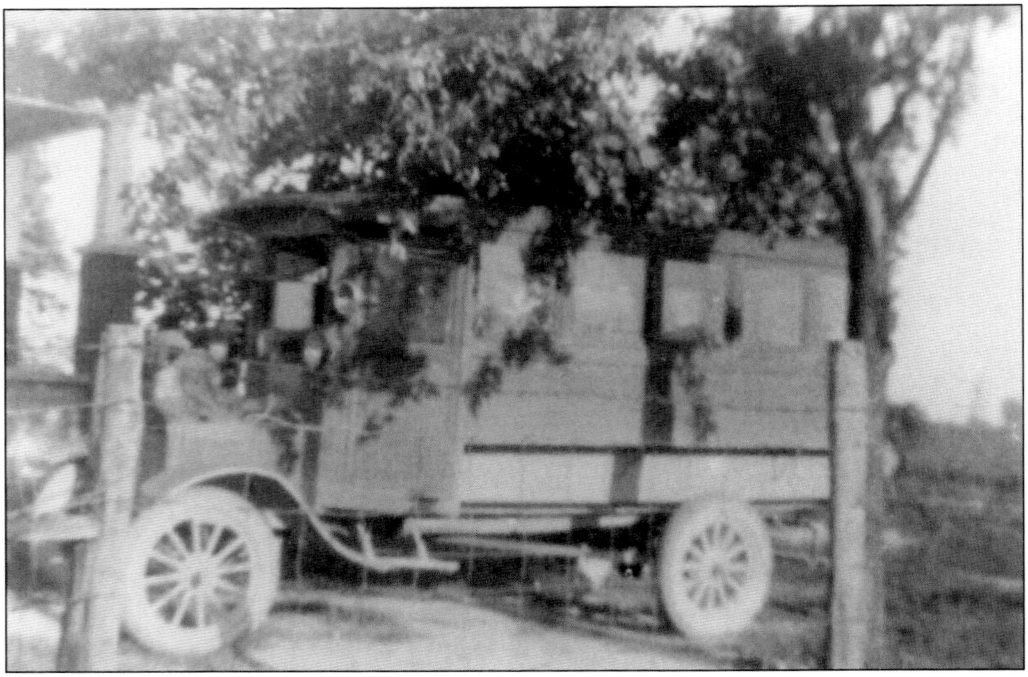

In the 1920s, J. Emil Sears owned one of the first school buses in Mount Pleasant Township; since Sears also owned a farm, the bus had the capacity of serving a dual purpose. In the summer months, the body on the back could be removed, making it usable as a farm truck. The bus had no heater, so the students would often wrap themselves in blankets during the ride to school. (Becky Monroe.)

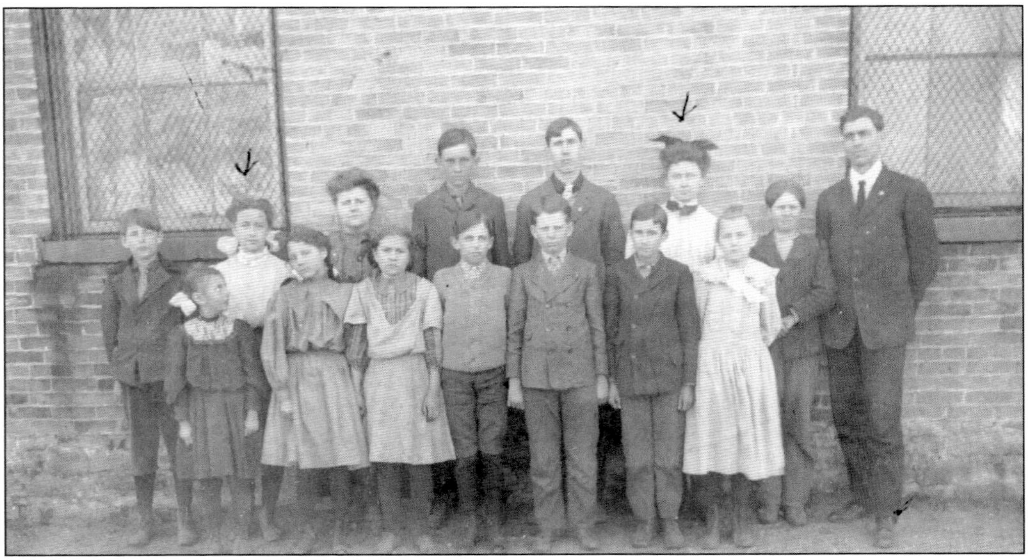

Kilgore School was situated southwest of Yorktown on State Road 32. Pictured here in 1908 are, from left to right, (first row) Nora Lang, Lucille Campbell, Kate Nelson, John Pugsley, Lester Campbell, Charles Henkle, and Ruby McWhirt; (second row) unidentified, Muriel Cunningham, Dessie Donovan, Josie McWhirt, Ralph Henkle, Edith Cunningham, Ben Nelson, and teacher Sam Pittenger. (YMPTHA.)

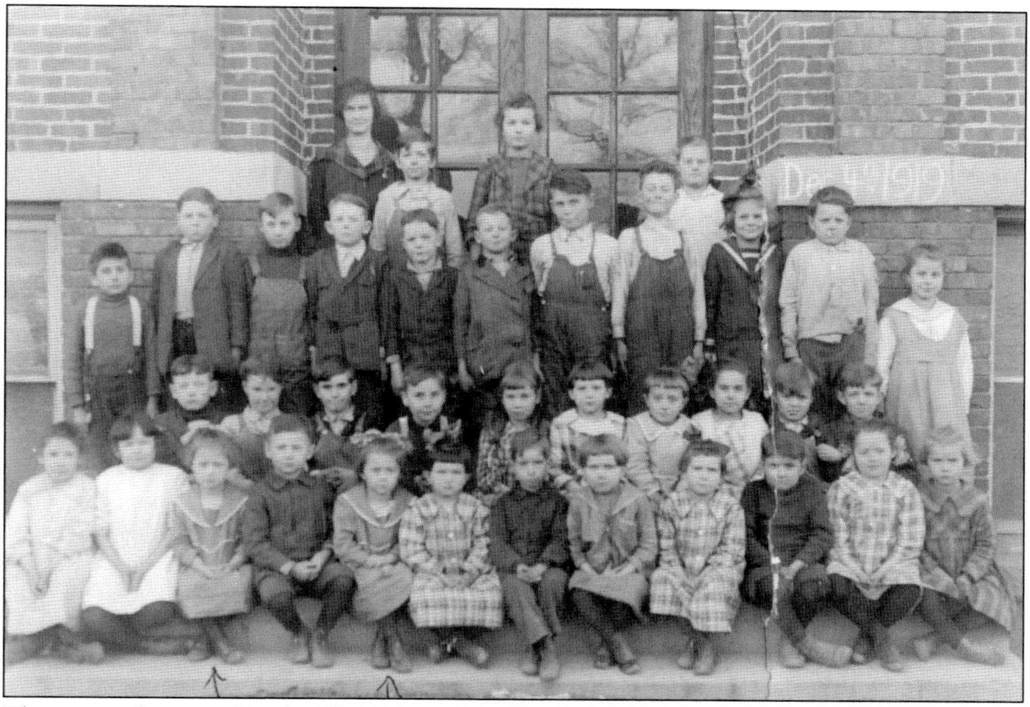

These two photographs of students outside Sycamore School indicate a good-sized enrollment through 1923. The above images dates from 1919; the below image, from 1923. Note that several of the same students appear in both photographs. Sycamore School was one of the last rural schools. (Both, Rhonda Williams.)

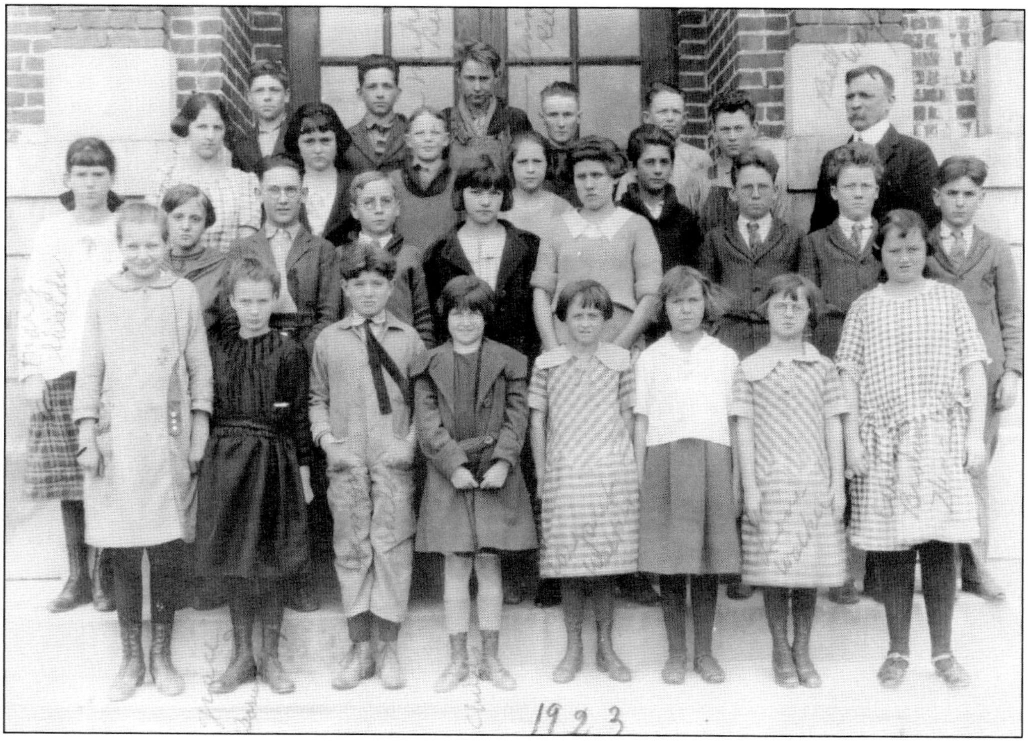

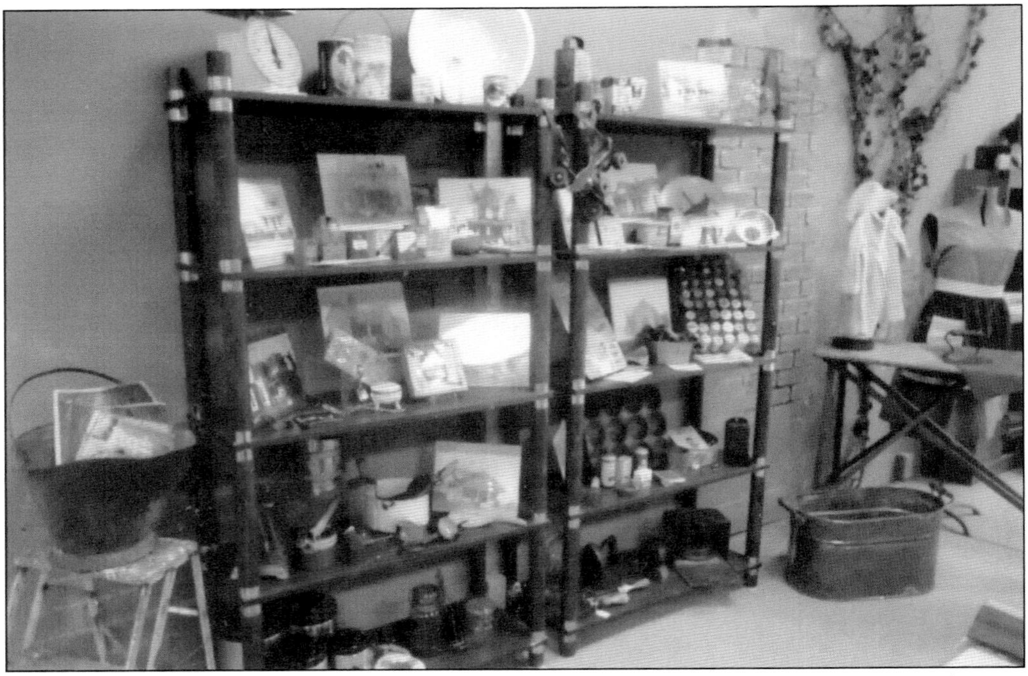

Both photographs on this page show some of the extra space the Yorktown–Mount Pleasant Township Historical Alliance has after the move in 2011 from the former township office to the new location at 9132 West Smith Street. The new site is owned by the local chapter of the Independent Order of Odd Fellows. After this location was secured, volunteers showed up in abundance to help move, paint, repair, and clean. The Historical Alliance provides local history from Yorktown's earliest days to more recent times. Informational meetings might include a virtual, pictorial walk down a local street to discover old buildings and the families or businesses who occupied them. Visitors will find everything from old photographs and common household or business items, to tools and information about local churches and cemeteries as well as family genealogies. (Both, YMPTHA.)

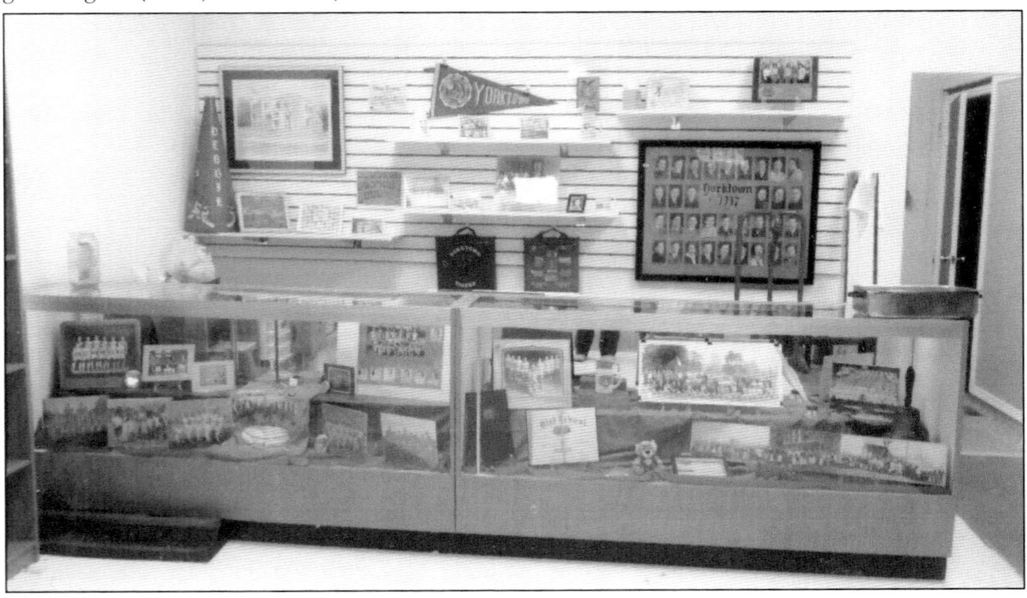

About the Yorktown–Mount Pleasant Township Historical Alliance

The Yorktown–Mount Pleasant Township Historical Alliance began as an idea in 2004 and became a reality in 2005. Becky Monroe brought together half a dozen people who were also interested in preserving and sharing the history of the community.

At first, the small group met in homes to share stories and memories, but it soon began to share items of interest from the past. Word spread, and others began attending these meetings until more space was needed. Judge Pat Ziebart generously offered her courtroom, and there the board of directors was developed. In 2006, the Historical Alliance became an official corporation and qualified for a 501(c)3, a not-for-profit organization. The organization quickly outgrew the courtroom and in 2008 acquired a room at the township building. There, the group continued to grow and was able to set up permanent displays.

After a period of time, the township building was sold to the school, and the organization was about to become homeless. The Odd Fellows lodge came to the rescue and leased a storefront in its building in downtown Yorktown. The space was larger than members were accustomed to, but it did not take long to fill it. The township trustee's office and the Yorktown Library both donated shelving units. Minor renovations were made; painting, electrical, and other jobs were all performed by members volunteering time and materials. The new location allowed better natural light from front windows and a more visible location to draw visitors. Members and other community people stepped in to pack, move, and unpack the collections. Funds given by the Yorktown Lions Club purchased a costly software program designed especially for museums.

This book could only materialize with the love of community and generous donations of time, information, talent, and many wonderful photographs provided by members of the community and members of the YMPTHA.

The YMPTHA is currently located at 9132 West Smith Street, Yorktown, Indiana.

Consistent with our mission to preserve history on a local level, this book was printed in South Carolina on American-made paper and manufactured entirely in the United States. Products carrying the accredited Forest Stewardship Council (FSC) label are printed on 100 percent FSC-certified paper.